SCENIC FORM IN
SHAKESPEARE

SCENIC FORM IN SHAKESPEARE

EMRYS JONES

OXFORD

At the Clarendon Press

1971

Oxford University Press, Ely House, London W. 1

GLASGOW NEW YORK TORONTO MELBOURNE WELLINGTON
CAPE TOWN SALISBURY IBADAN NAIROBI DAR ES SALAAM LUSAKA ADDIS ABABA
OMBAY CALCUTTA MADRAS KARACHI LAHORE DACCA
KUALA LUMPUR SINGAPORE HONG KONG TOKYO

TO BARBARA

Preface

THIS is a study of Shakespeare as a dramatist which focuses on a feature of his work which has received comparatively little attention: the *scene*. The first chapter introduces the scenic unit as the nucleus of Shakespearian drama; the following three treat related topics concerning scene and sequence, which are then given further application in the four chapters on individual plays. Except in the first chapter I have limited myself to the histories and tragedies: the two kinds are closely related and form a coherent body of material, while the comedies show an independent development which would require a separate study. (What I have to say in Chapter 3, for example, applies only to the histories and tragedies and not, with a few exceptions, to the comedies.) I have not included a chapter on *Hamlet*, since the loss of what was probably its source-play would have proved too great an obstacle to the approach adopted here.

Quotations from Shakespeare are from Peter Alexander's single-volume edition (1964 reprint).

I owe a very great debt to my wife, Barbara Everett: for encouragement and support, for criticism and innumerable discussions, and for substantial help at all stages in the writing of this book.

Magdalen College, Oxford
March 1970

Contents

PART ONE

1. *The Scenic Poet*

I T can be an illuminating experience to see Shakespeare acted in a completely unfamiliar language. A few years ago appeared a Japanese film version of *Macbeth*. The adaptation was very free, and the social order shown in the film, though recognizably 'medieval', was a long way from Shakespeare's Scotland. But the extraordinary vitality of some of the great scenes of the play survived with surprisingly little loss. One of them, the banquet scene, came across as a dramatic invention of the highest power; even without Shakespeare's words, the scene made a strong effect. The same can be said of the banquet scene as it occurs, sung in Italian, in Verdi's opera of *Macbeth*: although translated to a different artistic medium, it preserves a good deal of its force. When the scene is acted in English or read in its full poetic context in the play as Shakespeare wrote it, so much significance of a verbal and poetic nature claims attention that it is possible, perhaps even natural, to overlook or not to notice its basic structural shaping: that formal idea which gives the scene its dramatic unity and which was made to stand out in the film and opera. What Shakespeare has invented is something—a structure, an *occasion*—which may be said to be (however dangerous the phrase) independent of the words which are usually thought to give the scene its realization. This 'something' we may call a 'scenic form'.

Plays are made of scenes before they are made of words (although a play of Shakespeare's, like *Macbeth*, may be as great a poem as it is a play). The dramatist's first and proper task is to dramatize; and the scene is the primary dramatic unit, the unit in terms of which he will work out his play. If we look for a reason why Shakespeare's plays hold the stage as well as they do, and why so many of them have been acted continuously from his own time to the present day (as long as there have been theatres to act in), at least a partial answer will be found in his mastery of scenic construction. A play can hold an audience even though written without much verbal distinction; what it cannot overcome is defective scenic organization. For all its impressive qualities,

Timon of Athens, for example, is found in practice to be defective scenically, and it has never been a great success on the stage. When Shakespeare's contemporary Hugh Holland referred to him in the First Folio as the 'famous Scenicke Poet', he probably meant no more than that he was a dramatist, a poet of the stage. But the dramatist's concern with scene-making is such a vital part of his work as to make Holland's term worth reviving. In what follows I should like to show what it is to be a great 'scenic poet' in this more special sense: a poet of dramatic scenes, an artist in scenic form.[1]

I

If he is to be at all successful, the inventor of scenes requires an exceptional degree of insight into the relation between actors and audience. The forms assumed by his scenes will in fact be dictated by the peculiar, almost contractual, relationship between those acting and those for whom the performance is intended.

Dramatic writing is always a kind of metaphor, its essential principle one of mime, pretending that something is other than itself. The poor player impersonates a king, a plain chair serves for a throne, the acting space itself is anything required by the dramatist, a palace, a street, an island, or the entire world. What remains constant throughout these imagined transformations, underlying all the elaborations of plot which differentiate every play from all the others that have ever been written, is the literal truth of this theatrical situation: a group of persons being watched and listened to by a (usually) larger group of miscellaneously assembled people.

---

[1] It comes as a slight surprise to find that in the course of his notorious attack on Shakespeare, Tolstoy should remark that Shakespeare's 'masterly development of the scenes' constitutes his 'speciality'. See 'Shakespeare and the Drama', in *Recollections and Essays*, tr. Aylmer Maude (London, 1937, World's Classics edn.), p. 373. Tolstoy's remark is quoted by Peter Alexander in *Shakespeare* (London, 1964), p. 168. Another nineteenth-century novelist much interested in scenic construction was Henry James, whose novel *The Awkward Age* was entirely organized on a scenic principle. A passage from the Preface he wrote for the New York edition is very relevant to my argument and offers a precedent for my use of the term 'scenic'. James has been picturing each episode of the novel as a 'lamp': 'Each of my "lamps" would be the light of a single "social occasion" in the history and intercourse of the characters concerned, and would bring out the full latent colour of the scene in question and cause it to illustrate, to the last drop, its bearing on my theme. I revelled in this notion of the occasion as a thing by itself, really and completely a scenic thing . . .' (*The Art of the Novel*, ed. R. P. Blackmur [New York, 1953], p. 110).

This elemental theatrical situation is itself far from simple, and can be analysed in different ways. Indeed the resourceful dramatist can be said to be doing just that: he subjects this situation to a fresh analysis, choosing his subject and organizing his play so as to exploit certain aspects of it. The constituents of this theatrical situation are unchanging. In the simplest terms, the audience waits for something to happen. Time passes. Actors enter the acting space and leave it, meeting and separating from each other, and all the time in their words and actions pretend to be other people, in other places, in other situations. In this pretence the audience participates. The entire performance is a kind of conspiracy which involves the audience in looking, listening, and waiting.

The peculiarity of drama is its embodiment in actual human beings: the actors who provide the dramatist with his indispensable medium. Their activities are the language through which he must project his imitation of reality. Reduced to its barest minimum, what the actors do is to go into and out of the acting space ('They have their exits and their entrances'): so much in the way of 'action' we can expect from the least spectacular and most static of plays. But it is part of the resourcefulness of a dramatist (certainly of Shakespeare) to devise occasions for their meetings upon which scenes can be founded. What Shakespeare's characters do when they appear on the stage covers a wide range of situations (although compared with all the things people actually do in the course of their lives, it is of course a very narrow selection). They greet each other, question each other, exchange compliments, persuade each other, praise, denounce, accuse, or judge each other, bring good or bad news to each other, narrate events that have happened elsewhere, argue, quarrel, have wit-combats, deliver formal orations, have 'flytyngs' before battle, plead, threaten, curse, prophesy, and lament, invoke the gods, are silent, say things better left unsaid, converse informally, or in a courtly way, or in a foppish way, or in a rustic dialect or a foreign accent, take leave of each other, ceremoniously, or reluctantly, or brusquely. These are only a few of the things which the actors who impersonate the characters say and do when they are brought on the stage by Shakespeare. However, the meanings articulated by the actors' words, movements, actions, postures, and gestures cannot properly be considered in isolation from the other party to the theatrical contract: the audience. It is the presence of the audience that exercises a regularizing control over the activities of the actors. In devising action for the actors, the dramatist must obviously do so in deference to the capacities of the audience.

The audience has some strongly marked characteristics. Since it is likely to be anything between a few score and several thousand persons, an audience can hardly avoid having something in common with any crowd, any large assembly of people. Francis Bacon once observed that 'the minds of men are more patent of affections . . . congregate than solitary', and Shakespeare demonstrates the point in the Forum scene of *Julius Caesar*.[1] The peculiar responsiveness of a crowd is of course a commonplace of rhetorical, as of political, theory. A man may be intelligent, sensitive, and capable of critical discrimination and self-restraint, yet as part of an audience or a crowd he will become susceptible to feelings and inclinations which in other circumstances he might prefer not to acknowledge. But of course a theatre audience is not the same thing as a crowd or mob; and its influence on its individual members need not work in one direction only—that of simplifying or even coarsening their responses. In becoming a part of an audience a person need in fact lose nothing of his humanity; he may indeed have his sympathies enlarged if, as may happen, the mood of an audience is one of expansive geniality. A theatre audience is a *charmed* crowd: not only free of the mob's capacity for anarchic violence, but held in partnership by those on stage in an act of creative co-operation. The audience can, moreover, initiate its own positive contribution: it is always capable, by mere weight of numbers, of ceremonializing the theatrical occasion; and, particularly if it fills the audience space, its presence can be a cause of excitement not only to the actors but to itself.

The audience is a mysteriously endowed thing, in some respects slow-witted, in others shrewdly self-possessed and hard to deceive; having what may seem a simpler mental equipment than an intelligent individual, but with different powers and susceptibilities and a different emotional range. It is not necessarily obtuse: it can be quick to detect falsity or uncertainty of tone as well as technical incompetence. And it is quite capable of appreciating

[1] Bacon's remark is quoted by George F. Reynolds, 'Literature for an Audience', *Studies in Philology*, 28 (1931). The remark in full runs: 'And certainly it is most true, and as it were, a secret of nature, *that the minds of men are more patent of affections, and impressions, Congregate, than solitary*' (*De Augmentis*, tr. Gilbert Watts (1640), p. 107).

subtle effects. But the subtlety needs to be clearly prepared in advance, since an audience has to be led into position so as to be able to take the point; it cannot be addressed with the abruptness or inconsequentiality with which one individual can speak to an-other in the privacy of informal conversation. All this is of obvious relevance to the formal concerns of the dramatist. Especially relevant to the matter of scenic organization is the audience's taste—its appetite—for large, exuberant, even broad, effects. The point can be made by recalling two different uses of the term *scene* itself. In ordinary life a person given to 'making scenes' is commonly felt to be an embarrassing nuisance, while a big scene in a play can give considerable pleasure: what is felt to be too big, too simple, or too rigid for private life is the right size and shape for a theatre audience.

It seems true to say that during a performance of a play something comes into being which can be called, quite unpretentiously, an 'audience mind'—something to which actors respond as to a single entity: the corporate presence in the auditorium. This corporate being is composed of everything which the individual spectators have mentally in common. It is indeed precisely the fact that an audience can only be addressed in terms of what its members share that accounts for the characteristic forms of drama: those patterns and structural devices, and in particular those large scenic units which are characteristic of Shakespeare in his most robust stage plays. It is by means of these that a dramatist first unifies his audience and then engages with it. Before the performance has begun, the spectators may be no more than a collection of disparate individuals, possibly complete strangers to each other, though likely to be members of the same society. Only during the course of the play does the 'audience mind' come into being, and it does so when the individual spectators are made to *recognize* what is recognizable to everyone present. In the course of an entire play the members of an audience will be made over and over again to affirm their consciousness of their shared knowledge in response to what the dramatist shows them.

The dramatist's materials are therefore from one point of view very limited and concrete: living actors moving about and speaking from within a space visible to the audience. But his concern is also with something much more abstract: he must devise forms, of a bold and even hypnotically arresting kind, which will draw an audience, without its necessarily being aware of it, into a state of lively concern or excitement, and all the while carrying forward the plot, advancing the fortunes of his characters, and calling into being the world of the action. So that, while the spectators are being absorbed into the visible and audible world of the play, they are also being exposed to the influence of patterns which, though themselves neither visible nor audible, are none the less powerfully coercive. These patterns are in fact the means whereby the action of the play is carried deep into the audience's mind. Without them the details of the action would be heard as coolly and with as little involvement as one reads the synopsis of an opera.

At this point we can look at a particular scene, one which demands to be played before an audience, and see how it makes its effect.

*   *   *

Titus Andronicus was probably Shakespeare's earliest tragedy. The play has been a good deal despised and disliked, although in recent years a few critics have argued for recognition of its impressive qualities, while the production in 1955 by Peter Brook was a major piece of theatrical resuscitation. There is no doubt that the play was a great stage success in Shakespeare's day, and this is one reason for discussing a scene from it here. The one I have chosen is the great exhibition of passion in the third act (III. i). The scene is a remarkable one, although a reader may well be put off by its horrible physical circumstances, and it is probably true to say that it is greater in conception than execution. Moreover it needs great acting to bring out its full impact. But it is well worth considering as an example of what the dramatist can do to bring about a profound emotional experience in his audience.

What we see is the hero meeting a crushing series of misfortunes. Two of Titus' sons have been accused, wrongfully, of the murder of Bassianus and condemned to death, and the scene opens with a procession: '*Enter the Judges and Senators with Titus' two sons bound, passing on the stage to the place of execution, and Titus going before, pleading*'. Titus' pleading goes unheard: he is no longer the irascible warrior of the first act but an ageing father, vulnerable and weak. The second stage direction reads: '*Andronicus lieth down and the Judges pass by him*'; he is now literally a picture

of abject misery. He continues to appeal to the Judges and Senators even after they have gone, nor does he notice the entry of his
last remaining son brandishing a sword: Lucius has been banished
for trying to rescue his brothers. Titus' great passion scene now
properly begins.

The scene is carefully built in stages: a sequence of steps rising
to the climax. His brother Marcus brings to him Titus' daughter
Lavinia, hideously mutilated, and mute, and a passage of horrified
outcry and lament follows. Aaron the Moor now appears, and
tells Titus that if he consents to lose a hand and send it to the
Emperor the lives of his two condemned sons will be spared.
Titus tricks Marcus and Lucius so that they leave him for a
moment with Aaron, and his hand is severed. The brief episode
that follows seems to reach a climax of pain and misery—but that
is the point: it is *not* the climax, there is worse to follow. A messenger brings back the heads of Titus' two sons together with
his own severed hand. Now comes the climax. Titus has no tears
left, no more feeling or words. He bursts into a fit of laughter.
This is the turning-point of the scene and of the entire play: his
passion is over, and he now prepares himself for action. Titus
and the others swear a solemn vow of revenge and, finally, left
alone, Lucius announces his departure from Rome for the Goths.

The development of this scene could be described in various
figurative ways, but what is essential to it is the idea of tension
being increased to an almost intolerable point—the moment when
Titus bursts into laughter. The tension is then quickly lost, and
shortly after the scene closes. What is remarkable is the way tension is maintained through a long scene, and not only maintained
but increased; the dramatist's control over his audience is never
lost. In part this control is due to the author's training in rhetoric,
but part must also come from the actor Shakespeare's feeling for
audience response: in such a way we can try to account for his
ability to discriminate between degrees of misery, and for the
different but related ability to distribute climaxes in such a way
that the audience is not exhausted too soon—between every wave
is placed a trough, an interval, during which one can take breath
and relax. For although there is one major climax—Titus' laugh
—the scene proceeds through a number of clearly marked phases,
each of which has its high point which is then followed by a brief
lull. In this tensely controlled but undulating way the entire scene

moves through five or six actions: Titus' pleading with the judges; his exchange with Lucius; their reception of Marcus with Lavinia; Aaron's appearance, and the business leading up to the severing of Titus' hand; the messenger's appearance; the drying up of Titus' grief and its conversion into a will for revenge. Each of these actions is fairly short, and the longest of them, such as Titus' reception of Lavinia and his laments, are set out in highly formal rhetorical schemes. Titus' grief here, for example, is expressed in several brief exchanges with Marcus and Lucius and in three long speeches, each of which develops an elaborate image-pattern. There is no wandering or inconsequentiality; each unit of action has its own form which actors must be in possession of if they are to play the scene with the right tempo.

This last point is important. If the dramatist wants to develop, as he does here, a massively orchestrated movement, he must do it through carefully gradated stages, small units of action. Only in this way can he carry an audience with him, by degrees, up to the main climax of feeling. And once he has reached that point he must let it go; the audience must be given relief and allowed a brief interval of disengagement.

When the scene is acted, it seems to flow with an unpremeditated naturalness. Things seem to happen in this order for no particular reason. In reality, of course, the whole movement is deliberately planned so that everything occurs in the order best suited to the emotional effect. It is a long scene (300 lines); when the text is examined, it can be seen to fall into two equal parts. In the first part Titus laments, first, his two sons' condemnation to death; then the banishment of Lucius; thirdly, the rape and mutilation of Lavinia. In keeping with Shakespeare's usual method, these three actions are of very unequal weight and duration: the second is the briefest, the third by far the longest. The fully extended lamentations for Lavinia (66–149) mark the climax—a sort of high plateau—for this first part of the scene. The second part is opened with the appearance of Aaron (this is his first meeting with Titus), whose first line has a formality in keeping with the inauguration of a new phase:

Titus Andronicus, my lord the Emperor . . .

This is at line 150; we are half-way through the scene. For, although we may think we have reached a conclusion, this is in

fact only a half-way point; there is yet worse to follow. Before
Aaron appeared, the family group—Titus, Marcus, Lucius, and
Lavinia—had achieved a kind of stillness in misery. But with
Aaron's announcement the group is suddenly divided by a conflict in generosity: all three men strive to be the one who shall
sacrifice a hand. Shortly after Aaron's departure, the messenger's
appearance drives the action into its final phase, with grief yielding
to a fierce, and in the event insane, vengefulness. So the first part
of the scene (1–149) is marked by passive suffering and articulate
lament; the second (150–300) by violent and grotesque activity,
with a growing sense of the uselessness of words as well as of a
horrifying meaninglessness in the entire situation. In this way we
are prepared, well in advance, for the end of the road with Titus'
hysterical fit of laughter. (It is a laughter that acknowledges the
real element of farce which, prompted by Aaron's devilish detachment, one has already glimpsed out of the corner of one's eye.)

   Much of the scene's effectiveness is within the reach of an
imaginative reader's powers of re-creation. But one may doubt
whether even an exceptionally sensitive reader could realize the
force of some of the effects which performance will bring to life.
One of these is Shakespeare's use of the tongueless Lavinia.
Titus Andronicus is a play of strong and often fluent rhetoric. It
will certainly sometimes strike us as being altogether too fluent,
too verbose—the words come too easily. And yet at the centre
of this rhetorically sonorous play there is *silence*. Perhaps only in
performance can one judge the extraordinary impact of a character
who has been robbed of the power of speech. Lavinia's silence
helps to intensify to an almost intolerable pitch the emotion
generated by the situation—by suggesting that there is a limit,
quickly reached, to what words can do. The Senecan tag, so often
quoted in the sixteenth century, was no doubt felt to be relevant
here: 'Curae leves loquuntur, ingentes stupent.' So, later in this
scene, Titus is himself bereft of words. When the heads of his
sons are brought before him he is at first speechless, and then
says only

> When will this fearful slumber have an end?

After this, the spell is broken only when he bursts into laughter.
Such a use of silence is entirely of the theatre; its power is something a reader alone with the text will hardly give due value to.

The presence on stage of Marcus, Titus' brother, has a different kind of importance, but is one which, similarly, will only be fully realized in a performance. When Titus rages or yields himself up to grief, Marcus counsels restraint ('O, brother, speak with possibility, / And do not break into these deep extremes'; 'But yet let reason govern thy lament'). But at the climax of the scene, when Titus falls silent, Marcus urges him to give voice to his feelings: 'Now is a time to storm; why art thou still?' His role here is in part structural: he is always pulling in the opposite direction from Titus. In doing so he fulfils an important technical function: he helps to give definition to Titus' emotion, pulling what otherwise might be shapeless into shape. Without Marcus there would be a real danger that the more emotional passages might collapse into rant.

In this scene we have a very early specimen of Shakespeare's work. Yet even here Shakespeare shows himself to be a master of dramatic construction, an art which has nothing necessarily to do with such matters as the three unities of neo-classical critical theory. What is important is that he already had an unusually penetrating understanding of the psychology of a theatre audience and could arrange his materials in such a way as to produce a certain desired effect on that audience. A scene like this shows that he was already a formidably confident technician of the emotions, already possessing at least the rudiments of what Johnson called his 'knowledge of the passions'. I have not so far mentioned some of the touches which, despite its gruesome and repellent atrocities, make the scene so characteristic of Shakespeare. At its grimmest moment, the Messenger appears carrying the heads of the two sons and Titus' severed hand. But the Messenger's words are unexpectedly gentle and sympathetic. He concludes his speech:

> Thy grief their sports, thy resolution mock'd,
> That woe is me to think upon thy woes,
> More than remembrance of my father's death.

The Messenger is himself moved, and is prompted to a sense of *pietas*—he thinks of his own father. Marcus and Lucius cry out in horror, and a wordless action follows: '*Lavinia kisses Titus*'.

These moments of natural feeling suggest a final comment on this scene. This is that throughout it, as throughout the play, we are continually referred to a quality of normality in human nature.

We are made to *recognize*—acknowledge that we share—the humanity of the persons before us. The unnatural and at times almost diabolically cruel and malicious actions are measured against a standard of normal conduct and natural feeling. Everything that happens is made emotionally intelligible, so that by being kept in touch with natural feeling we also keep a sense of proportion and significance. This feeling for measure and proportion is of the utmost importance for Shakespeare's achievement as a dramatist (in this scene it is present, for example, in his use of Marcus). It is equally a sign of his human responsibility as an artist and of his sure structural grasp as a craftsman. This is one of those innumerable places in Shakespeare where, in examining the structure of his work, we are given an insight into its essential substance, since measure and proportion are as much attributes of the substance and meaning of his plays as of their structure.

II

If we look back for a moment to the scene just discussed, we can hardly fail to be struck by the bold simplicity of its shape. Titus is on stage almost throughout: he is the focus of consciousness and suffering. The actor playing Titus *carries* the entire sequence, and only a heroic actor is capable of such a feat. The scene opens on a high pitch, with Titus' pleading with the judges and his prostration of himself on the stage, but the intensity so soon established is not only maintained but increased to what in a powerful performance may seem like an unbearable extremity. Nothing is allowed to distract from the single-minded onward progression of the scene's movement (its continuousness is essential to the effect). The basic elements of this movement are, simply, repetition and accumulation. Titus is—as he himself says in one of his longer speeches—like 'one upon a rock' surrounded by the sea and lashed by an endless succession of waves. The process continues until something in him collapses and he becomes changed. This grandly simple design gives the scene its shape—this is how it comes across—and no one watching it performed can possibly miss its import.

Shakespeare's big scenes are usually founded on such powerfully simple devices as this. And the power exerted by such scenes is closely related to their simplicity. But the simplicity we are dealing with is of a special kind: it has nothing to do with banality or commonplaceness; it is much more like the densely suggestive simplicity of myth or legend. Indeed some of the greatest of Shakespeare's scenes do have something of the immemorial authenticity of myths—they seem hardly to have issued from the mind of one individual but to have been handed down in some ancient oral tradition. The banquet scene in *Macbeth* has an uncanny inevitability about it. Macbeth regrets the absence of Banquo from his feast, and turns to find him, or what seems him, sitting in his place. A second time he tempts fate; again he turns to find his place filled by Banquo's horrible blood-stained form. Crucial to the scene is its element of compulsive hypnotically predictable repetition, which is of a kind especially fitted to rouse an audience. It seems unlikely that a solitary reader of the text will respond to it to anything like the same degree, for the device underlying the scene can exert its full power only in the presence of large numbers.

Another powerful device used by Shakespeare is a pattern of human transformation from one polar extreme to the other. He will show a character being converted in point of view or opinion. Once the process of conversion has begun it continues before the eyes of the audience until it is complete: the protagonist moves with a satisfying clarity and completeness through 180 degrees. If he formerly loved he now hates, and if he formerly trusted he now not merely suspects but *knows* that what he formerly trusted was false. Othello of course exemplifies this best, and the scene of his transformation—the temptation scene—is, even for Shakespeare, a particularly grand example of scenic construction. The Forum scene in *Julius Caesar*, which may have been one of Shakespeare's immediate models for the temptation scene, similarly moves through a great arc, as Antony begins to work on the credulous plebeians so that they too, like Othello, end up in a position completely different from—indeed opposite to—the one they started in. These tragic scenes of conversion or persuasion are matched by the duping scenes of the comedies, as when Benedick in the arbour is surprised into eavesdropping on his friends, or when Malvolio is tricked by the forged letter. When such scenes are read, they may seem almost childishly obvious; the verbal wit can be appreciated, but the over-all drive of the scene is something to be intellectually assented to rather than felt—on the page it seems too loud, too insistently emphatic. But, like the figures in a ceiling painting which when seen in close-up appear crudely distorted, such scenes come into focus to release their energy when watched by a large audience; the presence of large numbers of spectators provides the psychic distancing.

The fourth act of *Richard II* is an ambitious example of another variety of big scene, the ensemble-scene, in which a massive effect is obtained by the presence on stage of a large number of actors, several of whom have prominent speaking parts. But the structure of the scene is quite unlike the passion scene of *Titus Andronicus*. Whereas Titus was on stage throughout the scene, leaving only just before the end, Richard is given a carefully delayed entry. The scene opens with a short episode involving angry petty squabbling: the quarrel between Aumerle and Fitzwater; which is followed by the excited throwing down of the gauntlets. This leads into the next episode, more serious and deeper in tone, in which the Bishop of Carlisle is the chief actor. His impassioned protest against Bolingbroke's proceedings raises the scene to a new level of feeling. Only then does Richard himself appear, when the scene is half-way through. The trial scene in *The Merchant of Venice*, also placed in the fourth act, is apparently modelled on the scene of Richard II's deposition. It too starts with short episodes of bickering and altercation which grow in vehemence, and, like Richard II, Portia makes a late appearance. The effect in both scenes is that Richard II and Portia appear just before the crest of the wave: they inherit the excitement worked up in the preceding episodes, and they dominate their scenes by riding the climax. In each case there follows a quick drop into low tension, and a short exchange follows of no great formal interest. The church scene in *Much Ado About Nothing*, also in the fourth act, seems to be a variant on the same basic model, but with interesting differences. We have nothing like the ground-swell of the former two, with gradually rising tension before the long-delayed appearance of the chief character. Instead we have a steep ascent within the first five lines to what seems at first to be a climax:

> *Friar Francis.* You come hither, my lord, to marry this lady?
> *Claudio.* No.

This long scene (about 330 lines) *starts* with an abrupt shock, and it does so because Shakespeare does not want to engage the

sympathies of the audience, at least not to any depth. By presenting
Claudio's rejection of Hero in this baldly unprepared-for way at
the very beginning of the scene, he goes some way towards
nullifying its impact. Claudio's accusations, couched in strong
though facile rhetoric, are followed by his departure; Leonato's
distress slowly dies away before the counsel of Friar Francis; and
the sequence ends with the prose colloquy between Beatrice and
Benedick. What the scene as a whole shows is the gradual super-
vention of wholesome feelings over poisonous ones, and the true
climax comes, not at the beginning with Claudio's brittle 'No'
(this is a false climax), but at the end, with the *entente* between the
newly declared lovers.

I have been insisting on the powerful simplicity of these big
scenes, and on the element of predictability usually present in their
development. We must know, or we must quickly get to know,
what is going to happen, so that the proceedings can be invested
with their full dramatic value. And the dramatist can do that only
by creating expectancy—an informed interest in what is going to
happen next. However, not all Shakespeare's scenes are built on
such a grand scale. Many scenes, particularly in the history plays,
have the more prosaic function of conveying information to the
audience, or of reminding them of the essentials of a historical
situation. What is interesting about these potentially dull passages
is that they are cast into such lively scenic patterns that the information is absorbed with little or no effort. The effect is of
watching a game or a group-dance; and indeed the choreographic
analogy is very obvious. So at the opening of the *Henry VI,
Part One*, for example, the scene invented by Shakespeare bears
no close relation to anything that actually happened in history.
The funeral procession of Henry V enters, and a dialogue follows
in which there are four speakers: Bedford, Gloucester, Exeter, and
Winchester. If we designate these speakers as A, B, C, and D, the
order of their speeches in the first part of the scene (1–56) is as
follows: A, B, C, D, B, D, B, A. That is to say, Bedford is the
'leader', who opens and closes this exchange. Gloucester and
Winchester are the fractious members of the group whose
quarrelling threatens to disrupt the formality of the occasion.
Exeter, in accordance with his role as the loyal watch-dog of the
commonweal, has only one speech: he knows his place and keeps
it. Thus, even in this short passage, each of the four speakers is

given a clear role: the chief spokesman or leader, the two quarrel-
lers, and the honest man—just as in any closed social group
different social 'roles' will tend to be distributed among its members. The rest of this opening scene is taken up with the entries of
three messengers from France and their bad news. Their appearances are treated as part of a single movement, which is made
rhythmical by ensuring that what they have to say is very unequal
in length: the second messenger is the briefest, and the third by
far the longest, so that any suggestion of the mechanical is avoided
and a strong climax is arranged (that is, they do not merely follow
an order of increasing length). Finally, the four main speakers
leave the stage in turn: first Bedford; next Gloucester; next
Exeter; then Winchester—in the same order as that in which they
initially spoke. If the actors are suitably arranged on the stage,
their relationships with each other together with the information
they are conveying about their situation can be rhythmically im-
parted to the audience with something of the ease and rapidity of
a rank of soldiers 'numbering off'. The patterns set going make
for easy comprehension, like a well-constructed sentence. The
comparable opening scene of *Henry VI, Part Two* is a larger
ensemble-scene: ten characters enter together at the opening and
all of them speak in the course of the scene, but after Margaret
has been formally received by the King they leave the stage at
intervals in threes, in pairs, or alone. The effect is of a large mass
dwindling to a point, since finally only York is left on stage. Again
the members of the group are differentiated, and hence characterized (since character is difference), with great speed, the secret
being in the use of repetition with rhythmical emphasis. We are
put in possession of a complicated situation with effortless ease.

  In such scenes as these we can observe Shakespeare's versatility
in the art of getting actors on and off the stage. He varies the process to make it interesting, so that the marchings to and fro which
take up a good deal of the *Henry VI* plays have an inventiveness
in them which shows a delight in the very mechanics of stage-
business. This delight can be felt in a brief scene (I. iii) in a later
history play, *Henry IV, Part Two*; it might easily be dismissed as
dull and flat, a mere necessary introduction to the historical
action, but this would be unjust. It is certainly a subdued piece
of writing, but designedly so, since coming between two of
Falstaff's scenes it furnishes contrast. Slight though it is, the scene

has its artistry. There are four speakers: the Archbishop of York, Mowbray, Hastings, and Lord Bardolph. If we call them A, B, C, and D, the order of their speeches for the entire scene is as follows: A, B, C, D, C, D, A; D, C, D, C, D, C, A; C, D, C, A; B, C. In this quartet the Archbishop is the 'leader'; Hastings and Bardolph carry the main burden of the argument; while Mowbray has only two speeches (the second in the scene and the last but one). The Archbishop's structural role is mainly to 'punctuate' the argument, so helping to mark off its stages, while Hastings and Bardolph oppose each other in argument. But the scene, although so brief, has a further principle of organization. Most of the speeches in this dialogue are short, but Bardolph's reasoned argument for caution is given fuller expression in a speech of over twenty lines (36–62). And towards the end of the scene the Archbishop's much more emotional plea for rebellion is similarly extended (85–108). These two long speeches are in fact the poles of the scene, the first arguing for caution, the second making a rhetorical appeal for what is in effect recklessness. The second wins. In short scenes which have no medial entries or departures and whose fundamental structure is therefore very simple, Shakespeare often uses this method of giving the dialogue rhythm and emphasis according to the order of the speeches. (Other examples are *Henry V*, III.v, and *Macbeth*, I. iii, I. iv.)

* * *

I want finally in this section to take a close look at another extended scene, but one very different from the passion scene of *Titus Andronicus* which I discussed earlier, and in some ways more like the brief expository scenes I have just been describing. This is the second scene of *Julius Caesar*. It has a further interest in that its historical basis in Plutarch allows us to inspect Shakespeare's way of converting his source materials into the clear, exuberant forms of drama. What I want to bring out is, once more, the scene's formal energy, its powers of enactment.

This scene introduces the main characters of the play: Caesar, Antony, Brutus, Cassius, and others. Caesar's procession pauses while he instructs Calpurnia to stand in Antony's way when he runs in the Lupercal. The Soothsayer warns Caesar of the Ides of March, and the procession passes across the stage, leaving Brutus and Cassius alone together. Cassius begins his long temptation of Brutus, while from the Forum, off stage, come the shouts of the people. Caesar's procession then returns across the stage, allowing time only for Caesar to comment on Cassius. Brutus plucks Casca out of Caesar's train; Casca gives his 'blunt' account of the events in the Forum; and finally, Cassius, left alone, plans the next stage in his seduction of Brutus to the conspiracy.

The scene communicates a good deal of information, about Caesar, Cassius, Brutus, and Antony, and their relationships with each other, about the political situation of Rome which is the play's starting-point, and about the direction in which the main action is going to move. And all this information is conveyed to us so easily and quickly that the play is well under way before we realize that Shakespeare has solved, or evaded, the usual problem of exposition. For the scene does much more than communicate information. It is also successful drama: a mechanism so contrived as to arouse interest and excitement. The main business of the scene, Cassius' highly rhetorical tempting of Brutus, is itself of a nature to arouse a high degree of concern and even anxiety. The occasion of Cassius' speeches is clandestine, their substance illicit and subversive. The two men have detached themselves from Caesar's train; and this in itself, this act of deliberate secession—opting out from what everyone else is doing—is a way of making visible on the stage the play's concern with public and private behaviour, and particularly with private behaviour that needs to be kept secret. Throughout Cassius' colloquy with Brutus we are kept uneasily and expectantly conscious of the goings-on off stage in the Forum through the shouts of the people and Brutus' anxious comments. With Brutus, we are kept in ignorance until Casca is in turn detached from Caesar's train and made to tell what happened. So the whole scene is punctuated by the two appearances of Caesar's procession, going to and returning from the Forum, and both its appearances help to establish an important part of the play's area of discourse—the public and private realms of conduct, the poles represented by Caesar the dictator and Cassius the arch-conspirator. And the fact that we, the audience, are detained with the private pair, Brutus and Cassius, rather than made to accompany Caesar's train, gives a strong sense of complicity. We are in the secret; we are one with the plotters.

There is something further to be said about the formal nature of this scene. Shakespeare's intensely theatrical imagination has invented the off-stage voices of the plebeians. They are used very economically: they are heard only twice, but this is enough to suggest a whole series, and their effect within the scene is far-reaching. In the first place, they help to establish a sense of the physical reality of the world of the play. The Rome of *Julius Caesar* is not evoked in much physical detail, but it convincingly extends beyond the stage space. We are made to feel that when Caesar and his train leave the stage they do not enter a void but, so to speak, go round a corner into the next street.[1] Secondly, the shouts make us aware of an action going on concurrently with the action on stage, and this also makes for imaginative solidity and for a stimulating suggestion of perspective. We are induced to imagine the actions of Caesar and Antony when they are no longer in front of us, so that we, with Brutus, strain to interpret the shouts and, later in the scene, the changed looks of the people in Caesar's train. Finally, the shouts are very much a part of the play's distinctive atmosphere: not only in the fact that the play makes notable use of its vociferous mob, but—a more elusively poetic matter— in its chilly spaces and its oddly disturbing long-distance acoustic effects (in her agitation before the killing of Caesar, Portia is to hear 'a bustling rumour, like a fray, / And the wind brings it from the Capitol'). This scene of two men exchanging dangerous confidences and interrupted by the distant shouts of the powerful mob forms a memorable and beautiful stage-picture—or rather a stage experience involving hearing as well as sight. It works imaginatively as a brilliant condensation of the entire dramatic action of *Julius Caesar* as Shakespeare has re-created it from Plutarch.

A glance at Shakespeare's sources for this scene in Plutarch's *Lives* shows how radically he transformed them. A number of stray remarks and observations in Plutarch came together in Shakespeare's mind, but the main sources are a paragraph in *The Life of Julius Caesar* which describes the Lupercalia and Antony's offer of the crown to Caesar,[2] and two passages in *The Life of Marcus Brutus*, of which the first is as follows:

But Cassius being a choleric man and hating Caesar privately, more than he did the tyranny openly, he incensed Brutus against him. It is

---

[1] Cf. *Julius Caesar*, III. ii. 3–4, where Brutus sends Cassius away with part of the crowd: 'Cassius, go you into the other street, / And part the numbers'.

[2] *Shakespeare's Plutarch* (Penguin Books, Harmondsworth, 1964), ed. T. J. B. Spencer, pp. 82–3.

also reported that Brutus could evil away with the tyranny, and that Cassius hated the tyrant, making many complaints for the injuries he had done him . . .[1]

The second passage is longer. It recounts a conversation between Brutus and Cassius after Cassius has been urged by his friends to persuade Brutus to join and lead their conspiracy:

Therefore Cassius, considering this matter with himself, did first of all speak to Brutus since they grew strange together for the suit they had for the Praetorship. So when he was reconciled to him again, and that they had embraced one another, Cassius asked him if he were determined to be in the Senate-house the first day of the month of March, because he heard say that Caesar's friends should move the council that day that Caesar should be called King by the Senate. Brutus answered him, he would not be there.

'But if we be sent for', said Cassius, 'how then?'

'For myself then', said Brutus, 'I mean not to hold my peace, but to withstand it, and rather die than lose my liberty'.

Cassius being bold, and taking hold of this word,

'Why', quoth he, 'what Roman is he alive that will suffer thee to die for the liberty? What, knowest thou not that thou art Brutus? Thinkest thou that they be cobblers, tapsters, or suchlike base mechanical people, that write these bills and scrolls which are found daily in the Praetor's chair, and not the noblest men and best citizens that do it? . . .'[2]

Possibly the sentence here—'Brutus answered him, he would not be there'—suggested to Shakespeare the idea of having Brutus and Cassius detach themselves from Caesar's train, so forming the germ of the scene. But otherwise, apart from supplying narrative material, Plutarch can have given him no guidance as to how to dispose the scene as a whole. Before the scene as we have it could come into being, Shakespeare needed to have a formal idea which would make the best of Plutarch's admirable but—from the dramatist's point of view—somewhat amorphous material.

Shakespeare probably had other 'sources' for his scene than the regularly cited Plutarch. One of my purposes in this study is to suggest (as I do in Chapter 4 and in the later chapters on single plays) that we often think too narrowly of 'sources' in terms of narrative substance, ignoring or neglecting the whole question of *structural* debts. A structural model for this scene may have come, I suggest, from a play which Shakespeare must have read or seen

[1] Ibid., p. 109.   [2] Ibid., pp. 111–13.

acted or may even have acted in himself. This was Greene's *James the Fourth*, and the scene in question the first of the first act. (*James the Fourth* was printed in 1598, in time for Shakespeare to renew his acquaintance with it for *Julius Caesar*, which was probably written in 1599.) This scene, like the one in *Julius Caesar*, shows considerable dexterity in handling a number of important characters and in getting the plot moving. The Scottish King, James IV, has just taken as his bride Dorothea, the daughter of the King of England. The scene is set for a ceremonious courtly occasion, as Greene's stage direction makes clear: '*Enter the King of England, the King of Scots*, Dorithe *his Queen, the Countesse, Lady* Ida, *with other Lords; and* Ateukin *with them aloofe*'.[1] First, Dorothea is crowned Queen of Scotland. Then the King of England takes his leave, and is accompanied to the harbour by Dorothea. The stage direction reads: '*Exeunt all save the King, the Countesse*, Ida, Ateukin, *in all royaltie*'. In a soliloquy James broods on his newly conceived love for Ida, the daughter of the Countess of Arran. After he has exchanged a few words with Ida, Dorothea returns: '*Enters the traine backe*'. A brief distracted exchange between James and his wife follows; then '*Exeunt all saving the King, and* Ateukin'. The villainous Ateukin, who has been silent until now, has been observing the King closely, and now offers his services. He undertakes to dispose of Dorothea and help the King to his new love.

If we abstract their totally different narrative circumstances from these two scenes and consider them as far as possible simply as dramatic structures, their resemblances will become apparent. What Shakespeare must have remembered (if Greene's scene was in fact his structural model) was the spectacular departure and return of the 'train'. The stage is first filled with splendidly dressed persons, is emptied except for the key characters, is filled a second time, and again emptied—except for the King and his villainous tempter. These movements repeated in this way set going a rhythm which greatly assists the dramatist in his task of getting the action moving while at the same time engaging the attention of the audience. The scene is in its way a skilful piece of work, and Shakespeare must have been struck by it so as to remember it, whether consciously or not, when he was working out the prob-

[1] Quotations are from *Plays & Poems of Robert Greene*, ed. J. Churton Collins (Oxford, 1905).

lem of getting the main action of *Julius Caesar* under way. In any
case the moral concerns of Greene's scene and Shakespeare's are
not unlike: in both scenes, between the two appearances of the
train, the hero undergoes the first stages of a temptation to
crime.[1]

The point I want to establish here is that, when converting his
source materials into scenic form, the dramatist must already
possess at least the rudiments of a dramatic vocabulary, a reper-
tory of expressive figures and devices which can be used in new
combinations according to his needs. Each of these scenic paradigms can act as a matrix for the new narrative material, just as
here Greene's Scottish and English court processions are given a
new life in the Roman dress of Caesar's train. Of course Shakespeare improves on Greene. His use of Caesar's train is much more
expressive than Greene's merely spectacular effect. Caesar's train
is made to seem an embodiment of the rule of the dictator, so that
it looks dangerous for Brutus and Cassius to remove themselves
from it for a private confabulation. And the use of the off-stage
shouts has already been discussed: Caesar's train has an off-stage
existence which Dorothea's does not. Still, Shakespeare owed
something to Greene—or whoever it was (if it was not Greene)
who first introduced this particular form to the Elizabethan stage.
As we shall see, he returned to it when he came to write *Othello*.

III

The scene just discussed from *Julius Caesar* is notable for the
degree to which it unfolds in terms of the stage space. It says what
it needs through the lineaments of the stage, through the movements to and fro of the actors, and the suggestion of action beyond
the stage's visible confines. The scene serves to show that drama
can unfold or extend in space and that the form of a good scene
may be almost visually perceived in terms of pattern and design.
But drama moves in time as well as space, and a description of the
scenic needs to take account of this temporal dimension. In this

[1] In another play of Greene's, *Alphonsus, King of Arragon* (printed 1599), occurs the
following: 'With such a traine as *Iulius Caesar* came / To noble *Rome*, when as he had
achieu'd / The mightie Monarch of the triple world' (I. i. 164–6). It may be that the
idea of Caesar's train as expressed here fused with the scene of Dorothea's train to
produce the basic form of I. ii. of *Julius Caesar*. Or possibly Greene is alluding to
another Julius Caesar play now lost.

last section I shall consider such time-conditioned qualities as rhythm and tempo.[1]

I remarked earlier that one inescapably obvious element in the theatrical situation was the passage of time. The audience waits for something to happen, and time passes. At a performance of any play we are *in attendance* (something which Samuel Beckett has in mind for the entire duration of *En attendant Godot*); and our expectation, together with the two or three hours which we have agreed to place at his disposal, are the dramatist's great opportunity. He must dispose his material with a view to exploiting our sense of expectation while we move through a more or less agreed period of time.

I want first to look at a very familiar scene which has to a marked degree the power to rouse an audience to excitement. This is the letter scene (II. v) from *Twelfth Night*. In it Malvolio discovers the letter supposedly written by Olivia which has in fact been planted on his path by Sir Toby and the rest.

Before the scene has even begun our expectations have been raised, and to a large extent we know what sort of thing is going to happen. In II. iii Maria had said: 'I will drop in his way some obscure epistles of love. . . . I can write very like my lady, your niece; on a forgotten matter we can hardly make distinction of our hands.' Sir Toby had replied: 'Excellent! I smell a device.' The scene itself is severely economical and purposefully shaped; as soon as it gets going the nature of the 'device' becomes obvious. Sir Toby, Sir Andrew, and Fabian appear first. Then Maria runs in to announce the approach of Malvolio, and runs out again. And Malvolio appears. The main business of the scene follows. Malvolio muses aloud, and in doing so discloses his ambition and his matrimonial designs on Olivia. He then notices the letter. He recognizes the handwriting. He interprets the rhyming riddle, and applies the letters MOAI to himself. He reads the main part of the letter. He is overjoyed at its import, and decides to obey its instructions. He then, and only then, notices a postscript. He reads it, and finally hurries away, crying: 'Jove, I thank thee. I will smile: I will do everything that thou wilt have me.' The three dupers emerge from their hiding-place, and are joined by Maria before they leave the stage.

[1] Cf. J. L. Styan, *Shakespeare's Stagecraft* (London, 1967), pp. 190–9. My section was written independently of his remarks on pace and tempo.

Like the other scenes which make a sharp impact in performance this one communicates a strong sense of shape; indeed we can visualize it in almost symmetrical terms. First the three dupers enter; then, briefly, Maria; lastly Malvolio. The main business of the scene follows. Malvolio leaves the stage to the dupers again, who are again joined by Maria, before they too leave. Such a sequence organizes a kind of dramatic space. We approach it, we enter it, and we emerge from it. Or we can see it as a pyramid: the dupers are on stage throughout, and Malvolio comes on and goes off, leaving them still there. Just before he comes and just after he goes, Maria appears. Shakespeare seems to use her to demarcate the central dramatic space formed by the scene. Without her two brief appearances the scene would feel less elegant a shape in our minds.

But the main observation I want to make about this scene concerns not spatial properties but temporal: the nature of its movement. For in performance a certain tempo is established akin to that maintained in an orchestra by the conductor's beat. The tempo of the scene is set by the utterances of Malvolio: slow, luxuriously indulged, fastidiously phrased. Some of his remarks form a single sentence, punctuated by pauses during which Sir Toby and the others *insert* their indignant comments. A long passage must be quoted to bring out the effect.

> *Fabian.* O, peace! Contemplation makes a rare turkey-cock of him; how he jets under his advanc'd plumes!
>
> *Sir Andrew.* 'Slight, I could so beat the rogue—
>
> *Sir Toby.* Peace, I say.
>
> *Malvolio.* To be Count Malvolio!
>
> *Sir Toby.* Ah, rogue!
>
> *Sir Andrew.* Pistol him, pistol him.
>
> *Sir Toby.* Peace, peace!
>
> *Malvolio.* There is example for't: the Lady of the Strachy married the yeoman of the wardrobe.
>
> *Sir Andrew.* Fie on him, Jezebel!
>
> *Fabian.* O, peace! Now he's deeply in; look how imagination blows him.
>
> *Malvolio.* Having been three months married to her, sitting in my state—
>
> *Sir Toby.* O, for a stone-bow to hit him in the eye!
>
> *Malvolio.* Calling my officers about me, in my branch'd velvet gown, having come from a day-bed—where I have left Olivia sleeping—

Sir Toby. Fire and brimstone!

Fabian. O, peace, peace!

Malvolio. And then to have the humour of state; and after a demure travel of regard, telling them I know my place as I would they should do theirs, to ask for my kinsman Toby—

Sir Toby. Bolts and shackles!

Fabian. O, peace, peace, peace! Now, now.

Malvolio. Seven of my people, with an obedient start, make out for him. I frown the while, and perchance wind up my watch, or play with my—some rich jewel. Toby approaches; curtsies there to me—

Sir Toby. Shall this fellow live?

Fabian. Though our silence be drawn from us with cars, yet peace.

Malvolio. I extend my hand to him thus, quenching my familiar smile with an austere regard of control—

Sir Toby. And does not Toby take you a blow o' the lips then?

Malvolio. Saying 'Cousin Toby, my fortunes having cast me on your niece give me this prerogative of speech'—

Sir Toby. What what?

Malvolio. 'You must amend your drunkenness'—

Sir Toby. Out, scab!

Fabian. Nay, patience, or we break the sinews of our plot.

Malvolio. 'Besides, you waste the treasure of your time with a foolish knight'—

Sir Andrew. That's me, I warrant you.

Malvolio. 'One Sir Andrew.'

Sir Andrew. I knew 'twas I; for many do call me fool.

(II. v. 28–75)

As far as Malvolio's part in it is concerned, this is a single speech, one which binds the whole of this passage together, giving it a tight elasticity which is reflected in Fabian's remark: 'Nay, patience, or we break the sinews of our plot.' The whole passage is strong in syntactical *sinews*—it has the tenseness of a spring. What we cannot fail to notice is an absurdly comic rhythm set going by the two sets of speakers: the slow measured pace of the 'turkey-cock' Malvolio, with his exquisite self-cosseting phrases, and, very different from it, the abrupt scuffling interjections of the concealed spectators, who supply a kind of comic bassoon accompaniment to Malvolio's unctuous 'cello. Each movement defines the other, and once set going the scene proceeds with a regard for timing musical in its strictness. It proceeds gradually—indeed with a positive show of gradualness, as if this were one of the rules of the game. Nothing is allowed to be rushed. When he finds the letter—'What employment have we here?'—Malvolio works forward, with a kind of leisurely, systematic thoroughness, first to the handwriting, then to Olivia's seal, then to the riddle, then to the contents of the letter itself, after that to his excited comments, and lastly to the postscript. In performance much of the rousing effect of the scene is due to this tantalizing rhythmically pausing progression. The dramatist seems to resist our crude inclination to rush it; he maintains—he enforces—a steady imperturbable pace.

Of course, like all eavesdropping scenes on the stage, this one infallibly arouses anxiety in the audience. Whether we like it or not, we are made accomplices. We suffer a comic agony when, for instance, Malvolio, hearing a sound, turns round and (as he has done in some productions) stares right at Sir Andrew without seeing him. Presumably our anxiety arises from the fact that such scenes create an uncomfortable division in our minds: we are identified with both the dupers and their victim, so that one part of us knows what the other part must not be allowed to know. When such scenes come to an end—when the victim leaves the stage as Malvolio does here, or when the concealed persons are discovered (as in the great duping scene in *All's Well that Ends Well* or in the screen scene in Sheridan's *School for Scandal*)—the sense of relief is correspondingly great: the conflict being staged in our minds gives way to a relaxing sense of wholeness.

What is interesting about this scene is its power to grip an audience. It uses the most tyrannical way of arresting our attention—telling us what is going to happen, and then making us wait for it. And when at last it comes, it exceeds expectation. But along with the element of predictability, the rhythmically pausing movement is essential to the scene's effect. We are tantalized and at the same time excited, amused but also agitated; and as likely as not, if the performance has been at all adequate, the audience will applaud Malvolio on his exit, quite as much as a way of discharging its nervous energy as of congratulating the actor. Such a scene makes a self-contained unit in itself, like a whole play in little—only more intense than a full-length play could ever be. No audience could endure such tension for two or three hours, and accordingly the letter scene is followed by a dialogue of little formal interest and low tension, which allows a short interval of respite.

A process of this kind—engagement followed by withdrawal, tension by relief—goes on throughout any successful stage play; but Shakespeare is particularly skilful (as an experienced actor would be) in knowing how far an audience can go in power of attention and when it must be given the chance to relax. His big scenes, like the one just discussed, are those parts of his plays which arouse most tension, and they seldom if ever last longer than about fifteen minutes. In his best stage plays the audience will be worked up and relaxed, starved and fed, over and over again. And such common conventions as disguise, mistaken identity, sustained hypocrisy (like Iago's), and such devices as the play-within-a-play, are infallible means of arousing a keen audience appetite and an anxiety which may sometimes be so fierce as almost to cease being pleasurable.

Shakespeare's concern with tempo is something he shares with any competent dramatist; but it is worth insisting on its importance. To a remarkable degree, his best plays bear repeated production; they can be seen repeatedly by the same playgoer. A comparison can be drawn with works of music, whether of concert hall or opera house, for there is something more than superficially 'musical' about such resilient theatrical works as *Richard III*, *Romeo and Juliet*, *The Merchant of Venice*, and *Hamlet*. When we see them performed what we enjoy is, in part, the process of 'going through' the work, taking pleasure in its texture and structure in a way which critical accounts which limit themselves to interpretation can hardly do justice to. This capacity for repeatedly enjoying the plays in performance comes out, for example, in the way we laugh at jokes (such as the grave-digger's in *Hamlet*) which when read in solitude can seem merely feeble. What makes them laughable in a theatre is their context in a shared communal activity; we laugh partly because we are psychologically induced to do so, just as we experience nervous tension in eavesdropping scenes despite our intellectual awareness of what is coming next in the plot. When the joke comes it feels new; it is in fact made new by being part of a new performance.

There is of course a strongly ritualistic element in theatrical performances. But it is not necessary to try to trace the origins of drama in religious ceremonies to account for this. Religious ceremonies and theatrical performances are cognate or parallel activities in that they make use of similar structural arrangements: both often exploit a predictably measured tempo. Malvolio's letter scene certainly makes an effect of comic ritual; it is as if a magic spell is being cast—'Nay, patience, or we break the sinews of our plot'—and in keeping with this we have the sense that nothing can be hastened or omitted, everything must be got right. Hence the unhurried, almost pedantic thoroughness of its mode of progression. But this scene is only one of many which are so designed as to dictate a certain tempo in their performance, with a consequent effect of ritualistic deliberation. The long scene in the last act of *Richard III* is a good example of this in a tragic style. It presents in one unbroken sequence the eve and morning of Bosworth. The tents of Richard and Richmond are raised on opposite sides of the stage; the leaders retire for the night, and one by one the ghosts of Richard's victims enter, first to curse Richard, then to bless Richmond: Prince Edward, King Henry VI, Clarence, then in a trio Rivers, Grey, and Vaughan, then Hastings, then the two princes murdered in the Tower, then Lady Anne, and finally Buckingham. What the particular ghosts actually say is of little moment; their words, highly conventionalized, have a ritual significance—conferring alternately ill will on Richard and good will on Richmond. But a steady, regular tempo is established by the appearance and disappearance of the eight separate parties, and their remorselessly imperturbable flow accumulates considerable power. In dramatic terms the scene is a convincing representation of the supernatural order: it comes across as a necessarily elaborate phase of denouement, a putting things right which had been awry and disordered. The result is that Richmond's victory at Bosworth can be imaginatively accepted as what had to happen; Richard is already a lost man before he takes to the field. The procession of the ghosts—no mere item of pageantry—with its insistent regularity of tempo helps to persuade us of this.

Some of Shakespeare's finest 'ritual' passages occur in his recognition scenes. (Scenes of formal recognition have a long history in Western drama; the tradition goes back to Greek tragedy.) In these scenes we move towards a foreseen point of climax, the moment (usually) when a person's identity is discovered or revealed. Once we have entered such a set piece we know, or quickly guess, what the end will be, but we are allowed to reach it only at the slow pace set by the dramatist. The great recognition scene in the *Iphigenia in Tauris* of Euripides is the prototype of all the others. In Shakespeare, Lear's awakening to Cordelia, the discovery of Marina by Pericles, and the statue scene in *The Winter's Tale* are the fullest examples, but there are also less developed recognition scenes in *The Comedy of Errors* and *Twelfth Night*. In all of them we proceed in a tense but measured pace, as if keeping time to a conductor's beat. At the climax of the statue scene, Paulina actually does call for music, and her words assume a charged formulaic brevity:

> Music, awake her: strike. (*Music*)
> 'Tis time; descend; be stone no more; approach;
> Strike all that look upon with marvel. Come;
> I'll fill your grave up. Stir; nay, come away.

There are here eleven pauses in four lines. But the entire scene has been conducted at a measured tempo: only by carefully marked stages and finally as if step by step are we led to the moment of highest feeling when the statue moves. The essential beauty of these scenes lies in their deployment of time; they are entirely a matter of fulfilled expectations.

It is only a short step from measuring time in this way to actually counting it, and in some scenes this step is taken. The effect is irresistibly coercive to the imagination. This can be shown by glancing at the great Boar's Head scene (II. iv) in *Henry IV, Part One*.

This tavern scene gives the actor playing Falstaff his great chance; no other shows off Falstaff's genius to more comic advantage. When performed, it seems a wonderful exhibition of spontaneous high spirits (with, of course, some ominous darker notes in its second half); but when examined, it is seen to be not at all a meandering effusion but a controlled structure, a skilfully threaded series of small firm units. Despite its considerable length (over 500 lines), nothing is allowed to flag or get out of hand.

The scene is in two main parts, with a bridge passage between them. The first part is restrospective (it looks back to the Gadshill robbery); the second is anticipatory (it looks forward to the Prince's coming interview with the King). It proceeds through a number of short dialogue-units. First, Hal speaks with Poins, and they tease Francis the drawer (on the printed page, at least, a feebly unfunny effect) (1–75); Hal declares his high-spirited mood, and Falstaff's entry is announced (76–109); as soon as he appears,

Falstaff starts boasting of his prowess at Gadshill, and eventually
he is exposed (110–274). This is the main business of the first part
of the scene. Now the Hostess enters, and Falstaff goes out to see
the 'nobleman of the court', while Peto and Bardolph tell Hal
of their stratagems (275–316). This is the bridge passage which
effects a complete change of subject. Falstaff returns and announces
the northern and Welsh rebellions (317–62). Falstaff and Hal then
rehearse the Prince's coming interview with the King, and Hal
warns Falstaff of his impending overthrow (363–464). This is the
main business of the second part. The sheriff knocks at the door,
Falstaff hides, and, after the sheriff's departure, Hal and Poins find
him asleep; they pick his pockets and leave to prepare for the
coming military engagement (465–531).

A sense of expectation is aroused by Hal's own excitement and
high spirits as well as by Falstaff's late entrance: nearly a fifth of
the scene goes by before he is allowed to appear. When he does
appear, tension rises, and one reason why it does so is that the
dialogue suddenly acquires a marked formality. Not that the diction becomes elevated, but that Falstaff's speeches are heavily
marked by repetition. His first remark sets the key: 'A plague of
all cowards, I say, and a vengeance too!' Since Falstaff's own
cowardice has been unmistakably displayed in the Gadshill
robbery scene (II. ii), and since Hal and Poins are merely biding
their time before they expose him, his choice of topic is, from a
comic point of view, the best he could make. Through the next
fifty lines, the 'plague of all cowards' sentiment becomes a *leit-
motiv*, for he repeats it, or variations on it, half a dozen times.
When the repetitions have acquired a sufficient weight of porten-
tousness, Shakespeare makes a transition to Falstaff's account of
the exploit itself, and in doing so he enters into the second of the
formal schemes which support this part of the scene. But this
second one carries the element of formality even further, since it
uses not only phrasal repetition but an ascending series of
numbers.

> *Prince.* Pray God you have not murder'd some of them.
> *Falstaff.* Nay, that's past praying for: I have pepper'd two of them;
> two I am sure I have paid—two rogues in buckram suits. I tell thee
> what, Hal, if I tell thee a lie, spit in my face, call me horse. Thou
> knowest my old ward: here I lay, and thus I bore my point. Four
> rogues in buckram let drive at me—

Prince. What, four? Thou saidst but two even now.
Falstaff. Four, Hal; I told thee four.

(182–91)

In a few moments he goes up from two to four, to seven, to nine, to eleven, when Hal intervenes to expose him. The whole episode is of course triumphant comedy, but the use of a numerical series fixes the attention in a remarkable way and charges the exchange with a mysterious power. It is as if we were assisting at some immemorial comic rite, the comic equivalent of the compulsively repetitive ritual of the banquet scene in *Macbeth*. What is interesting here is the emotional power generated by the use of numbers, for this passage not only amuses, it excites. The numbers seem to contribute a rigid formality which is, on the face of it, completely at odds with the free play of the comic spirit. We are, I think, delighted by the way the apparently freely random course of the dialogue suddenly acquires a pattern so fixed in its intervals as to seem almost mechanically predetermined.

Another scene which uses a numerical series to powerful effect is that in the second act of *King Lear* before Gloucester's castle. Here the numbers in question are those of Lear's knights. Lear's train has already been reduced from a hundred to fifty; and now, in the course of this scene, his daughters propose that it should be cut down from fifty to twenty-five and even further:

Goneril. Hear me, my lord:
What need you five and twenty, ten, or five,
To follow in a house where twice so many
Have a command to tend you?
Regan. What need one?

The over-all effect, accelerated here at the climax, is of a countdown: from fifty to nought. The numerical references reinforce the already taut structure of the scene and give it a grimly rigorous inevitability. It seems right that Falstaff's comic scene in the Boar's Head should use an ascending series of numbers: we feel that it could go on indefinitely, as long as Hal and Falstaff want to keep up the joke. (In its absence of a limiting bound it recalls the way in which Coleridge tried to define comedy: 'poetry in unlimited jest' which entails 'the apparent abandonment of all definite aim or end, the removal of all bounds in the exercise of the mind', a 'display of intellectual wealth squandered in the wantonness of

sport without an object'.)[1] It also seems right that the scene in
King Lear should use a descending series, with a final terminus, a
fixed point which signalizes the presence of tragic necessity.

Like all works of art, plays are organized basically on principles
of repetition (even contrast, of which Shakespeare is so great a
master, makes its effect through repeated alternations). What
distinguishes these highly wrought scenic units from the rest of
the plays in which they occur is that in them the repetitions come
with much greater frequency. It is this muted, insistent drumming
—which may not be at all consciously perceived—which causes
the audience's mounting agitation. One of the effects of the slow,
deliberate, pausing movement already noted is to awaken an
awareness of repetition: it calls attention to the passage of time by
dividing time into small segments. We advance a little and stop;
advance a little further and stop; and so on. The use of numbers
simply makes manifest a metronomic quality latent in such measured deliberate movements. In such a scene as the statue scene,
for example, we know, or quickly guess, that the action has a
certain terminus: the moment when the statue will move. So the
interval between the beginning of the scene and this moment is
divided into as many of the narrow segments as are needed to
traverse the intervening space. It is precisely the impression we
have that the characters are going through a pre-ordained number
of movements and antiphonal responses which are all taken at a
certain appropriate tempo which makes us want to call such a
scene ritualistic.

* * *

The scenes mentioned so far in this section have a certain kind
of tempo in common. They all proceed slowly and pausingly, as
if reluctant to reach the obvious destination; and this has the effect
of arousing impatience and excitement. In these scenes it might
be said that our wish is to accelerate; we want to hasten the passage
of time. In the scenes I now want to consider the reverse happens:
we want to slow down the passage of time. The dramatist has
so shaped his material that we want to linger within the precincts
of a particular situation.

The balcony or orchard scene in *Romeo and Juliet* (II. ii) is the
most famous scene of the play, and largely because of it

[1] Coleridge, *Shakespearean Criticism* (London, 1960), ed. T. M. Raysor, vol. i,
p. 152.

Shakespeare's lovers have achieved their legendary status in the popular imagination. But structurally it is quite different from the tense cumulative scenes I have been describing. It is not without its own tension—when performed it induces a keen suspense, a highly wrought state of feeling; but it does not move towards a strongly anticipated, long-delayed end. Instead, our first impression may be that it hardly moves at all.

Certainly little enough happens in the scene. Romeo has climbed over the wall into the Capulet's orchard, and seeing Juliet at her window he soliloquizes. Juliet apostrophizes him, and he reveals himself. This occupies about the first third of the scene. The middle third is taken up with their first tentative exchanges, with Juliet's fears for Romeo, and their troth-plighting. Then the last third of the scene—or rather more than a third—is given to their leave-taking. Juliet says good-night, and repeats it several times until the end of the scene (at one point she says, 'A thousand times good-night'). Three times a voice off stage—the voice of the Nurse—calls her to go within. At last she goes—only to reappear almost immediately after. And finally, when they have arranged to meet next day, their leave-taking comes to an end.

Of the scene's three phases (which merge imperceptibly into each other), the first culminates in the direct mutual addresses of the lovers. The third part is given to the protracted leave-taking. It is only in the brief second part that we have any sense of the lovers simply meeting, simply confronting each other; but this feeling of fulfilment (for such it is) lasts only for a few moments: Juliet begins saying good-night, and the Nurse begins calling her. The effect of this is to make us aware of the unwelcome but unrelenting passage of time. (Here the use of the voice off stage calling Juliet is a particularly powerful and beautiful one. It is rather like the use Wagner makes of Isolde's confidante Brangaene in the love scene of *Tristan and Isolde* and Shakespeare's scene may be the 'source' here.) The scene, one might say, has a clear beginning, middle, and end, but the end is by far the longest part of it.

Part of what Shakespeare is doing here can be seen by attending to the small detail of the orchard walls (his own invention) which Romeo has to climb in order to get into the garden. (They are of course present only imaginatively; they are 'off stage'.) Their function is partly to help isolate the lovers and emphasize the privacy of their meeting. But they also work to demarcate the scene and establish a strong sense of interiority, so prompting the audience to imagine a charmed enclosed space—a *locus amoenus* or Keatsian 'haven of intenseness'—whose precincts we are ourselves reluctant to leave. But we are compelled to go; hence the long final movement of the scene, with its lingered-out good-nights.

Shakespeare is here making resourceful use of time. But he is also making use of the visual aspect of the scene, so that the tableau formed by Juliet on her balcony and Romeo standing beneath becomes deeply etched on the audience's visual memory. The scene is after all quite long, yet it is almost entirely static. Little happens on stage, except that the lovers look at and speak to each other. The extraordinary *raptness* of the scene is epitomized in the moment when Romeo, standing still, hears Juliet call him and exclaims

> How silver-sweet sound lovers' tongues by night,
> Like softest music to attending ears!

The apparent self-consciousness with which he for a moment steps outside the situation is in fact a way of framing and distancing it: we become aware of a moment as perfect in its stillness and fulness as music heard in a mood of absorbed intensity. At this point Juliet returns:

> *Juliet.* Romeo!
> *Romeo.*   My dear!
> *Juliet.*   ˎ   At what o'clock to-morrow
>   Shall I send to thee?
> *Romeo.*   By the hour of nine.
> *Juliet.* I will not fail. 'Tis twenty years till then.
>   I have forgot why I did call thee back.
> *Romeo.* Let me stand here till thou remember it.
> *Juliet.* I shall forget, to have thee still stand there,
>   Remembering how I love thy company.
> *Romeo.* And I'll still stay, to have thee still forget . . .

Even while they make their arrangements for marriage the next day, they feel that time no longer exists. The present moment has become indefinitely prolonged; the repeated terms—'stand here', 'still stand there', 'still stay'—repudiate (or try to) all distracting thoughts of past and future. The way the scene conveys this feeling of a prolonged present moment is one of its remarkable achievements and helps to explain why in performance it carries with it such a profound sense of occasion—one awe-inspiring in its beauty and poignancy. It persuades us that we are witnessing something happening *now*, in the moment of performance— something unique, marvellous, and tragically unrepeatable.

The way this scene lingers as if unwilling to come to an end is matched in a scene in *The Merchant of Venice* which is also one in which lovers confront each other. This is the last of the casket scenes (III. ii), in which Bassanio chooses the lead casket and wins Portia. It is a long slow movement, which is set off by the scenes which precede and follow it: both are short, brisk, and active, with Shylock appearing in both. The tempo is set by Portia's long opening speech, with its hesitations, its involutions, its reluctance for Bassanio to commit himself to what may be a fatally wrong choice. She begins:

> I pray you tarry; pause a day or two
> Before you hazard; for, in choosing wrong,
> I lose your company; therefore forbear a while. . . .
> I would detain you here some month or so
> Before you venture for me . . .

The feeling is of pained unwillingness for the scene to begin (Romeo and Juliet had been unwilling for their scene to end). She ends her speech:

> I speak too long, but 'tis to peize the time,
> To eke it, and to draw it out in length,
> To stay you from election.

She wants to 'peize the time': put weights on it, slow it down. Then later, when Bassanio has chosen the lead casket and Portia has become his betrothed, the moment's emotion is not relinquished but held still; as in the balcony scene, the present moment seems prolonged:

> *Bassanio.* So, thrice-fair lady, stand I even so,
>   As doubtful whether what I see be true,
>   Until confirm'd, sign'd, ratified by you.
> *Portia.* You see me, Lord Bassanio, where I stand,
>   Such as I am . . .

The present tenses and the choice of verbs ('stand', 'am') strengthen the effect of stasis which works to arrest the scene's movement. We are made to contemplate neither action nor passion but a state of being, and for a few moments the lovers enjoy a rich happiness. (A comparable effect of brimming stillness is achieved in another fine scene in the same play: the homecoming of Portia in the last act.)

What distinguishes these scenes from the earlier ones I discussed is that, while they last, we wish (we are induced to wish) that the time would pass more slowly than it does. We want, not to hasten the action, but to retard or delay it: 'to peize the time, /To eke it, and to draw it out in length'. The scenes of the first group might be called dynamic; those of the second group static —or as nearly static as the dramatic form will allow (of course, a literal full stop is impossible). These scenes are a way of bestowing value on the present moment, enriching the instant of experience. They are contemplative; and what they present for our contemplation is something unusual for its emotional warmth or its beauty. If our first impression is that these scenes are in some way structurally defective, our impression is misleading: they are firmly shaped, although there may be nothing corresponding to the openly insistent pressures, the quickening repetitions of the other type of scene. In some cases the pressures which give shape to the scene are, in verbal terms, entirely implicit: we must seek them in the dramatic situation as a whole and in the larger concerns of the play up to that point. Such a scene is one from *Henry IV*, *Part Two*, with which I shall close this opening survey of some of Shakespeare's scenic devices.

The last interview of Prince Hal with the King resembles the balcony scene of *Romeo and Juliet* and the scene just discussed from *The Merchant of Venice* in that it induces the audience to put up a resistance to the passage of time. This interview has been prepared for by the whole of the preceding play; indeed from the beginning of *Part One* we have known of the King's belief in his son's degeneracy and his fears for the kingdom when his son should succeed him. Now, in the fourth act of *Part Two*, in a carefully composed sequence, Shakespeare prepares us for the final interview. Two circumstances arouse concern: the King's approaching death, and his misunderstanding of his son's true nature, which now or never must be corrected. The sequence opens (IV. iv) by showing the King with his younger sons Clarence and Gloucester;

he asks where Hal is, and urges Clarence to study Hal's disposition
and try to control it. He is then suddenly taken ill, asks to be left
alone, and places the crown on his pillow. He falls asleep, and at
this point Hal enters. Seeing his father asleep, he jumps to the
conclusion that he is dead, and goes into the next room taking the
crown with him. The King awakes, and seeing the crown gone
calls for his sons and counsellors. He discovers that the Prince of
Wales has been there, and that it was he who must have removed
the crown. He exclaims bitterly:

> See, sons, what things you are!
> How quickly nature falls into revolt
> When gold becomes her object!

Hal returns, the others leave, and he faces his father. The sequence up to this point can be said to recapitulate the course of
the entire play as far as the King and the Prince are concerned.
The unluckily timed entry and exit of Hal—which aroused the
King's suspicions—are a means of re-enacting their whole relationship, and especially the father's rooted misunderstanding of
his son. They have, so to speak, kept on missing each other all
their lives. At last, and for the first time in *Part Two*, they are
alone together.

In performance this scene comes with what is perhaps a surprisingly weighty impact; it feels as if it is the climax of the whole
play. Together with the rejection of Falstaff, it is what nineteenth-
century theorists of the drama would have called a *scène à faire*,
one which the logic of the plot obliges the author to supply. We
know that a scene of this sort must at some point take place, and
when at last it comes it brings with it an almost oppressive sense
of occasion. It opens as follows:

> *Prince.* I never thought to hear you speak again.
> *King.* Thy wish was father, Harry, to that thought.
> I stay too long by thee, I weary thee.
> Dost thou so hunger for mine empty chair
> That thou wilt needs invest thee with my honours
> Before thy hour be ripe? . . .

The simplicity of the diction attests to the speakers' depth of
feeling. But, further, there is a tone here which makes the occasion
express something of general import, so that for a few moments
the characters become not only King Henry IV and the Prince

of Wales but Father and Son—all fathers and all sons. When the King reproaches Hal—

> Thy life did manifest thou loved'st me not,
> And thou wilt have me die assur'd of it

—his voice assumes a more than personal note. He seems to speak with the bitterness of fathers generally, who come to realize that their children will in time *happily* survive them. The King has already exclaimed to his other sons, who on the face of it are blameless, 'See, sons, what things you are!' And now, in this declaration to the Prince, which has a painful intimacy rare even in Shakespeare, something universal is suggested about human nature. The bitterness of disappointed love which the King expresses here is soon dissipated by the Prince's protestation that follows, and the rest of the interview is given to political matters: the dying King, at last reconciled to his heir, presses on him heartfelt advice. But what gives the scene its warmth is the King's very human distress and the new understanding between father and son. The scene is, in its way, quite as much a love scene as those between Romeo and Juliet and Portia and Bassanio. In this often sour and sardonic play, in which all relationships seem feebly halfhearted or frustrated, it gives much-needed expression to natural feeling; in performance, even more than in reading, it brings relief of an immensely refreshing and invigorating kind.

But there is something else which makes the scene relevant to the present subject: Shakespeare's way of instigating in the audience a resistance to the passage of time. Prince Hal thought his father dead when he was only asleep. It looked as if he had lost him for ever. His discovery that he is in fact alive gives the few moments he now spends with him something of the nature of a priceless second chance, as if the King had been—against all probability—reprieved from certain death, or almost as if he had actually come back from the dead:

> I never thought to hear you speak again.

It might be said that the King, thought dead by the Prince and about to die in fact, is almost as good as dead—a 'living dead man' among the living.[1] He can now lose nothing by being frank about his political procedures, while the Prince must at all costs

---

[1] The phrase 'living dead man' is from *The Comedy of Errors*, v. i. 241.

put the record straight about his own nature. Everything combines to make their last desperately sincere conversation one which
needs more time than can in the circumstances be given. The King
is cut off by weakness:

> More would I, but my lungs are wasted so
> That strength of speech is utterly denied me

—so that no sooner has he discovered the truth about his son
than he dies. 'More would I': as with the balcony scene, we reach
the end unwillingly—which is only to say that Shakespeare has
again exploited the elementary fact that time passes.

2. *Time and Continuity*

I

A T the end of the last chapter I considered the ways we experience time (in the form of timing or tempo) within scenes. It is often thought that we experience time in a rather larger sense during a play as a whole. The term 'time-scheme' was invented to denote the imagined duration of the action; and where there were discrepancies in the evidence that supplies this impression of duration, more complicated 'double-time schemes' were devised to account for them. I want in this chapter to expose some of the fallacies in this approach. I shall argue that the Shakespearian use of time is best understood if we hold on to the principles already outlined : we must think of time in terms of a more illusionist and mimetic system in which the prime concern is not duration but continuity, and above all continuity of scenes.

Beginning in 1849 with John Wilson (who wrote under the pseudonym of 'Christopher North') and, independently of Wilson, N. J. Halpin, several nineteenth-century critics gave a good deal of attention to Shakespeare's use of time. The two just mentioned were followed by Charles and Mary Cowden Clarke, P. A. Daniel, and Sir Mark Hunter.[1] A. C. Bradley and Harley Granville-Barker took much of their work for granted and added to it, and they are still referred to in the work of such contemporary scholars as J. Dover Wilson. What interested John Wilson and Halpin particularly was the duration, or apparent duration, of the action of Shakespeare's plays. Wilson examined *Macbeth* and, more extensively, *Othello* from this point of view, and Halpin *The Merchant of Venice*. Both writers are subtler than a summary will suggest, and Wilson especially is hard to pin down since he expresses his views in several dialogues in which his opinions are distributed

---

[1] John Wilson, *Blackwoods Magazine* (November 1849; April, May 1850); N. J. Halpin, 'The Dramatic Unities of Shakespeare', in *The New Shakspere Society's Transactions* (1875–6); Charles and Mary Cowden Clarke, *The Shakespeare Key* (1879); P. A. Daniel, 'A Time Analysis of the Plots of Shakspere's Plays', in *The New Shakspere Society's Transactions* (1877–9); Sir Mark Hunter (ed.), *Julius Caesar* (Madras, 1900).

between several speakers and not necessarily limited to the speeches of 'Christopher North'. The theory associated with these critics is that of (in Wilson's words) 'Short Time and Long Time'. They argue that a straightforward attempt to compute the duration of Shakespeare's plays (at least, of some of them) is doomed to frustration, since it will be found that Shakespeare works according to two mutually incompatible 'clocks'. According to the Short Time clock the action will be found to fill a relatively short time, usually not more than a few days. But on the Long Time clock the action is much more protracted: it may seem to take several weeks or months or years. So in *The Merchant of Venice*, Halpin argued, if the sequence of scenes is closely observed, the action seems to take no more than two or three days; everywhere the stress is on haste and the need for instant action. Yet from another viewpoint a much longer period of time seems to elapse, since Shylock's bond was to expire only after two months, and by the end of the third act Antonio is being hustled into prison. Wilson noticed the working of a similar 'double time' in *Macbeth* and *Othello*, while thirty years later the Cowden Clarkes applied the test to all Shakespeare's other plays and found evidence of the same phenomenon. These critics all agree, however, that the discrepancies discovered by the minute reader will pass unnoticed in performance, and probably even the casual reader will not notice anything amiss. Only occasionally will a reader be bothered by what amounts to two sets of incompatible information. *Othello* is the extreme case of this, and here indeed Shakespeare seems to run the risk of making his play fundamentally implausible. 'Christopher North' summed up the case in a pair of mutually contradictory statements:

Verdict: DESDEMONA MURDERED BY OTHELLO ON THE SECOND NIGHT IN CYPRUS.
Verdict: DESDEMONA MURDERED BY OTHELLO HEAVEN KNOWS WHEN.

But in performance, it is agreed, the bifocal vision afforded by simultaneous Long and Short Time dissolves these apparent impossibilities.

John Wilson, Halpin, and the others take it for granted that the questions they ask about the duration of the action and the way they go about answering them are critically permissible. They were writing at a time when the novel, with its often highly naturalistic assumptions and conventions, had become a thoroughly familiar form. Novelists like Richardson, Jane Austen, and a (to them) contemporary writer like Emily Brontë evidently used calendars or almanacs to compute the exact chronological sequences of their narratives. It was, therefore, a natural impulse that prompted them to look for similar concerns in writers of earlier periods. Of course they were not naïve: they brought to their reading an informed historical sense; but there seems little doubt that they were to some extent the victims of their own rationalism. When they examined the texts of Shakespeare's plays they often found a closely articulated plot sequence in which event followed event with what seemed like a constant pressure that left no interstices for unaccounted-for intervals of time. The evidence for computing the passage of time seemed to them objective enough; it was to be sought in the references to time distributed throughout each play: verbal expressions like 'tomorrow', 'last night', and so on, and such indications of particular days passing as scenes set at night or morning or any other specified time of day. What they looked for was always evidence of continuity, scene-by-scene linking, and they undoubtedly found what they wanted. But when it also became clear that there was a good deal of evidence of another kind—which showed that in some ways Shakespeare conceived his action as filling a much longer period than was consistent with the period covered by the linked scenes—it seemed to them as if nothing but a system of 'double-time' could possibly account for the facts. Much of what they discovered about Shakespeare's constructive methods is true and useful, but their theory of 'double-time' needs a sceptical examination, and in particular that part of it which computes 'Short Time'.

Julius Caesar can be taken as an example of the way the theory is applied. (The duration of its action was fully discussed by Sir Mark Hunter in his 1900 edition of the play; his arguments are closely based on those of John Wilson and the Cowden Clarkes.) From the opening scene to iv. i Shakespeare shows remarkable care to keep the action continuous. The first two scenes clearly follow on one another without a break: in the first Flavius and Marullus remonstrate with the plebeians for their fickle behaviour, and in the second we witness or are told of the main events on this public holiday, the Feast of Lupercalia. In his soliloquy which

44 TIME AND CONTINUITY

closes this second scene Cassius, who has begun his temptation of Brutus, announces that he will 'this night, / In several hands, in at his windows throw, / . . . Writings' (i. ii. 314–17). Since the following scene takes place at night, it seems natural to suppose, as most editors do, that it is the night of the day which has seen the events of i. i and i. ii. There is no hint in the dialogue that a period of time has elapsed, but in any case our attention is drawn away from the immediate past to the immediate future. Cicero says

Comes Caesar to the Capitol to-morrow?

(i. iii. 36)

—and 'to-morrow' is the main concern in this and the following two scenes. These scenes all show what takes place in this same night: Cassius and Casca set off for Brutus' house; in the next scene (ii. i) they and the other conspirators arrive there; and they finally leave for Caesar's house. In ii. ii we see them welcomed by Caesar before they all set out for the Capitol. In Act Three the assassination of Caesar, the funeral speeches of Brutus and Antony in the Forum, and finally the fury of the mob, follow one another without possibility of interval. In reading these scenes, and certainly in performance, it seems as if we are being shown the events of two successive days; certainly the series 'Day-Night-Day' is one powerfully persuasive to the imagination. According to the Short Time clock therefore—such is the argument used—the first act takes place on 'Day One', while Act Two, Act Three, and the first scene of Act Four take place on 'Day Two'.

Julius Caesar deals of course with historical events, with in fact one of the most famous episodes of classical history. We know, just as Shakespeare and many of his audience knew, that the events which are dramatized in these first three acts did not take place on two successive days. The Lupercalia occurred on the Ides (13th) of February, and the assassination of Caesar on the Ides (15th) of March. Did Shakespeare mean his audience to think that only two days spanned Cassius' first approach to Brutus on the subject of Caesar, and Caesar's assassination? The answer, it seems clear, is that he did not expect his audience to think this. Despite our smooth passage from one day to the next, we are not intended to make any inference about the actual period of time which these events historically occupied. The terms just used—'actual', 'historically'—point to the nature of the imaginative process with which we are concerned. Shakespeare's play, dealing as it does with a series of famous historical events, is an *imitation* of an action. It presents us not with the real thing but with an enactment of the real thing. The play enacts the historical episode in accordance with the principles of drama, or more particularly, with the principles of Shakespeare's theatre. (Especially important was the freedom with which the dramatist could choose either to give his action a precise location or to leave the location unspecified.) What we see when we watch the play acted is not only an immensely speeded-up version of what, according to Plutarch, historically happened; we see also a version of history which has been subjected to a process of rigorous selection and artistic rationalization. Everything has been made simpler and clearer to our understanding than it would have been in actuality (or even than it is in Plutarch). Complex historical processes—such as they would appear to a historian—are presented on the stage embodied in real persons, and events which historically were quite separate or even remote from each other are fused by the dramatist as if they formed part of the same occasion. (Shakespeare does this in the opening scene by combining Caesar's triumph that celebrated his victory over Pompey's sons—October 45 B.C.—with the Lupercalia—February 44 B.C.) The historical events are rearranged into a highly stylized form in the interests of drama; there is not the slightest pretence that what we are watching is anything other than an evocation of historical realities. We see the first day leading to the day of the assassination with only a night between them because this makes a compelling dramatic sequence, with its own internal system of anticipation, long-drawn-out suspense, and finally a sustained climactic movement (III. i–iii) which more than satisfies the expectations that have been aroused in the foregoing scenes. We are always expected to understand that, since the dramatist has only about two hours at his disposal, it would be absurd to pretend that such an enactment of an action which historically lasted for at least several months could be anything more than a symbolic or token representation. We see 'what may be digested in a play' (*Troilus and Cressida*, Prologue, 29), and we instinctively obey the injunction of the Chorus in *Henry V*:

Piece out our imperfections with your thoughts

(Prologue, 23)

—'Minding true things by what their mock'ries be' (*Henry V*, Act IV, Chorus, 53)—as we do, of course, with any play we see.

To be aware of these matters is only to admit the 'artificiality' of a play like *Julius Caesar*—that we are, after all, experiencing a work of art, with its understood and accepted conventions. If we now return to the question of double time, it seems safe to say that the Long Time part of the theory is more or less acceptable, since an impression that a longish period glides by in the course of the play—in this case, the first three acts—is quite consistent with the duration implied by Plutarch's narratives and with what we otherwise know of the historical reality of which the play is a representation. But it is quite otherwise with the Short Time part of the theory. The carefully interlinked scenes (e.g. the way Cassius leaves for Brutus' house at the end of I. iii and arrives there near the beginning of II. i, and the way the conspirators leave for Caesar's house at the end of II. i and arrive there near the end of II. ii to set out then for the Capitol which they have reached by the opening of III. i, etc.) which carry us without interruption from the opening of the play to IV. i are a method of dramatically articulating the narrative source materials; they are a form of dramatic syntax whose aims are wholly consistent with the stylistic aims of other Renaissance forms of writing: clarity and force. But they do not, it seems, carry with them any obvious implications of temporal duration. We are free to admire the way in which Shakespeare has so organized his material into a smoothly flowing sequence of scenes that each episode follows its predecessor with an appearance and 'feel' of a wholly convincing emotional logic, but we are not encouraged to think in terms of calendar time, and especially when watching a performance we shall almost certainly not think—not be free to think—in such terms at all. What we shall be doing is contemplating an action in which the processes of cause and effect will have been made unusually clear. And whether this action took place in one or two months or one or two years will be immaterial. In this particular case we happen to know the answer a historian would give; but in other plays, in which the historical or fictional source will not be known to most of the audience, this sort of external check will not be available—but neither will it be at all relevant unless the dramatist wishes to make it so. And if he does find it relevant he will supply the information within the play itself.

The point to note is that Shakespeare is evoking time dramatically, and this entails using terms like 'day' and 'night' with some metaphorical as well as literal application. The important thing about the sequences of days and nights is, precisely, their sequence and not (as is so often thought) their duration. The 'night', for example, in which Brutus joins the conspiracy is an ordinary literal night, but it also has a strongly metaphorical or emblematical character. It is marked by Brutus' sleeplessness, in contrast to the slumber enjoyed by the boy Lucius, by the guilty stealth of the conspirators' approach, by the dankness and unwholesomeness of the night airs—in short, by the traditional associations of Night with evil, crime, and danger to which Brutus refers immediately before the conspirators are admitted:

> O conspiracy,
> Sham'st thou to show thy dang'rous brow by night,
> When evils are most free?
>
> (II. i. 77–9)

Moreover, as if to show more clearly the more than naturalistic nature of this night, Shakespeare seems to distinguish with some care the night of I. iii and of II. ii from that of the present scene, II. i. For the night scene in Brutus' orchard is one of stillness and quiet: the boy Lucius is asleep and Brutus is restless and uneasy, but in a mood of quiet introspection. The scenes preceding and following it, which appear to take place on the same night, are tumultuous with storm and preternatural portents. In performance the audience probably notices nothing odd about this sequence, and it is indeed perfectly acceptable. But it is hardly susceptible of a straightforward naturalistic interpretation. There was, after all, no pressing reason other than an imaginative one why Shakespeare chose to place the conspiracy scene (II. i) at night. He presumably chose to make it a night scene simply because night was appropriate to such enterprises as a plot to murder Julius Caesar. But this does not license us to make Short Time calculations. Time in that measurable sense does not enter into the matter. This night is, if we choose to say so, as much a place as a time of day: it is an appropriate *setting* for this conspiratorial phase of the action. (But there is also another dramatic reason why Shakespeare chose to give extended treatment to the night scene in Brutus' orchard. It is that the night before a great event—the

eve of the great day—is an obvious dramatic occasion; it may be
even more dramatically interesting than the day itself. In *Richard
III* we are given an extended treatment of the eve of Bosworth,
and in *Henry V* the eve of Agincourt. So when plotting a play on
the death of Julius Caesar and deciding which occasions to
dramatize Shakespeare would naturally be drawn to the night
before the crucial event.)

But there is another consideration, and this too can have its
importance in interpreting a play. It is often assumed that, however drastically time may be compressed in so far as it affects
characters off stage (e.g. movements from place to place which
occur between scenes), the time actually represented in dialogues
on stage must have a literal value. That is to say, if the playing
time of a scene is ten minutes, then ten minutes must be assumed
to elapse in the imagined world of the play. This alleged rule is
occasionally put forward as if common sense demanded it. But
it is certainly not a safe assumption as far as Shakespeare is concerned. In the second scene of *Julius Caesar* there are, for part of
its length, two simultaneous actions, one on stage, the other off
stage. On stage Cassius tempts Brutus, while off stage a great
public ceremony is performed and Caesar in the presence of the
people is three times offered a crown. If we ask how long these
simultaneous actions last, it may seem easy to provide an answer:
as long as it takes the actors playing Brutus and Cassius to perform
their colloquy. This could no doubt be worked out from the
number of lines they have to speak: say, about fifteen minutes.
But if this is so, can we assume that the off stage action also took
no more than fifteen minutes? A moment's reflection will make it
clear that the elaborate ceremonies in which Caesar took part and
which Casca later in the scene describes must have taken considerably longer than a mere quarter of an hour. The truth is, of
course, that it is not possible to calculate their duration from the
playing-time of Brutus and Cassius' colloquy. The ceremonies
undergo, in Shakespeare's treatment, a stylized abbreviation, which
is clearly quite unnaturalistic. But the colloquy between Brutus
and Cassius is no more naturalistic either. Their dialogue is highly
rhetorical and formalized. Cassius' first broaching to Brutus of
his discontented thoughts, which in 'real life' would have been
more tentative and inconclusive, altogether less well shaped and
less eloquent, and would moreover probably have been spread

over several distinct occasions, is here worked up into a single splendidly purposeful and climaxed scene. It has been translated into the language of the drama (they converse in blank verse), and is certainly not capable of any simple naturalistic interpretation, nor can we legitimately make such a comment on it as 'Brutus and Cassius had a ten- or fifteen-minute conversation', for it is not possible to make any such simple quantitative conversion into the units of real-life clock-time. The *duration* of their talk together is simply not a material consideration.

All this may seem very obvious, but it is perhaps worth insisting even further on the unnaturalistic mimetic nature of Shakespeare's drama, since when it concerns the passage of time it is (as we shall see) clearly possible to forget it. A play of Shakespeare's is an imitation of an action, so designed as to bring out the essential moral lineaments of that action. The plot is so constructed as to make clear the connection between an act and its consequences. Accordingly, the plot of *Julius Caesar* is an unbroken chain leading from Cassius' temptation of Brutus in I. ii to the end of the play with Brutus' death and the victory of the triumvirate. We are given an understanding of what happened and how it happened. But questions about how long it took to happen have no place. Shakespeare's stress on haste, which has frequently been noticed especially in comparison with his source materials, is quite distinct from a concern with duration; it is indeed essential to distinguish them. Haste in his plays has more than one function. It has an obvious dramatic value: it helps to generate interest and excitement. But it may also be seen as an aspect of that concern with plot, with the inexorable relation between an act and its consequences, which has just been mentioned; for the constant pressure of events helps to bring out the connections between scene and scene, so helping the audience to master the significance of what they are witnessing. But the element of haste has only a relative temporal value; it tells us nothing positive about the duration of what happens.

If, finally, we look once again at the beginning of the night sequence in *Julius Caesar*, we can see—though only by examining the text of the play—how Shakespeare managed to compress the events of over a month into what seems like two successive days. At the end of I. ii Cassius announces (in lines already quoted) that he will throw documents into Brutus' house. The phrase 'this

night' (314), placed near the end of the scene, is powerfully premonitory; it throws our expectation forward to the next scene,
so that when that scene opens with Cicero's words 'Good even,
Casca', which are later supported by Casca's 'never till to-night,
never till now' (9), it seems obvious that this must be the night
on which Cassius was going to work on Brutus—and sure enough,
a little later in this scene Cassius appears. Later still, in II. i, we
learn that the boy Lucius has picked up a document which had
been thrown in at the window. In this way the sequence makes its
effect in performance as well as in reading. But what Shakespeare
has done is simply to join two 'nights' together, so that the night
of the Lupercalia merges imperceptibly into the eve of the Ides of
March. It is a piece of expert stitching, and is not meant to be
noticed. By means of it we glide magically from one great occasion,
the Lupercalia, to the next, the eve of the assassination. Or another
way of putting it would be that we move from the initial act
(Cassius' temptation) to the first consequence (Brutus' mental
disorder that is both a cause and a consequence of his decision to
join the conspiracy). Fusions of this sort are part of Shakespeare's
usual technique of converting his source materials into dramatic
form. Chronological veracity is sacrificed in the interests of a
different kind of significance : the transformation is one of history
into poetry.

II

It is in keeping with this process of translation into an essentially poetic form that numerical references are usually of a symbolic nature. The historically accurate but often arbitrary numbers
which occur in Shakespeare's sources (such works as histories and
biographies) are usually omitted, probably because they were felt
to be unassimilable into the essentially symbolic mode of poetic
drama in which all details aspire towards meaningfulness. If the
age of a person is mentioned in the plays, it is an age which is felt
to be capable of interpretation : so Juliet is fourteen, and in the
graveyard scene we learn that Hamlet is thirty; Lear is four-score
and upward. Periods of time which are explicitly mentioned are
usually of a round conventional sort. The number twenty-three
occurs a few times (three times in *The Winter's Tale*), but it was
possibly felt to have a symbolic value : being one short of twenty-

four it is expressive of a state of being *almost* complete and is comparable to the expression 'the eleventh hour'. (Twenty-four, the number of completeness, is the number of years Doctor Faustus was given in which to exercise power before forfeiting his soul; the twenty-four years pass like twenty-four hours, and the play ends appropriately at midnight, the twenty-fourth hour of the day.) It is true that some of the early historical plays are occasionally blemished by violations of what was to become Shakespeare's working principle in this matter. In *3 Henry VI* (II. i) Edward of York tells Warwick that his father the Duke of York has met his death. Warwick replies:

> Ten days ago I drown'd these news in tears . . .
>
> (104)

Here the precise reference to ten days previously has a noticeably jarring effect: far from making the episode convincingly realistic it threatens to break the illusion by refusing to be assimilated into the smoothly stylized time-convention we have hitherto accepted. For elsewhere in the play such precise references to calendrical time have been avoided. In *I Henry VI* a messenger relates the capture of Talbot, beginning

> The tenth of August last this dreadful lord . . .
>
> (I. i. 110)

Again the reference seems excessively precise, although in this case, since the reference is to events which took place before the opening of the play, little harm is done to the time-illusion. In later plays Shakespeare showed more imaginative tact in avoiding such arbitrarily fixed and hence unassimilable details. In *Antony and Cleopatra*, for example, ten years of historical time are condensed with extraordinary skill into an intricate yet smoothly continuative sequence which never jars by introducing the awkward fixed quantities—the arbitrary numbers—of a chronicle narrative.

What we find most often in Shakespeare in temporal contexts is the use of extremely common terms like 'tonight' and 'tomorrow' or 'last night' and 'yesterday'. When taken in their dramatic context, such words have, or can be invested with, a considerable emotional pressure. We can go further and hazard a generalization: as a dramatist Shakespeare is primarily interested in

the immediate future and the immediate past, for only those
parts of time which are continuous to the present moment can
have much imaginative reality for the theatre audience. 'To-
morrow' and 'yesterday' are, after all, words with a powerful
emotional charge, to which Shakespeare is as responsive as anyone. During a performance of a play, however, what most concerns us is the immediate future, what is going to develop out of
the present moment. As Susanne Langer has observed, 'it is only
a present filled with its own future that is really dramatic'.[1] Compared with the immediate future, any other temporal consideration
—the remoter future or the past, which may often be referred to
in the dialogue—will be much less compelling. Indeed words like
'tonight' and 'tomorrow'—far more than their corresponding
terms, 'last night' and 'yesterday'—become valuable structural
devices, serving to throw our expectation forward to the next
phase of the action. So in *Macbeth* at key points in the play we find
such lines as the following:

> The King comes here to-night
>
> (I. v. 28).
>
> To-night we hold a solemn supper, sir . . .
>
> (III. i. 14)
>
> I will tomorrow,
> And betimes I will to the Weird Sisters . . .
>
> (III. iv. 132–3)
>
> To-morrow, and to-morrow, and to-morrow . . .
>
> (V. v. 19)

And as I have already suggested, all scenes which are set on the
eve of a great event—Bosworth, Agincourt—derive much of their
power from the implicit *leit-motiv*: 'To-morrow is the day'
(*Antony and Cleopatra*, IV. iii. 1).

Shakespeare's treatment of time is marked by a brilliant ex-
pediency. He will introduce his *to-nights* and *to-morrows* when it
suits him dramatically and with little or no thought for what the
nineteenth-century critics would have called duration. Occasionally, however, the nature of the story he is dramatizing
obliges him to give it at least some consideration. This happens
in the middle scenes of *Romeo and Juliet*. Until the middle of the
play—until III. iii, to be precise—we have been aware of haste, but
not of duration. But with the killing of Mercutio and Tybalt and

---

[1] Susanne K. Langer, *Feeling and Form* (London, 1953), p. 307.

the banishment of Romeo, the play takes second wind and we
return to a matter broached in the second scene of the play but
allowed to rest forgotten until now: Paris' suit to marry Juliet.
In III. iv Paris reappears, and Capulet conceives his plan to marry
Juliet to him—an ill-fated plan which is to bring about the
catastrophe. Romeo and Juliet are to die as a result of mistiming,
and accordingly, at the point in the play where the marriage to
Paris is introduced, references to time and to duration become
noticeably prominent:

> *Capulet.* But, soft! what day is this?
> *Paris.*   Monday, my lord.
> *Capulet.* Monday! ha, ha! Well, Wednesday is too soon.
>   A Thursday let it be; a Thursday, tell her,
>   She shall be married to this noble earl.
>
> (III. iv. 18–21)

In the following scene (III. v) Juliet is told of her father's decision;
she resolves to tell the Friar. The next scene (IV. i) opens with the
Friar saying to Paris:

> On Thursday, sir? The time is very short.

And later in the scene, broaching his plan to Juliet, he says:

> Wednesday is to-morrow;
> To-morrow night look that thou lie alone . . .
>
> (90–1)

This unusual particularity is necessitated by the plot, since at this
point matters of timing are crucial. Therefore in this whole
sequence leading up to Juliet's apparent death (III. iv to IV. v) we
can properly speak of a time-scheme, since Shakespeare goes to
some pains to work up an illusion of several specific days passing:
Monday to Thursday. It should be noticed, however, that he
makes it quite clear in advance what he is about to do. We are
first told explicitly by Capulet and Paris that it is Monday when
the plan is conceived, and after that we are reminded several times
that the wedding is fixed for Thursday. This is the practice which
Shakespeare usually adopts. If the story he is dramatizing turns
on matters of time and timing, he brings the fact clearly to our
attention beforehand. In *The Comedy of Errors*, for example, it is
made clear in the opening scene that if Ægeon is not reprieved he
will die at sunset on that same day. But if there are no such explicit

references to time which prompt us beforehand, then a 'time-scheme' does not exist—any more than it does in *Julius Caesar*. With these considerations in mind we can now turn to the problematical case of *Othello*.

III

Ever since John Wilson's dialogues on the play (published in 1849–50), *Othello* has attracted attention from those critics who believed that duration was a factor to be seriously reckoned with in an interpretation of Shakespeare's plays. It is still a common-place of *Othello* criticism that without reference to double-time the play will hardly make sense. For, as I have already mentioned, the exponents of double-time maintain that we are provided with two mutually contradictory sets of facts. The action of Acts Two to Five, they argue, is strictly continuous; in Bradley's words:

> . . . it seems clear that the time between the arrival in Cyprus and the catastrophe is certainly not more than a few days, and most probably only about a day and a half: or, to put it otherwise, that most probably Othello kills his wife about twenty-four hours after the consummation of their marriage![1]

This is the Short Time scheme of the play. For the Long Time scheme Bradley's words will again serve:

> Now this idea that Othello killed his wife, probably within twenty-four hours, certainly within a few days, of the consummation of his marriage, contradicts the impression produced by the play on all un-critical readers and spectators. It is also in flat contradiction with a large number of time-indications in the play itself.[2]

He goes on to list such things as Bianca's complaint that Cassio has kept away from her for a week, Iago's suggestions that Desdemona has become tired of Othello and that she has re-peatedly committed adultery with Cassio, as well as his story that he slept with Cassio 'lately'—all of which suggest, as Bradley says, that 'some little time has elapsed, probably a few weeks', since the arrival in Cyprus. Another critic who accepts the double-time theory, Granville-Barker, is quite clear that the action of the last three acts takes place on a single day, and he points out the

---

[1] A. C. Bradley, *Shakespearean Tragedy* (London, 1905), p. 424.
[2] Ibid., p. 425.

references at appropriate points in the dialogue to morning (III. i), midday dinner-time (III. iii), supper-time (IV. ii), and night (IV. iii to V. ii). By the opening of Act Three we have, he says,

> reached the morrow of the arrival in Cyprus and of the consummation of the marriage. This is plain. It is morning. By the coming midnight or a little later Othello will have murdered Desdemona and killed himself.[1]

The double-time theory has reached such proportions in discussions of *Othello* that the play is made to appear as a rather dubious special case, as if without the special licence granted it by Long and Short Time it would be seen to be a tissue of absurdities. Like everyone who writes on this matter, Bradley concedes that 'I do not think anyone does notice the impossibilities either in the theatre or in a casual reading of the play',[2] but he seems nevertheless uneasy, for if Shakespeare relied on his audience's not noticing anything amiss, then he 'did in *Othello* what he seems to do in no other play. I can believe that he may have done so; but I find it very hard to believe that he produced this impossible situation without knowing it'.[3] There seems to be a suspicion of something meretricious in Shakespeare's procedure; and even when a critic intends to praise his technical resourcefulness the terms in which he does so seem to call the strategy in question; so J. Dover Wilson praises Shakespeare for resorting to a piece of 'dramatic legerdemain, the most audacious in the entire canon' and observes that 'as every conjuror knows it is when the attention of an audience is deeply engaged that a sleight of hand has its best chance of success'.[4] But if, as I believe, the double-time theory is itself at fault, it should be possible to remove from *Othello* the damaging imputation of trickery which has been, however reluctantly, made against it.

The main issue is easy to formulate. It is whether it is true that the Cyprus scenes fall within two successive days, so that we have the extraordinary situation of Othello murdering his wife for adultery (many times committed) on the night after their marriage was consummated. Some of the arguments of the double-time

---

[1] Harley Granville-Barker, *Prefaces to Shakespeare* (two-volume reprint, London, 1958), vol. ii, pp. 24–5.
[2] Bradley, op. cit., p. 428.
[3] Ibid., p. 429.
[4] New Cambridge *Othello* (1960), pp. xxxi, xxxv.

critics look formidable on paper, particularly as Granville-Barker
formulates them—but they have one insuperable flaw. They all
agree that the Short Time action of the final three acts is confined
to a single day (or as Bradley, with characteristic caution, puts it,
'most probably . . .'), yet they also agree that when the play is
acted this is *not* the impression made on the audience. When
Granville-Barker enumerates the apparently systematic indications
that we are proceeding through a single day—early morning
music, midday dinner, evening supper, night, midnight—the
reader is tempted to feel that the case is proved. But a theatre
audience, we are informed—and anyone can test this for himself
—thinks otherwise. It is surely clear whose response is more to
be trusted. They cannot both be right, as these critics (rather
surprisingly) believe: the audience must be right, the critics
wrong.

The reasons for this have been formulated earlier in this chapter. An audience can only be alerted to a 'time-scheme' if the
dramatist brings it clearly to its attention beforehand. This is what
Shakespeare did in *The Comedy of Errors* and in the middle scenes
of *Romeo and Juliet*. In both these plays the plot turned on matters
of timing and mistiming. In the case of *Othello*, on the other hand,
there is nothing corresponding to the time fixed for Ægeon's
execution or the wedding between Juliet and Paris on Thursday.
While watching the last three acts of *Othello*—the scenes of
Othello's collapse into jealousy and violence—we do not reflect
'How many hours, or how many days, or how many weeks, is
Othello taking to succumb to jealousy?' These questions do not
come into our heads because the dramatist never at any point
prompts them. While watching the play we contemplate a process to which such matters are irrelevant.

However, it may be fairly objected that there is at least one part
of the play where we are pointedly made to think about the
passage of time: the third scene of the second act. This is the first
night on Cyprus, the wedding night of Othello and Desdemona,
and the night in which Cassio gets himself cashiered for drunkenness. It is one of those scenes—there are other examples in Shakespeare—which give us the illusion of passing through an entire
night: through the earlier then the later stages of the evening,
midnight, the small hours, first light—a series of small actions all
conceived as part of a single continuous movement and orches-

trated with a bold economy. Since this is clearly a nocturnal movement, we naturally endow it with the duration which nights
usually have in our experience, and to this extent thoughts of
duration can be said to enter our minds. Moreover Shakespeare
carefully prepares us for this time-conscious movement. Near the
end of II. i Iago instructs Roderigo how he is to anger Cassio and
stir up a 'mutiny'. We are in this way clearly apprised of the
shape of the coming episode. Next (II. ii), the Herald reads his
proclamation and pointedly refers to the time by the clock: 'there
is full liberty of feasting from this present hour of five till the bell
have told eleven.' This reference to the time makes its contribution
to the scene that follows (early on, Iago tells us "Tis not yet ten a
clock,' II. iii. 13–14), for it sets going in our minds an imaginative
equivalent to a clock which is essential to the movement which
now begins from evening till dawn. (Comparable to it is another
all-night scene: v. iii of *Richard III*, the night before Bosworth.
Again we are informed of the time: *Richard*. 'What is't o' clock?'
Catesby. 'It's supper-time, my lord. / It's nine o'clock.' This mention of the time sets a timepiece going during the long nocturnal
movement that follows.) However, with the coming of morning
in III. i and the start of the main action of the play—the destruction
of Othello and Desdemona—we enter a new structural phase with
its own quite new rhythm. Unlike the movement just discussed,
the new movement is not inaugurated by any indications of time,
except for one or two details which make it clear that the new
scene begins on the morning after the night of Cassio's disgrace.
(*Iago*. 'You have not been abed, then?' *Cassio*. 'Why, no: the day
had broke before we parted.' III. i. 30–1.) This absence of any
clear indications of a time-scheme governing the new movement
is important, for it means that we are in effect entering upon a
phase of the action which is, for dramatic purposes, unspecified
as to its duration. The mistake of the critics is to suppose that,
since for a special limited purpose we are adverted of the passage
of time in II. ii and II. iii, we are also to keep the time in mind
throughout the three remaining acts. The truth is, however, that
the fall of Cassio should be kept formally distinct from the much
greater fall of Othello which follows it. The first is accomplished
within the limits of a single night; the second is, as we shall see,
altogether more indefinite. In the first, considerations of time and
duration are relevant; in the second, they are not.

Before we look more closely at the last three acts it should be noticed that Iago's plan to destroy Othello and Desdemona—announced near the end of Act Two—still has something vague and indistinct, even impracticably grandiose about it:

> ... And out of her own goodness make the net
> That shall enmesh them all.
>
> (II. iii. 350–1)

This is quite different from the more limited objectives which were behind his plan to get Cassio drunk and disgraced. The new moves against Othello and Desdemona have not been clearly thought out; there is a great deal of scope for improvisation, and we do in fact embark with Iago on his great effort of Act Three without much sense of what shape it is going to take. This in itself is a sign that we are entering upon a phase of unspecified duration: the indefiniteness of his plans is consistent with a vaguely protracted period of time. It is, moreover, significant that Iago has *not* informed us that he intends to accomplish his ends within a single day. If he had, there would be no problem for the time-critics. But he has not; and his (or Shakespeare's) silence on the extraordinary rapidity of Othello's downfall is one of the main reasons for disbelieving in it. For no one in the last act of the play draws our attention to the fact (if fact it is) that Othello has murdered his wife on the night after they had consummated their marriage. Instead, as everyone agrees, the impression we have is that some time has elapsed between their first day together and their deaths—but exactly how much time is impossible to say, because we are not told. The 'clock' which is set going in II. ii and which continues to tick—though with stylized speed—throughout II. iii, fades out of hearing at the beginning of III. i. Indeed Iago's remark

> By th' mass, 'tis morning!
> Pleasure and action make the hours seem short
>
> (II. iii. 366–7)

glances retrospectively over the entire previous movement and announces, in effect, its imminent cessation. For with the entry of Emilia (III. i. 40), who promises to help Cassio to forward his suit, our attention is taken up with the intricacies of Iago's schemes to the exclusion of any continuous awareness of the passage of time.

But what of the apparent indications, listed by Granville-Barker,

of a chronological progression through a single day: morning
music, dinner at midday, supper, and the rest? These references
undeniably appear in an order which makes the reading of the
Short Time critics at least superficially plausible. It seems to me
that two factors contribute to their mistake. In the first place, the
absence of a sub-plot or a secondary action has the effect of
focussing attention on the sustained continuativeness of the
sequence of scenes. (Roderigo does not appear between II. iii and
IV. ii, so that in the middle scenes of the play there is nothing to
distract us from the main action.) In other plays, *The Merchant of
Venice*, *As You Like It*, or *King Lear*, for example, the alternating
threads of action work to distract attention from the deliberately
vague indications of time. But a reader of *Othello* who is determined to find a time-scheme may be encouraged to do so by the
single-minded continuativeness of all the Cyprus scenes. As in
Julius Caesar, however, the fact that a dramatic action has been constructed with a view to maximum scenic continuity does not, or
need not, imply that in any simple sense it took place within forty-
eight hours.

Secondly, the action of the middle scenes of *Othello*, and especially those in which Desdemona appears, has a conspicuously
domestic atmosphere. When in III. iii Shakespeare has her appear
to fetch Othello to dinner—

> Your dinner, and the generous islanders
> By you invited, do attend your presence
>
> (284–5)

—the point is not to remind us of the time of day, which is immaterial, but to show Desdemona performing her domestic con-
jugal role. (It also has the technical function of getting Othello
off stage for a while, so that during his absence Iago can gain
possession of the handkerchief.) Her reference here to dinner is in
keeping with her previous concern with inviting Cassio to a meal
(the whole passage, III. iii. 58–84, is a good example of Desdemona's domestic ambience, the 'house affairs' (I. iii. 147) which
are her proper domain).[1] The domestic setting suggested by such

[1] The way Desdemona appears in order to invite her husband to dinner is paralleled in other plays, all of them comedies. In *The Merry Wives of Windsor*, Anne Page
comes to announce dinner at the end of I. i, and at II. i. 140 Mrs. Page says to her
husband: 'You'll come to dinner, George?' Cf. *Comedy of Errors*, II. ii. 205, and *Much
Ado*, II. iii. 224. In all of them the women are shown performing an appropriate

details as these may admittedly have the effect of bringing to mind ordinary everyday ways of measuring time. But we should not make the mistake of supposing the play to be more naturalistic than it really is. For despite these domestic touches the action is as highly stylized as it ever is in Shakespeare; we are not watching a piece of late nineteenth-century realism. When Desdemona comes to invite him to dinner, Othello goes off with her, but forty lines later he returns—presumably, if we wish to say so, having dined—although forty lines' playing-time might seem rather inadequate to cover the interval during which Othello as Governor of Cyprus and his guests sat through a formal meal. Of course we hear nothing more about this dinner, but the way it is used at this point helps to show that this scene is not to be taken as a naturalistic representation of events as they would have happened in 'real life'. F. R. Leavis's remarks on the speed with which Othello succumbs to Iago's insinuations, based on the number of lines spoken by the actors, are equally wide of the mark.[1] What we see in a performance of *Othello* is, as with *Julius Caesar*, an imitation of an action. The imitation—the play itself—may last only two or three hours, but the action which it imitates has an unspecified duration.

But even if all this is granted, it may still be objected that the references listed by Granville-Barker—morning music, dinner, supper, etc.—fall into a suspiciously apt order, so that it might still be maintained that Shakespeare was thinking in terms of a single day. It is, after all, undeniable that Act Three begins with morning and Act Five takes place at about midnight. In the first place, the impression made on the minute reader (though not on an 'uncritical' one, or on an audience) that a single day has passed may not be intentional on Shakespeare's part as far as the concluding night sequence is concerned, since his plot required him to end with a night scene if Othello was to murder Desdemona in their marriage bed. That is to say, the fact that the play ends with a night scene may not—I think it does not—have anything to do with a time-scheme involving the passage of a single day. There are, in fact, three night sequences in *Othello* (the others are in Acts

domestic role. Only in *The Comedy of Errors,* where there is in any case a single-day time-scheme extending through the entire play, is there any suggestion that the summons to dinner has a secondary function of indicating the time of day.

[1] F. R. Leavis, 'Diabolic Intellect and the Noble Hero', in *The Common Pursuit* (London, 1952).

One and Two), but they are all apparently introduced for pragmatic dramatic reasons (as was the case with the conspiracy scene
in *Julius Caesar*), not because a time-scheme required them.
Secondly, the series of references to activities appropriate to
evening and night which are purposefully worked into the dialogue
from iv. i. 156 and 177 onwards (*Bianca*. 'An you'll come to supper
to-night, you may'; *Othello*. 'Ay, let her rot, and perish, and be
damn'd to-night') are there in order to knit the sequence together
with exceptional tightness so as to increase anticipation and suspense. There are further references at iv. i. 200, 203, 206, 258, iv.
ii. 105, 170, 216, 232, and 240—all of them are to 'this night' or
'to-night', when Cassio will 'sup' with Bianca, when Lodovico will
'sup' with Othello and Desdemona, when Iago and Roderigo
will make their murderous attempt on Cassio, and when Othello
will suffocate Desdemona. Of this sequence (iv. ii to v. ii) at least
we can say that it takes place on a day and the night following it,
for whether in reading the play or in seeing it acted the reiteration
of phrases reminding us of what is to happen on the coming
evening and night is unmistakable. But we should not, and in
performance we do not, make any retrospective links with the
earlier scenes of Act Three so as to say that *all* these events happened on the same day.

An analogue may be found in *As You Like It*. The middle scenes,
those set in the Forest of Arden from iii. ii to v. i, take place in a
quite unspecified time; we are agreeably free from any sense of
temporal pressure. The beginning of the end comes with the arrival
of Oliver in iv. iii—not that he brings anything but good will,
but that his appearance in a morally converted state seems to be the
first move towards the complex denouement of the play's end.
Then, in v. ii, Shakespeare begins working into the dialogue
precise time references: 'Let your wedding be to-morrow', says
Orlando to Oliver (v. ii. 12), and from this point until the next
scene the word 'to-morrow' sounds repeatedly (cf. v. ii. 39, 45,
62, 66, 106, 108, 110, v. iii. 1, 2—all of them references to the
weddings that are to take place on the next day, in the play's
final scene). The way in which a sense of time becomes particularized in this penultimate phase of the play is exactly analogous to
what we have in *Othello*, with 'to-night' corresponding to 'to-
morrow', and the appearance of Lodovico in Cyprus (iv. i)
matching the appearance of Oliver in Arden. Similarly too, just

as Orlando expresses weariness with his wooing game with
'Ganymede' ('I can live no longer by thinking', v. ii. 47), thus
preparing for the denouement, so in his last colloquy with Iago,
Roderigo also betrays impatience, which we feel to be a signal of
the approaching end: 'Faith, I have heard too much; for your
words and performances are no kin together' (IV. ii. 183). What
matters to Shakespeare is the shape of the play, the effect it has
on the audience, not the maintenance of time-schemes. Towards
the end of IV. i of *As You Like It* Orlando takes his leave of
Rosalind saying he is to 'attend the Duke at dinner' and that he
will return at two o'clock. Here the exceptional reference to a
precise time (otherwise 'there's no clock in the forest') is entirely
pragmatic: it has nothing to do with a time-scheme, but merely
provides Orlando with a reason for taking his leave, while in
IV. iii his failure to keep his appointment is explained by the
new turn taken by the plot.

   If it is accepted that the traditional application to *Othello* of the
double-time theory is mistaken, then some points of interpretation
which depend on it will have to be revised. It is often said that one
reason for the rapidity or impetuosity of the action in its middle
and later phases is that Iago's intrigues would be discovered if
the time were long drawn out. So Granville-Barker asks: 'If
Othello were left time for reflection or the questioning of anyone
but Iago, would not the whole flimsy fraud that is practised on
him collapse?'[1] The answer to this must be that, if the action takes
place during an unspecified period of time, then Iago is in no
particular hurry or fear lest his lies should be exposed. There is in
fact no suggestion in the third and fourth acts that Iago feels that
time is against him. And this, I think, accords with what one
feels at a performance. The effect postulated by Granville-Barker
belongs to another play than *Othello* and one quite inferior to it.
Similarly when J. Dover Wilson says that Shakespeare 'used Short
Time to prevent the audience realizing that Othello's acceptance
of Iago's tissue of falsehood was in reality absurd', he is, as elsewhere in his Introduction to the play, conceding that *Othello* is
essentially nothing more than a melodramatic thriller.[2] But in fact
Iago's 'tissue of falsehood' is not absurd, given the unspecified
time of the action. Again, Kenneth Muir remarks: 'If Othello

---

[1] Granville-Barker, op. cit., p. 26.
[2] J. Dover Wilson, New Cambridge *Othello*, p. xxxiv.

were capable of rational thought at this point [i.e. III. iii. 417–30], he would know that Iago and Cassio had had no recent opportunity of sharing a bed.'[1] But if this colloquy between Othello and Iago does not take place on the day after their arrival in Cyprus, then Othello is not being excessively irrational in listening to Iago's story. At a performance of the play we do not, I think, respond in the way which Muir's remark would suggest. We know that Iago is lying, but it is not an impossible lie. When he says

> I lay with Cassio lately,
> And, being troubled with a raging tooth,
> I could not sleep . . .
>
> (III. iii. 417–19)

what strikes us is Iago's audacity and cunning, his brilliantly telling choice of circumstance, not the impossibility of his fabrications, nor Othello's incapacity for thought.

The conclusion we are drawn to is that the action of *Othello*, like that of its narrative source, Cinthio's *novella*, extends through a considerable, though unspecified, period of time, and consequently that there is no need to resort to a double-time theory to account for features of the play which in any case do not exist for an audience at a performance.[2]

IV

However we may wish to modify the theories of the nineteenth-century time critics, they did at least draw attention to one important feature of Shakespeare's dramaturgy: namely, the close connections between scene and scene—what John Wilson more than once called 'the consecution of the scenes'.[3] A good example of their work is the section on Time in the Cowden Clarkes'

[1] New Penguin *Othello* (1968), ed. Kenneth Muir, pp. 27–8.

[2] It will be apparent that I am unable to accept Ned Allen's theory that *Othello* was composed in two separate parts, comprising the first two and the last three acts, and that the time-indications of each part are internally consistent but mutually incompatible. See 'The Two Parts of "Othello" ', in *Shakespeare Survey*, vol. 21 (1968).

[3] A similar phrase is used by Glynne Wickham; he remarks of Elizabethan drama: 'From the Miracle Cycles the new plays received their structural form, a consecution of scenes'. See *Early English Stages*, vol. ii, Part 1 (London, 1963), p. 36.

Shakespeare Key, which is still a useful survey of this aspect of
Shakespeare's technique. A later critic, T. M. Raysor, has suggested some interesting reasons as to why Shakespeare was so
concerned to maintain scenic continuity. In his view the plays
were designed for continuous performance, with no intervals;
and after a close inspection of all the plays he found that 'Shakespeare's solicitude to fill every time-interval is a striking characteristic of his art. . . . I find that he habitually indicates an interval
of time by means of an intervening action, apparently even when
the choruses such as those in *Henry V* would sufficiently bridge
the gap without supplementary dialogue. The most impressionistic
methods are observed, so that a five-minute action on the stage
may be used for an action off stage (or merely a blank interval of
time) which would require hours, or days, or months. But in all
cases the intervals were supplied with some sort of action on the
stage.' For example, when a character departs in order to make a
journey or to perform some action or other, another scene intervenes so that when the character reappears his journey or action
can be imagined as having taken place during his absence from
the stage. This is a very obvious mimetic principle, but Shakespeare is unusually sensitive to the proportions and rhythms
necessary to secure imaginative belief in the concurrent passage
of time and traversing of space. Raysor concludes: 'The flowing
continuity of his plays, like that of music, is an achievement de-
pendent upon his consciousness of time and shows a profound
understanding of the nature of drama and of the human consciousness in general.'[1] Raysor's shift of stress on to the consciousness of
the members of the audience is a sound one; so too is the suggestion he makes that the continuous performance of a play
establishes 'a theatrical unity of time': it accords with what
we have already seen of Shakespeare's habitual concern with
audience control, his constant awareness of the actual time elap-
sing during the performance of a play as opposed to the fictitious
time passing in the imagined world of the action.

In his 'solicitude to fill every time-interval' Shakespeare reveals
himself as a writer of modified neo-classical sympathies. That is

---

[1] T. M. Raysor, 'The Æsthetic Significance of Shakespeare's Handling of Time',
Studies in Philology, 32 (1935), and 'Intervals of Time and their Effect upon Dramatic
Values in Shakespeare's Tragedies', *Journal of English and Germanic Philology*, 37
(1938).

to say, he usually favoured an extended sequence involving more than the 'single day' of strict neo-classical theory, but he combined it with a neo-classical insistence on tight connection, strong dramatic syntax; the result was a lucid sequence which illustrated cause and effect. A similar concern is noticed by K. O. Myrick in his study of Sidney's revised *Arcadia*. He shows convincingly that Sidney revised his *Arcadia* in accordance with the epic theory of the Italian critic Minturno: 'in each book of the *New Arcadia* he keeps his narrative continuous from beginning to end'; 'he has learned to keep his story unbroken in exciting scenes'. And speaking of the narrative sequence in terms of a journey he remarks: 'the occasions when Sidney has interrupted the journey with even the most trivial break are far outnumbered by those, too numerous to mention, when he takes pains to have us follow a character from one scene to the next. Especially noteworthy are the nameless messengers with whom we often travel, and whose prominence is hard to understand except as a device for connecting two incidents.'[1] At the time when Shakespeare wrote *Julius Caesar*, the *Arcadia* must have seemed easily the most ambitious and impressive work of contemporary English literature. The full extent of its influence on Shakespeare has yet to be described, but it may be that not the least of Shakespeare's debts to Sidney lay in this matter of scenic continuity.

Shakespeare evolved his own freer version of what French neo-classical theorists were to call *liaison des scènes*. He has nothing, of course, of the systematic regularity with which the French practice was later formulated; but his care to maintain continuity, which is to be observed especially in the arrival and departure of characters, is a sign of the same desire for unity and coherence of design.

[1] K. O. Myrick, *Sir Philip Sidney as a Literary Craftsman* (Cambridge, Mass., 1935), pp. 136–7, 144, 145. Cf. Alwin Thaler, *Shakespeare and Sir Philip Sidney* (Cambridge, Mass., 1947), for the possible influence on Shakespeare of Sidney's *Apology for Poetry*.

3. The Two-Part Structure

I

MODERN editions of Shakespeare regularly present the plays in the five-act arrangement first applied to the whole of Shakespeare by Nicholas Rowe in his edition of 1709. Rowe worked on the neo-classical assumption that the division of plays into five acts was the correct and natural scheme of things. But he was not, as is sometimes thought, simply imposing an Augustan scheme on plays written according to a different plan. The First Folio (1623) had led the way by showing a similar concern for neo-classical regularity. All the comedies in the First Folio are divided into five acts, some of them into scenes as well. The histories and tragedies are more irregular, but some (*King John*, *Richard II*, *1* and *2 Henry IV*, *Richard III*, and *Henry VIII*; and *Macbeth*, *King Lear*, *Othello*, and *Cymbeline*) are divided into acts and scenes, although sometimes the division goes astray; others are divided into acts only (*Henry V*, *1 Henry VI*, *Coriolanus*, and *Julius Caesar*); while *2* and *3 Henry VI*, *Troilus and Cressida*, *Romeo and Juliet*, *Timon of Athens*, and *Antony and Cleopatra* have nothing marked after an opening 'Actus Primus, Scoena Prima'. *Hamlet* is exceptional, with the first three scenes of Act One and the first scene of Act Two marked, but nothing else.

Shakespeare died in 1616, and the First Folio was set up for the press during the years 1621–3. It may be that the editors of the Folio wanted to emulate the dignified classical appearance of Jonson's *Works*, which had appeared in the year of Shakespeare's death. Even so it is strange that the labour which they seem to have expended on marking act and scene division did not extend to all the plays. But the important question concerns Shakespeare's own attitude to his work. Would he have accepted the five-act division for his plays? Did he think in terms of this structural scheme when he was composing a play? These questions are pertinent, since none of the Quartos (with the exception of the 1622 Quarto of *Othello*) has any act or scene division, so that those versions of his plays which were printed during his lifetime (including the Good Quartos) bear none of the editorial marks of division which any modern reader of Shakespeare takes for granted. A recent book has been devoted to the subject of act division in Elizabethan and Jacobean drama, and the following is part of the author's conclusion on Shakespeare:

> On a closer study of these plays, it becomes apparent that in every case where there were two different 'good' texts of a play (Quarto and Folio), the earlier text was undivided and showed less trace of interpolation from either stage adapter, prompters, scribes or editors than did the later text, which was divided. It was also interesting to note that two texts which appeared for the first time in the Folio were undivided, and also were among the closest to the author's original: *Antony and Cleopatra* and *Timon of Athens*. It appears very doubtful, therefore, that any of the divided plays were originally marked with act headings (except perhaps in the case of *The Tempest*), and that Shakespeare made no regular practice of act division except by means of choruses in *Henry V*, and, possibly, in *Romeo and Juliet* and *Pericles*. The division in his Folio texts appears to have been added later, often as a result of a history in the theater, but sometimes by an editor.[1]

This conclusion about act-division in the printed texts of the plays and possibly also about Shakespeare's practice in his own manuscripts is not necessarily incompatible with the position of T. W. Baldwin, who has argued that Shakespeare learned early in his life how to construct a play after the Terentian pattern.[2] The Terentian commentators, following Donatus, analysed Terence's comedies into five acts which corresponded to five distinct stages in a comic intrigue or action. This method of construction, once learned, could be applied to any play, comic or tragic. In any case the tragedies of Seneca fell naturally into five divisions, and so English neo-Senecan tragedies such as *Gorboduc* were laid out in the expected five-act scheme. Most, though not all, critics would agree that many of Shakespeare's plays observe the five-act arrangement. The act-divisions are particularly clear in some of the comedies, in such tragedies as *Titus Andronicus*,

[1] Wilfred T. Jewkes, *Act Division in Elizabethan and Jacobean Plays 1583–1616* (Hamden, Conn., 1958), pp. 97–8.
[2] T. W. Baldwin, *Shakespere's Five-Act Structure* (Urbana, 1947). Baldwin's thesis was attacked by Henry Snuggs in *Shakespeare and Five Acts* (Washington, 1960). For a sensible compromise position see the review of Snuggs by J. R. Brown (*Modern Language Review*, 57 (1962), 411).

King Lear, and *Macbeth*, and in *Henry V*, where the Chorus appears at all the inter-act divisions. In some other plays it may well be that Shakespeare bore the five-act arrangement in mind, using it as a kind of clock so that the allocation of time to the various parts of his material would be proportionate, and yet doing so in such a free and unsystematic way that the finished play does not very obviously suggest five clearly marked stages. Such a play is *Antony and Cleopatra*, which in the Folio, our only text, has no divisions.

There might have been no harm in marking the act- and scene-divisions in Shakespeare's plays if the task had been carried out with a scrupulous concern for each play's real structure. In a number of cases one can have no quarrel with the Folio's placing of divisions or with Rowe's extension of the method to plays neglected by the Folio. But there are other cases, and those involving some of Shakespeare's best work, where the act-divisions are so placed as to obscure the structural lines of the play. In such cases the loss of the play's real structure can entail failure to see where Shakespeare is stressing meaning. *Hamlet* and *Antony and Cleopatra* are two such cases, and it is possible to argue that *Julius Caesar*, *Othello*, and *Coriolanus* suffer some injury from incorrect act-division.

What a play's true structural lines are would be determined to some extent by the practice of Shakespeare's company in the theatre. It seems clear from internal evidence that Shakespeare was exceptionally careful to maintain continuity; this has made some argue that his plays were written to be acted without an interval or interruption of any sort. In the absence of firm external evidence any generalization about his theatrical practice must be no more than conjecture; nevertheless, a hypothesis concerning the history plays and tragedies may be ventured. (It may also be applicable to such tragicomedies—if the term is warrantable—as *All's Well that Ends Well*, *Measure for Measure*, and *The Winter's Tale*; but the comedies as a whole are not included in this generalization.) It is that a play will usually be found to divide into two unequal movements (corresponding roughly to the first three acts and the last two acts) and that the division between them is such as to make it likely that in performance a major interval took place. It is true that a few plays have their break after the second act, while in others the dividing point is arguable.

But enough plays can be accommodated by this hypothesis to make it seem worth considering.[1]

It has of course not escaped notice that some of Shakespeare's tragedies divide into two parts or movements. In his lecture on 'Construction in Shakespeare's Tragedies', A. C. Bradley describes what he sees as the characteristic pattern in terms of a rising and falling movement, or an action followed by a counteraction:

> Shakespeare's general plan . . . is to show one set of forces advancing, in secret or open opposition to the other, to some decisive success, and then driven downward to defeat by the re-action it provokes.[2]

He notes that some time must elapse between the crisis—the climax of the first action—and the counteraction:

> What seems necessary is a momentary pause, followed by a counteraction which mounts at first slowly, and afterwards, as it gathers force, with quickening speed.[3]

He notes too that the 'decided slackening of tension'[4] that results will usually be found in the fourth act. In his *Prefaces to Shakespeare* Granville-Barker is firmly committed to the view that in ideal circumstances the plays should be acted without any interval; even so, he several times considers where the main interval or intervals should come, on the assumption that complete abstention from them is impracticable. More recently, in a very suggestive essay, the distinguished theatre historian G. F. Kernodle has argued that 'a twofold structure with a new beginning at Act Four, is one of the basic patterns of Elizabethan drama'.[5] And he points out the occasional use of parallelism of motif or situation between the opening of the first and fourth acts; for example (what Bradley had already noticed), the appearance of the Weird Sisters at the opening of the fourth act of *Macbeth*, which parallels their appearance at the beginning of Act One.

Readers of Shakespeare are unlikely to trouble themselves with such matters as intervals; but stage producers, as Granville-Barker

---

[1] A Court performance of *Pericles* in two parts is recorded for 1619; the interval occurred after the second act. See New Arden *Pericles* (1963), ed. F. D. Hoeniger, p. lxvi.

[2] A. C. Bradley, *Shakespearean Tragedy*, p. 55.

[3] Ibid., p. 56.   [4] Ibid.

[5] G. F. Kernodle, 'The Symphonic Form of "King Lear" ', in *Elizabethan Studies* presented to George F. Reynolds (Boulder, Colo. 1945), p. 185.

concedes, must give it some thought. They have to determine the best place or places for a pause in the performance, a stopping-place where actors and audience can rest; and in doing so they are likely to find, if they are at all competent, the true lines of continuity and break within the text. The obvious guide here will be the system of linked scenes which was referred to in the previous chapter. It will often be found that only one or two places in the text definitely indicate a break, a place where the usual tight continuity is for some otherwise unexplained reason relaxed. In *Hamlet* and *Othello* there may at first appear to be two such breaks or pauses; in both these plays the first apparent break occurs after the first act, where in *Hamlet* there is or seems to be a lapse of time, and in *Othello* a change of location from Venice to Cyprus. But it is highly unlikely that at a point so close to the beginning of the play an interval would be arranged. It looks as if what may at first seem slight breaks in continuity in these plays after the first act are simply the result of unusually well-defined expositions. The change of location in *Othello*, for example, is well prepared for in I. iii, and taken up in the usual well-knit way at the beginning of II. i. In *Hamlet*, as in *Othello*, there is probably only one place for a major interval, and it occurs in the usual position : at about the end of the third act.

That there is often a marked break in this position can probably be taken as established. But the critical implications of this arrangement have not been by any means fully explored. The aim of this chapter is to consider some of them.

II

We have seen in Chapter 2 that it is because Shakespeare is so exceptionally attentive to matters of continuity and causality that he is able to manipulate the audience's consciousness of time in such a masterful way. Indeed to the reader who has leisure to analyse how the illusion is effected, it can seem nothing less than audacious. When it suits his dramatic purposes Shakespeare will introduce his 'nights' and 'mornings' so that we have, at odd intervals, a vague sense of the passage of ordinary time, with its days and nights and with occasional specific hours of the day thrown in. At the same time we sense the lapse of much longer periods, although their duration is usually kept tactfully indefinite. Hours,

days, years are all evoked; and it is in part due to the illusion we
have that different time units are concurrently passing that the plays
(or the greater ones) can make such a deep impression on us:

> For 'tis your thoughts that now must deck our kings,
> Carry them here and there, jumping o'er times,
> Turning th' accomplishment of many years
> Into an hour-glass . . .

(Henry V, Prologue, 28–31)

Such plays are, among other things, dense and complex images of
time.

Shakespeare's concern with continuity is the most obvious
means whereby he casts his spell on the audience, so ensuring that
they accept his boldly imaginative treatment of time. Each long
concatenation of scenes habituates us to an imagined system or
world; but once the continuity is broken, as it must be if the play
has an interval, the imaginative system is dissolved and another
one must replace it when the play is resumed after the interval.
T. M. Raysor's notion of a 'theatrical unity of time', referred to
earlier, is relevant here.[1] Such a unity, he maintained, could be
established only by continuous performance. But if a play were
divided into two by an interval, then it would also divide into two
distinct systems, each with its own 'theatrical unity of time'.
This is, I think, what we find in many of the histories and tragedies; for within the larger imaginative unity of the play as a whole,
each of the two main parts has its own lesser unity which will be
best appreciated in continuous performance. Raysor's comparison
of the 'flowing continuity' of these plays to that of music is
entirely apt. It follows that their natural intervals need to be
observed in performance at least as scrupulously as the pauses
between movements in symphonic works.

If this suggestion concerning the imaginative unity of each of
the two parts is accepted, several others lead on from it. An interval will have the effect of releasing us from the powerful dramatic
illusion which has been established during the first part of the
play. What Shakespeare often does is to treat the interval as a
licence to himself to make considerable changes in the substance
and presentation of his material, changes which otherwise—that

---

[1] T. M. Raysor, 'The Æsthetic Significance of Shakespeare's Handling of Time',
Studies in Philology, 32 (1935), 202.

is, without an interval—might seem inadmissibly abrupt. Characterization, for example, can be radically modified. But also affected will be such things as tone and mood, quality and range of feeling, indeed the whole nature of the audience's involvement with the events on stage. If we fail to notice the purposeful contrasts in the dramatic substance before and after the interval, we shall probably respond less clearly to what is in front of us (as if one had not noticed that a sonnet was divided into an octave and a sestet). However, these general remarks can be best tested by considering particular plays.

Richard III is a comparatively early and unusually clear example of Shakespeare's structural method in this matter of the two parts. The interval comes where stage producers usually put it: at the end of the third act. The first three acts have had a single main concern: Richard's struggle to get the Crown. The first act, largely fictitious, deals with the disposal of Clarence; a subsidiary matter is the wooing of Anne. The second act is closer to history: King Edward dies, and his boy-heir is brought to London where his uncle Gloucester awaits him as Protector. Act Three sees a marked acceleration of events: the last obstacles to Richard are removed—Hastings and others—and finally the citizenry of London are manœuvred into offering Richard the Crown. At this point there is a sense of completion and fulfilment, and the play pauses. This is the natural place for an interval—indeed the way Shakespeare has disposed his material seems to require it. For the final two acts have a quite different orientation from the first three. Richard is now King; he is no longer murdering his way to a throne. The subject of these two acts is quite simply his fall, ultimately at the hands of Tudor Richmond. Richmond's name is therefore pointedly brought into the text: twice in the first scene of the fourth act (IV. i. 43, 92), again in the following scene, this time six times (IV. ii. 89, 97, 100, 101, 107, 111), three times in the following short scene (IV. iii. 40, 46, 49), and so on. We are repeatedly made to recall Richmond and the outcome at Bosworth. The second part of *Richard III* is Richmond's, although his stage role is very limited and kept well subordinated to Richard's. The over-all structural lines of the play are clear: the first part might be called 'Getting the Crown', the second 'Losing it'.

The characterization of Richard is in keeping with this sharply differentiated two-part arrangement. In the first three acts he is overpoweringly energetic, resourceful, witty, and sardonically amusing. Above all, he enjoys the peculiar close *rapport* with the audience which stage characters of his type inherited from the early Tudor 'Vice'. However much our moral feelings may protest, Richard makes exhilarating stage company as he 'bustles' (his word) about the stage, manipulating the other characters, devising 'scenes' in which he will act the star part, and deploying his brilliant gifts of mimicry in a chain of clearly recognizable stage roles—affectionate brother, wilfully dominating wooer, honest 'plain' man, dutiful son, and finally in the third act a punctiliously moral and primly pious cleric, a kind of latter-day Henry VI. But in the last two acts he is divested of his boisterous and savage gaiety; no gleam of humour is allowed him, and he no longer has any use for mimicry. He is now the Tyrant, ripe for overthrow, grim, sleepless, friendless, and, on the night before death, anticipating God's judgement. Shakespeare has of course given Richard enough consistency of personality throughout all five acts to make him a convincing character, and in performance the actor will carry the audience with him; but there is unquestionably a sharp change after the third act, which affects the tone of the entire play, so that the first part might be described as in a large sense comic and upward moving (despite such isolated but powerful episodes as the death of Clarence), and the second part as tragic and declining.

There is, however, a further structural feature, well exemplified in *Richard III*, which is clarified by being seen in the setting of a two-part structure. This is the placing of an elaborately developed climactic sequence in the third act. Bradley had noticed that such scenes or sequences tended to occur at this position: in *Julius Caesar* the assassination of Caesar and the Forum scene, in *Hamlet* the play scene and its consequences, in *Macbeth* the banquet scene. But he had not related this feature with the possible occurrence of an interval shortly after it. In Shakespeare's two-part arrangement the exciting material of his third acts was no doubt a highly satisfactory way of leading up to a break in the performance. We have reached a point of partial fulfilment and rest (a provisional ending), but the situation is rich in unrealized potentialities (a provisional beginning). The same explanation accounts for the low tension of many of the fourth acts. The play now makes a fresh start; the dramatist has to re-engage his audience's interest, in some cases win their sympathy for an unfamiliar group of characters or a new kind of dramatic material. Of course the audience will want to know what happens next; they will have an interest in the hero's fortunes which the dramatist can at this point take for granted; but Bradley's observation still holds : there will sometimes be 'a decided slackening of tension' in the fourth act, although this is not the same thing as a falling-off in real interest.

In *Richard III* the main object of the first part of the play—getting the Crown—has reached a crisis in Act Three. In the first half of the act Richard clears the stage for himself: the young Prince Edward is lodged in the Tower, the Queen's kinsfolk are executed at Pomfret, and finally Hastings too is brought to a sudden and ignominious end. Then the second half of the act presents Richard himself as a main actor, paradoxically now taking an ostensibly passive role—the pious recluse, bitterly reluctant to take upon himself the cares of kingship. It is in this last phase of his climb to royal power (III. v to III. vii) that Shakespeare devises a sequence so extravagantly histrionic in conception as to seem like a half-acknowledged play-within-a-play. The theatrical metaphor is certainly in Shakespeare's—and Richard's—mind:

> *Gloucester.* Come, cousin, canst thou quake and change thy colour,
> Murder thy breath in middle of a word,
> And then again begin, and stop again,
> As if thou were distraught and mad with terror?
> *Buckingham.* Tut, I can counterfeit the deep tragedian;
> Speak and look back, and pry on every side,
> Tremble and start at wagging of a straw,
> Intending deep suspicion . . .

(III. v. 1–8)

And the sequence that follows till the end of the act has a peculiarly heightened, histrionic intensity. This is largely because in earlier scenes Richard had usually been the sole 'actor'; he had assumed roles hypocritically and played them before audiences ignorant of the deception. But now he has engaged Buckingham as a fellow actor, and this establishes the atmosphere of true theatricality: a group-assumption of roles devised and rehearsed beforehand.

A sequence of this kind, highly elaborate, and often with a distinctly self-conscious or histrionic colouring, is a feature which Shakespeare favoured for his third acts and which he used at all stages of his career from the *Henry VI* plays to *Coriolanus* and *Timon of Athens*. (The trial of Hermione in *The Winter's Tale*, III. ii, makes a similar effect.) In *Henry VI, Part Two*, for example, the climactic third act presents, first, the baiting of Duke Humphrey by the Queen and her allies (III. i), then in a tableau the murder of Humphrey which is followed by a weighty court scene (III. ii), and finally the immediate consequences of the murder in the remorseful death of Cardinal Beaufort (III. iii) and the banishment and killing of Suffolk (IV. i). (Here the Folio act-division is questionable—though it may be right—since Suffolk's death is arguably part of the sequence which began in III. i. If an interval were placed after Suffolk's death, the second movement of the play would open with the fresh interest supplied by Jack Cade, who enters in the following scene.) In *Henry VI, Part Three* the alternative arrangement is used: the break in the action occurs earlier, at the end of the second act. For the play falls into two movements whose chief contents are indicated in the Quarto's title: *The True Tragedie of Richard Duke of York, and the death of good King Henrie the Sixt* . . .[1] The first act culminates in the death of York at Wakefield, and the second in the major defeat of the Lancastrians at Towton and the death of Clifford. At II. vi. 31 the victorious Yorkists enter, and Edward, now king, announces what seems the conclusion of hostilities ('Now breathe we, lords: good fortune bids us pause / And smooths the frowns of war with peaceful looks'). It sounds almost as if we are at the end of the play; a break in the performance seems called for. The sequence that follows makes a fresh start, and establishes an altogether different rhythm: Henry VI, now in Scotland, is captured (III. i); Edward woos Lady Elizabeth Grey, while Richard Gloucester announces, in a tremendous monologue, his designs on the crown (III. ii); and then, in France, Warwick indignantly joins with Margaret on hearing of Edward's totally unexpected marriage (III. iii). From now on Warwick supports Henry. The first movement of *3 Henry VI*, therefore, shows Warwick with the Yorkists, the second with the Lancastrians. In the first movement the Yorkist leader is killed (*'The True Tragedie of Richard Duke of York'*), in the second the Lancastrian (*'the death of good King Henrie the Sixt'*). The final scene

---

[1] This break in the action is pointed out by E. W. Talbert in the course of an excellent analysis of *3 Henry VI*. See *Elizabethan Drama and Shakespeare's Early Plays* (Chapel Hill, N.C., 1963), pp. 218–20.

of the play shows Edward IV with his brothers, again victorious, just as II. vi had done. And again the note is one of confident— though, as we know, precarious—stability. This large structural device—having the two parts conclude on a similar note (it may be considered as a kind of structural rhyme)—is one which Shake- speare returned to more than once in later plays.

He uses it in *Julius Caesar* and *Hamlet*, although in both cases his design has been obscured by misleading act-division. *Julius Caesar* is a particularly clear example of a play designed in two parts, with the division coming at about the end of the third act. The first part of the play concerns the conspiracy against Caesar and his assassination, with its immediate consequences in the Forum. The second part shows the defeat of the conspirators. The first part is set in Rome, the second in the 'field' (Sardis and Philippi). The planned differences between the two parts extend to such matters as characterization and the nature of the emotional response elicited from the audience. In the first part of *Julius Caesar* Shakespeare deliberately baffles our feelings and sym- pathies; it is hard to feel warmly about any of the characters and impossible to identify oneself with any of them for long. But in the second part the play makes a strong and successful bid for our sympathies on behalf of Brutus and Cassius. The quarrel scene (IV. iii), the farewell scene (V. i), and the deaths of the two friends have a strong 'sentimental' interest which brings out by contrast the relative coldness and the critical distancing with which nearly all the characters have been presented in the first part. Cassius, for example, shows (so to speak) a different profile in each of the two parts. In the first, in keeping with his conspiratorial role, we are made to observe his envy of Caesar, his restlessness, and the way he coolly goes about the task of working Brutus into a suitably discontented frame of mind. But in the second part he is the vulnerable, even weak, 'shortsighted', faithful friend, who has even undergone a modified form of religious conversion—his earlier Epicureanism is discarded: 'now I change my mind, / And partly credit things that do presage' (v. i. 77–8). As with Richard Gloucester, there is of course a real consistency of personality persisting throughout these changes which makes us accept them as developments rather than violations of his character. Neverthe- less there is a marked difference, indeed contrast, between the two profiles of Cassius in the first and second parts of the play.

I suggested that *Julius Caesar* makes use of the device of 'structural rhyming'—the two parts of the play having like endings—and that this feature had been obscured by wrong act-division. The First Folio ends the third act with the scene of the poet Cinna's death at the hands of the mob. The first scene of Act Four shows the triumvirate working out their list of proscriptions. This is the first time that Octavius has appeared. Although he is quietly ushered on to the stage, his appearance needs a discreet emphasis, for it is Octavius who, historically, is to survive all the other main characters of the drama, including Antony. His presence in the play, though not on the stage, is first announced immediately after Antony's soliloquy, spoken over Caesar's body in III. i: Octavius' servant enters announcing that his master is 'within seven leagues of Rome'. He is next mentioned at the end of the Forum scene (III. ii. 263 ff.), when a servant again enters to Antony announcing, 'Sir, Octavius is already come to Rome', and the scene ends with a further reminder of their coming encounter: 'Bring me to Octavius'. The following brief scene shows the killing of Cinna, and the next (IV. i) the meeting of Antony, Octavius, and Lepidus, which opens with the ugly words: 'These many, then, shall die; their names are prick'd.' These actions seem plainly part of a sequence which requires continuous performance if the ironies of its scenic juxtapositions are to be realized.[1] The scene after this one (IV. ii) shows Brutus and Cassius in their camp near Sardis; this makes a sharp break from what has gone before. It does not connect with anything before it in Shakespeare's usual closely knit manner; the last that we had heard of Brutus and Cassius was merely that they had 'rid like madmen through the gates of Rome' (III. ii. 270). The present scene in the camp initiates a new sequence, that of the second part of the play. If this is so, the Folio's IV. i might be better numbered III. iv. Its detachment from its true position as the last scene in the sequence following Caesar's assassination is analogous to the Folio's placing of the scene of Suffolk's death in Act Four of *2 Henry VI*. If *Julius*

[1] There is perhaps a slight difficulty. Antony says he will meet Octavius and Lepidus at Caesar's house (III. ii. 266); but editors give the locality of IV. i as 'Antony's house'. This is because at IV. i. 7 Antony says: 'But, Lepidus, go you to Caesar's house; / Fetch the will hither . . .' J. Dover Wilson notes: 'Sh. forgets (i) that acc. to 3.2.266 the triumvirate should be meeting there (Caesar's house), (ii) that acc. to 3. 2. 130 Ant. himself had taken the will therefrom' (New Cambridge *Julius Caesar* [1949], p. 169).

Caesar, then, is considered as a play with a two-part structure, the first part ends with the triumvirate—or rather (for Lepidus is sent packing early on in the scene, just as he was historically) with the two strong men Antony and Octavius. But the last scene of the second part of the play also ends with Antony and Octavius: they have the last two speeches of v. v just as they have the last two speeches of iv. i. It is of course appropriate that these two should occupy this conclusive position, because they had the last word over the assassins of Julius Caesar (just as Richard Gloucester, later Richard III, in effect had the 'last word' in the two parts of *3 Henry VI*). It is, further, just as appropriate that Octavius should in both parts of *Julius Caesar* have the last speech of all, despite Antony's seniority in age and experience, since he ultimately survived Antony. The formal elegance of *Julius Caesar*, which reveals itself in this 'structural rhyming', is therefore by no means empty of significance.

The same is true of *Hamlet*, probably the next tragedy after *Julius Caesar* to be written. In the modern standard editions Rowe's act-divisions have a particularly unfortunate effect. They do nothing to help the reader to see how the play is shaped. Partly as a result of this, it is not uncommon for *Hamlet* to be thought lacking in the patterning devices more readily discernible in some of the other tragedies. Rowe placed the end of Act Three after the closet scene (iii. iv), but this point could hardly be less well chosen, as subsequent editors often have observed (Granville-Barker called it 'cobbling of the clumsiest'). For this is not really the end of a scene at all. Hamlet tugs off the corpse of Polonius, leaving the Queen on stage; the King enters to her, and the dialogue continues. The Folio has it as follows:

Hamlet. Good night Mother.   *Exit Hamlet tugging in Polonius.*

Enter King.

King. There's matter in these sighes.
These profound heaves
You must translate; Tis fit we understand them.
Where is your Sonne?

If the exit of Hamlet is obviously not the place requiring a break in the performance, where is such a break to be located? The first and second acts, as divided by Rowe, make distinct stages: the first concludes the business of the Ghost with Hamlet's 'O cursed spite, / That ever I was born to set it right!', and the second with his soliloquy 'O, what a rogue and peasant slave am I!' But the third act seemed to pose Rowe with a problem, since the sequence of scenes set going by the performance of the play-within-a-play (III. ii) is so exceptionally long that he probably thought it disproportionate. But this sequence is at the same time so close-knit that any interruption of it must obviously thwart Shakespeare's intentions. The play scene ends with the Queen's summons to Hamlet, announced by Polonius, and with Hamlet's soliloquy ''Tis now the very witching time of night'; the next (III. iii) is the King's prayer scene, which is followed by Hamlet's interview with his mother (III. iv). This scene continues with the King's appearance to the Queen (Rowe marked this IV. i), his discovery of Polonius's death, and his orders to Rosencrantz and Guildenstern to find Hamlet. The following two scenes show Hamlet being fetched before the King and dispatched to England. The next brief scene (IV. iv) sees Fortinbras with his army on their way to Poland. In the Second Quarto, though not in the First Folio, Hamlet appears while Fortinbras and his army march away; he soliloquizes for the last time: 'How all occasions do inform against me.' The next scene (IV. v) opens with the Queen, Horatio, and a Gentleman. The Queen says, 'I will not speak with her.' And Ophelia's mad scenes follow, with the return of Laertes into the action. It is surely plain, as Granville-Barker noticed, that the sequence here allows only one interruption: that after IV. iv, the scene of Fortinbras's appearance and—in the Second Quarto—of Hamlet's soliloquy. If an interval is placed here, it admittedly makes the first part of *Hamlet* exceptionally long—but there is no getting away from the mere length of *Hamlet*. The play must have been drastically cut, as it usually is in modern productions. But if it is acted through without interruption from I. i to IV. iv (as it was in Peter Hall's production at Stratford-upon-Avon in 1965 and 1966), it comes across with unusual clarity.[1]

[1] In his detailed study 'Play Abridgement', in *Shakespeare and the Homilies* (Melbourne, 1934), Alfred Hart argues that 'all plays exceeding 2,300 to 2,400 lines in length would be liable to abridgement and usually would be abridged' (p. 120), and that consequently 'only the seven shortest of Shakespeare's plays would have been acted without abridgement' (p. 134). Hart gives the number of lines in the received text of *Hamlet* as 3,762.

The two parts of *Hamlet* formed by this division need to be compared if the expressive purposes behind Shakespeare's design are to be appreciated. If we ignore all the detail of circumstance and consider only the essential lines of action, then the first part of the play presents us with a sequence as follows. Hamlet accepts the Ghost's command to revenge him; the arrival of the players gives him an opportunity to act, and by the end of this first part (IV. iv) he has abandoned himself to a course of passionate action. But his sole concrete achievement is to have killed Polonius, an act which serves only to deliver himself into the King's hands, and he is dispatched to England. The second part of the play opens with a new situation, an ironical reversal of the first. Laertes is now the injured son, whose father has been murdered; Hamlet is now, from this point of view, the murderer who must be put to death. Moreover Shakespeare has again made use of the device of 'structural rhyming': each of the play's two parts ends with Fortinbras. Fortinbras is mentioned early in the first scene (I. i. 95 ff.); Claudius' business with Norway concerning Fortinbras is twice introduced in succeeding scenes (I. ii. 27 ff., II. ii. 58 ff.), but thereafter he is allowed to be forgotten until his first appearance on stage in the final moments of the first part of the play. Hamlet just misses meeting him, if we accept the Second Quarto's version; in the Folio Hamlet does not appear at all, but the very brief scene of Fortinbras's army passing over the stage is left to make its own quietly eloquent point. The effect is not unlike the quietly emphatic first appearance of Octavius in IV. i of *Julius Caesar*. The second appearance of Fortinbras is at the very end of the play, pointedly matching his scene at the end of the first part—and again Hamlet just misses him. In the context of this exceptionally full and copiously written play, Shakespeare's use of Fortinbras is notable for its economy and reticence.

Closer examination of *Hamlet* would show the differences in characterization, tone, mood, and so on, between the two parts. All Hamlet's soliloquies occur before the interval; when he returns from his sea voyage (the observation is of course a commonplace) he is a changed man—although what precisely constitutes the change may not be agreed. An important character, Polonius, has no part to play after the interval; and this too is a feature of some of the other histories and tragedies—namely, that an important character has his role confined to the first part of the play (e.g. Duke Humphrey, Mercutio, Julius Caesar, Lear's Fool and Cornwall, Banquo). This sometimes has the effect of making the second part of the play seem less complex, lighter, or even thinner in texture. But more positively, it sometimes allows Shakespeare to narrow the emotional range with a view to tragic effect: characters like Mercutio and Polonius are, among other things, a source of laughter; when they are dead, their respective plays are free to move with a more unrelieved gravity to the catastrophe.

III

Most of Shakespeare's other histories and tragedies gain in clarity if they are considered as plays conceived in two unequal movements. Some plays—*Coriolanus* and *Timon of Athens* among them—are so evidently designed in this way that it is not necessary to do more than state the fact. Coriolanus is first a Roman among the Romans, and then a Roman among the Volscians; Timon is first inside the city walls, and then out in the wilderness. In *Coriolanus* the Folio act-division does what it can to obscure this clear contrast, for the sequence of Coriolanus' banishment ends in IV. ii, after which there is a marked break. It would clarify the design if the fourth act were to begin with what Rowe marked IV. iii, the encounter between a Roman and a Volsce which initiates the second movement.

In other plays the division between the two parts is less conspicuous, indeed more open to question altogether. In *Romeo and Juliet* the admirably sustained plot allows of more continuity than usual between the first part of the play and the second. But even so, the conclusion of the third act is a good point for a performance to pause at, if it has to, for an interval. This is at Juliet's soliloquy 'Ancient damnation! O most wicked fiend!' (III. v. 236–43), in which she dismisses the Nurse from her confidence and, in a weightily charged final couplet, looks foward to the play's tragic ending:

> I'll to the friar to know his remedy;
> If all else fail, myself have power to die.

In *Romeo and Juliet* the differences in tone and mood, in the emotional claims made on the audience, before and after the interval, are suggested by the role of the Friar. His counsels of moderation are all confined to the first part; after the interval he resorts to desperate remedies (IV. i. 68 ff.) and for the first time mentions his death-simulating drug. The first part of the play is exuberant, energetic, and various; there is a great deal of humour, with important contributions from Mercutio and the Nurse. The second part is more unrelievedly distressful: Mercutio is dead, the Nurse's role is greatly reduced, and Romeo and Juliet never meet until just before their deaths.

The genre of *Troilus and Cressida* is still in dispute, but at least in structure it has much in common with the tragedies. An interval might well have occurred after III. ii. This is the scene in which Pandarus brings Troilus and Cressida together. The dialogue rises to a sonorous formal chant, as the three characters self-consciously invoke their fame in after-times. The scene ends with the sense of an achieved ritual:

> *Pandarus.* Go to, a bargain made; seal it, seal it; I'll be the witness. Here I hold your hand; here my cousin's. If ever you prove false one to another, since I have taken such pains to bring you together, let all pitiful goers-between be call'd to the world's end after my name—call them all Pandars; let all constant men be Troiluses, all false women Cressids, and all brokers between Pandars. Say 'Amen'.
> *Troilus.* Amen.
> *Cressida.* Amen.
> *Pandarus.* Amen. Whereupon I will show you a chamber and a bed; which bed, because it shall not speak of your pretty encounters, press it to death. Away!
> > And Cupid grant all tongue-tied maidens here,
> > Bed, chamber, pander, to provide this gear!

It makes a perfect conclusion to the first movement of the play. Troilus' immediate object has been achieved: Cressida has relented. And Pandarus' final couplet addressed to the audience fittingly rounds off the movement with an air of finality. It feels as if the action was planned to pause here for an interval. The following scene (III. iii) is set in the Greek camp and introduces an entirely new topic: Cressida's father, Calchas, appears for the first and only time to plead with the Greek lords that Cressida should be exchanged for Antenor. This request initiates the second move-ment of the play, as far as Troilus and Cressida are concerned. Furthermore, the second part ends, like the first, with Pandarus, who again addresses the audience in rhyming couplets (v. x. 45 ff.).

A much earlier play, *King John*, has often been criticized for apparently changing its subject about half-way through. After a short first act which introduces the Bastard Faulconbridge, the action moves to France and centres on the siege of Angiers. It continues in France until the end of the third act, after which it returns to England. *King John* is certainly not very satisfyingly constructed, and no amount of special pleading could conceal its episodic progress. But if one imagines Shakespeare disposing his somewhat intractable material in two unequal parts, the play can be said to gain something in coherence and lucidity. The first part of the play (Acts One to Three) is largely satirical in tone, and the Bastard's presence as a sardonic commentator is all-important. The scene is one of powerful unprincipled politicians making and breaking alliances and oaths, together with their helpless victims and pawns; all provide matter for the Bastard's sermon on 'Com-modity'. But after the interval, if this is placed after iii. iv, the moral concerns of the play are differently orientated. The change is prepared for in iii. iii, with John's suborning of Hubert to murder the child Arthur, and in iii. iv, in which Constance is shown mad with grief. The fourth act opens with the scene set for the blinding of Arthur—which is of course not carried out. His subsequent death and its political consequences, and then the French invasion of England, are the main concerns of the rest of the play. In these last two acts there is no rumbustious satire; the episode of Arthur's death is treated with a grave moral concern, and the Bastard's speech on finding Arthur's body is crucial for the tone of this part of the play:

> Go, bear him in thine arms.
> I am amaz'd, methinks, and lose my way
> Among the thorns and dangers of this world.
> How easy dost thou take all England up!

(iv. iii. 139–42)

And the remaining scenes concerning the French invasion, al-though rather perfunctorily treated, catch something of the

Bastard's national feeling. *King John* as a whole is not perhaps very profoundly unified, but what unity of feeling and tone each of its two parts has is focused in the person of the Bastard. In the first three acts he arouses critical laughter at the expense of the politicians. But in the last two acts his role is sharply modified; his moral passion remains, but the mood is now tragic rather than comic or satirical.

None of the other history plays so far undiscussed divides as clearly as *King John*. The two Parts of *Henry IV* present a special structural problem, as Harold Jenkins has suggested.[1] If Jenkins is right, Shakespeare changed his intentions while in process of writing what we know as *Henry IV, Part One*. Instead of bringing the Hotspur business to a quick conclusion in Act Four and dealing with the King's reconciliation with the Prince and with the rejection of Falstaff in Act Five, he decided (so the argument runs) that his material warranted much fuller treatment; hence the addition of a Second Part. But this meant that he had rather more space than he needed; and the last two acts of *Part One*, as well as much of *Part Two*, are in places uncomfortably diffuse. In *Part One* an interval would be well placed after the third act, which ends with Prince Hal and Falstaff in the Boar's Head Tavern about to move off towards Shrewsbury to meet the rebels. The last two acts are set in the 'field' and show the defeat of Hotspur and his allies. The play is so rich in dramatic matter in its first part that the second part seems a distinct falling-off; but Jenkins's theory of changed intentions may help to account for this. *Henry IV, Part Two* is less lucidly organized; again, the explanation may be that, faced with an insufficiency of historical material, Shakespeare was forced to improvise in the comic scenes. The best place for an interval would seem to be after III. i, but an argument might be made for one after III. ii. The former seems preferable, since the first part of the play would then conclude with the King's appearance. This is his first appearance in the play, and this in itself—his entry so late into the play that bears his name—would be eloquent of the disorderliness of his reign. This argument is strengthened by the fact that the scene is quite unnecessary in terms of plot. Its function is purely thematic: the King appears '*in his nightgown, with a Page*', and the whole scene is in fact a tableau illustrating

---

[1] Harold Jenkins, *The Structural Problem in Shakespeare's 'Henry the Fourth'* (London, 1956).

the line 'Uneasy lies the head that wears a crown'. The mention of Rumour at 97–8 ('Rumour doth double, like the voice and echo, / The numbers of the feared') recalls the appearance of Rumour as the Prologue to the play; and the King's desire to go to the Holy Land, stated in the final couplet, contributes to a system of *leit-motivs* in both Parts of *Henry IV* (first sounded in *Part One*, I. i. 19 ff., and I. i. 101–2, and taken up again in *Part Two*, IV. iv. 1 ff., IV. v. 210–11, IV. v. 235–41). This short scene's functions are many, and Shakespeare makes the most of its contribution by placing it—if an interval did in fact occur here—at the end of the first movement. The next scene (III. ii) introduces a new set of characters: '*Enter* Shallow *and* Silence, *meeting*; Mouldy, Shadow, Wart, Feeble, Bullcalf, *and* Servants, *behind*'. Shallow's speeches inaugurate a new rhythm, and even his opening words, with their early morning references, suggest that the play is entering on a different movement:

> Come on come on, come on; give me your hand, sir; give me your hand, sir. An early stirrer, by the rood! And how doth my good cousin Silence?

IV

Shakespeare used the two-part structure at all stages of his career. It is present in *Titus Andronicus* as well as in such a late tragicomedy as *The Winter's Tale*. (I shall discuss four of the mature tragedies from this point of view in later chapters.) But it is not for a moment suggested that he invented this structure. A division into two parts can be traced in some of the longer of the early Tudor plays. Medwall's *Fulgens and Lucrece* (written before 1500), the earliest extant secular comedy in English, was frankly written in two parts, for the first was to be acted before dinner, the second after dinner. To go back earlier still, to the early part of the fifteenth century, *The Castell of Perseverance* has a dual action: Humanum Genus is tempted and falls; he repents; he is tempted and falls a second time, and is again saved. Between the first repentance and the second fall into temptation he becomes an old man, and it may be, again, that an interval at this point— in what is a very long play—would have facilitated the marked shift in attitude.

To return to the Elizabethan drama: some of Marlowe's plays show signs of a two-part structure, as G. F. Kernodle points out in his remarks on *The Jew of Malta*.[1] In *Doctor Faustus* Marlowe seems to have used a five-act structure,[2] but this does not rule out the possibility that the play was divided into two parts for performance. A good place for a break would be shortly after the show of the Seven Deadly Sins; and this elaborate set-piece accords with what was said earlier about Shakespeare's tendency to have such set-pieces shortly or immediately before the interval. *Edward II* has often been criticized for having an apparently invertebrate structure; the action seems to change its nature about two-thirds of the way through. But this is another case where the supposition that Marlowe was using a structure of two unequal parts can be of help: such plays as *Edward II* are not incompetently broken-backed but rather deliberately designed in two stages, and the hypothesis that actors and audience required an interval helps to clarify the author's intentions. So the first part (in modern editions the first three acts) presents Edward's love for Gaveston, and concludes with Gaveston's death. The second part shows a more aged, more vulnerable Edward, persecuted by a now hostile Queen and Mortimer; the King now elicits sympathy, whereas before he was treated with a cool detachment. This is not to claim that Marlowe uses his two parts as skilfully and resourcefully as Shakespeare does even in the comparatively early *Richard III*; Marlowe's structural gifts were limited. But there is, as several critics have recently shown, more artistry in his plays than had been suspected.

Kyd's *Spanish Tragedy* is written in four acts, with an induction and epilogue. But here too it is useful to see the play as designed for performance in two parts. The place intended for an interval may well be after III. vii (the German critic Biesterfeldt, writing from another point of view, suggested an additional act-division at this point).[3] The situation is as follows. The previous scene (III. vi) had shown the climax and conclusion of the episode of

[1] Kernodle, op. cit., p. 186.
[2] See G. K. Hunter, 'Five-Act Structure in "Doctor Faustus" ' in *Tulane Drama Review* (1964).
[3] See the note to III. viii. i in Philip Edwards's edition of *The Spanish Tragedy* (London, 1959). Edwards notes that P. W. Biesterfeldt argued that there was a break in the action here; he also notes that some editors have marked a new act (Act IV) at this point.

Pedringano and his comic-macabre death by hanging. Pedringano had faced his execution brazenly, in the confidence that his pardon was contained in the box which a page standing near by was holding. But the villainous Lorenzo has betrayed his servant, and the execution is carried out. The following scene (III. vii) shows Hieronimo in a state of frenzy at his own inactivity and ignorance of his son's murderers. At once the Hangman comes in with a letter which he has just found in Pedringano's pocket; it is addressed to Lorenzo and makes it plain beyond doubt that Lorenzo and Balthasar were Horatio's murderers. Hieronimo's emotional frustration now bursts out in a torrent of rage against the killers. His soliloquy is very long, but divided into short stages of not more than ten lines, each of which ends with a rhyming couplet. The emotion of the speaker is therefore clearly articulated, and the actor can plan the whole long tirade in stages, working up to a climax. The speech certainly offers the actor a great opportunity—and this is the speech which seems intended to be followed by an interval. (The effect is not unlike Richard Gloucester's long soliloquy in III. ii of *3 Henry VI*; and Shakespeare may have been indebted to Kyd for the idea of placing a vehement monologue at a roughly comparable point in the play.) This is an excellent point to break off the performance. Hieronimo is now certain of the identity of the murderers; accordingly, the second part of the play concerns his revenge. Moreover—and this is important for Kyd's over-all design—Hieronimo's role is clearly differentiated before and after the interval, assuming an interval to take place here. Before it he is, though grief-stricken, sane; after it he is, however we qualify the term, essentially mad. But this marked contrast is quite independent of the four-act division.

Some of Shakespeare's successors also made use of the two-part structure. Among the clearest examples are Tourneur's *Revenger's Tragedy*, Ford's *'Tis Pity She's a Whore*, and, in comedy, Jonson's *Epicoene*. Tourneur's play is quite clearly in two parts: in the first (Acts One to Three), Vindice assumes the role of a court pander; in the second he disguises himself as a malcontent. The penultimate scene of Act Three is an elaborate set-piece in which the Duke is poisoned. Ford's play uses a form of 'structural rhyming': near the end of Act Three the Cardinal appears for the first time; he is also present in the last scene of Act Five, when he speaks the play's concluding speech. In performance *Epicoene* comes across as an obvious two-part play, with the final scene of Act Three making a noisy climax as the tormenting of Morose reaches its height. This marks a point in the play where, in modern performances at least, an interval seems essential.

4. *The Growth of Scenes*

I

LIKE any prolific artist who works continuously in a single medium over a large number of years, Shakespeare made abundant use of his own earlier work. The early history plays in particular (the three Parts of *Henry VI*, *Richard III*, and *King John*) became rich repositories of structural paradigms which he was to draw on when he embarked on the series of tragedies which began with *Julius Caesar*. Indeed, to an extent which has not been appreciated, many of the structural sources of the mature tragedies are to be found in the early history plays. The scenic forms and larger structural units in question are, it is true, often so transformed or put to such different use from that of their original context that it may at first be doubted whether Shakespeare was in fact remembering his own earlier work; but further examination will, I think, establish that the early plays contributed in a number of specific ways to the composition of the great tragedies.

It may be best to begin with a fairly circumscribed example of self-borrowing. The most famous and most ceremonious oath-taking in Shakespeare is probably that at the end of the temptation scene in *Othello*. The long colloquy between Othello and Iago is just reaching its conclusion. Iago has produced his last and culminating 'proof' of Desdemona's infidelity—the words of Cassio, muttered in his sleep, of their secret love—and on top of this he ventures one more tormenting disclosure: he has, on that same day, seen Cassio wipe his beard with the handkerchief which Othello gave Desdemona. At this point Othello comes to a decision. The scene loses its onward movement and seems to pause for the solemn act that follows:

> *Othello.* O that the slave had forty thousand lives!
>   One is too poor, too weak for my revenge.
>   Now do I see 'tis true. Look here, Iago—
>   All my fond love thus do I blow to heaven.
>   'Tis gone.
>   Arise, black vengeance, from the hollow hell.

    Yield up, O love, thy crown and hearted throne
    To tyrannous hate! Swell, bosom, with thy fraught,
    For 'tis of aspics' tongues.
Iago.   Yet be content.
Othello. O, blood, blood, blood!
Iago. Patience, I say; your mind perhaps may change.
Othello. Never, Iago. Like to the Pontic sea,
    Whose icy current and compulsive course
    Ne'er feels retiring ebb, but keeps due on
    To the Propontic and the Hellespont;
    Even so my bloody thoughts, with violent pace,
    Shall ne'er look back, ne'er ebb to humble love,
    Till that a capable and wide revenge
    Swallow them up. (*He kneels*) Now, by yond marble heaven,
    In the due reverence of a sacred vow,
    I here engage my words.
Iago. (*Kneeling*) Do not rise yet.
    Witness, you ever-burning lights above,
    You elements that clip us round about,
    Witness that here Iago doth give up
    The execution of his wit, hands, heart,
    To wrong'd Othello's service! . . .

                                    (III. iii. 446–71)[1]

The ceremonious formality of this act of swearing makes it one
of the two or three most *rousing* passages in *Othello*. The long
temptation scene is itself one of the most brilliantly devised—and
in performance most agitating—in the whole of Shakespeare,
but it needed some further device which would raise its closing
moments to an even higher level of theatrical power. After Iago's
long process of insinuation and suggestion and Othello's
fluctuating responses, the decision to put an end to doubt and to
undertake a definite course of action comes as a great relief. But
more than that: it brings a sense of instant fulfilment, because it is
itself a kind of action. The oath-swearing, with its threat of de-
vastating and annihilating violence, has a way of working which
is equivalent to what J. L. Austin has termed a 'performative

    [1] The words 'Like to the Pontic sea . . . heaven' do not appear in Quarto, only
in Folio. It has been suggested that, along with several other passages found only
in the Folio, they were later added by Shakespeare. See Nevill Coghill, *Shakespeare's
Professional Skills* (Cambridge, 1964). As Kenneth Muir temperately remarks: 'Actors
would be unlikely to omit the lines' (New Penguin *Othello*, p. 205).

utterance'.[1] The utterance has the force of an action; in performance we feel that something has been done as well as said; and the
magnificent formality with which the decision is raised into ritual
communicates a sharp pleasure.

In fashioning this climax Shakespeare seems to have had present
in his mind a scene of *Julius Caesar* which at first sight has little in
common with the temptation scene of *Othello*. This is the scene
(v. i) in which the conspirators and their army face their opponents,
Antony and Octavius. It is relatively short (125 lines) and is made
up of several actions: in a brief opening dialogue Antony and
Octavius bicker irritably and show signs of their later hostility;
then the conspirators' army enters led by Brutus and Cassius,
and a 'flyting' ensues of a kind which often precedes battles on the
Elizabethan stage; in the middle of it Octavius ceremoniously declares war on the assassins of Caesar; and finally, left to themselves,
Brutus and Cassius take their 'everlasting farewell' of each other.
The whole scene is remarkably various in its dramatic forms and
at the same time economical; it treats a number of topics and
touches on a wide range of feeling. The part of it relevant to
Othello's oath-taking is Octavius' declaration of war. Like the
passage quoted from *Othello* it marks an abrupt change from mere
verbal exchange to the vivid here-and-now of dramatic action:

> *Octavius.* Come, come, the cause. If arguing make us sweat,
>   The proof of it will turn to redder drops.
>   Look,
>   I draw a sword against conspirators;
>   When think you that the sword goes up again?
>   Never till Caesar's three and thirty wounds
>   Be well aveng'd, or till another Caesar
>   Have added slaughter to the sword of traitors.
>
> (v. i. 48–55)

Octavius' diction has nothing of Othello's magnificence; nor
is his speech placed, as Othello's is, at the climax of a long scene.
But its value as dramatic action should not be underestimated
by the reader. The physical act of drawing the sword, and so

---

[1] See J. L. Austin, 'Performative Utterances', in *Philosophical Papers* (Oxford, 1961):
'if a person makes an utterance of this sort we should say that he is *doing* something
rather than merely *saying* something.' He gives a few examples: 'Suppose, for
example, that in the course of a marriage ceremony I say, as people will, "I do"—
(sc. take this woman to be my lawful wedded wife). Or again, suppose that I tread
on your toes and say "I apologize" . . .' (p. 222).

inaugurating the civil war, is signalled by the one word 'Look' and the long pause that follows it. Both the action and the silence are arresting ways of ceremonializing the moment. Indeed the fact that the means are non-verbal is intensified by their contrast with the rather feeble and futile word-slinging of the previous exchange ('Words before blows', Brutus has just said). Octavius' 'Look' is matched by Othello's

> Look here, Iago—
> All my fond love thus do I blow to heaven.
> 'Tis gone.

The moment is similarly ceremonialized. There is of course no sword-drawing, but Othello invents a comparable gesture, a symbolic renunciation of his love, made real by a mysterious but expressive physical movement, as if he were releasing a bird into the sky: the actor can make it shoot up out of sight. ''Tis gone': a long pause follows, to mark the movement; and then the oath begins. The emphatic use of 'Never' (always a powerful dramatic word, with its suggestion of the absolute and the irrevocable) is much better placed here than in Octavius' speech, and is fortified by the imagery of freezing hardness and the strong syntactic curve of the following speech. In everything Shakespeare is improving on himself. But it is necessary to take the account one stage further back: this time to *Henry VI, Part Three*.

Act Two, Scene Three of that play presents an interlude during the battle of Towton. The scenes preceding it have shown some of the worst atrocities of the English civil wars: the murder of the child Rutland and the long-drawn-out tormenting of his father York at the hands of Clifford and Margaret. In the present scene the Lancastrians seem to be winning; and one by one, the leaders of the Yorkist side stagger on to the stage to take respite: first Warwick, then Edward, then Clarence, and last Richard. The quadruple patterning of the entries is pointed. Richard announces that he has just seen Warwick's brother die (the Quarto makes the death Warwick's father's), and the news rouses Warwick from despair into a desperate defiance. Warwick's change of mood affects the others, and finally all four return to the battle with renewed heart and put the Lancastrians to flight. This short scene of the lull in the battle has a pronounced pattern: the four men— three of them brothers—are brought on like the members of a dance-group. But the scene makes its strongest effect at the moment of Warwick's change of heart, when it changes direction and tempo. Richard finishes his account of Warwick's brother's death, and the following passage occurs:

> *Warwick.* Then let the earth be drunken with our blood.
> I'll kill my horse, because I will not fly.
> Why stand we like soft-hearted women here,
> Wailing our losses, whiles the foe doth rage,
> And look upon, as if the tragedy
> Were play'd in jest by counterfeiting actors?
> Here on my knee I vow to God above
> I'll never pause again, never stand still,
> Till either death hath clos'd these eyes of mine
> Or fortune given me measure of revenge.
> *Edward.* O Warwick, I do bend my knee with thine,
> And in this vow do chain my soul to thine!
> And ere my knee rise from the earth's cold face
> I throw my hands, mine eyes, my heart to Thee,
> Thou setter-up and plucker down of kings,
> Beseeching Thee, if with Thy will it stands
> That to my foes this body must be prey,
> Yet that Thy brazen gates of heaven may ope
> And give sweet passage to my sinful soul.
> Now, lords, take leave until we meet again,
> Where'er it be, in heaven or in earth.

And the leave-taking between the three brothers and Warwick follows.

If we take this scene along with the one immediately preceding it (II. ii), which includes the 'flyting' between the Lancastrian and Yorkist leaders, we have the model for the whole sequence of brief actions which makes up the scene in *Julius Caesar* just discussed. It includes the solemn leave-taking of Brutus and Cassius, given of course a Roman as distinct from a Christian colouring. The middle part of this sequence—Octavius' declaration of war—does not have any close equivalent in *Henry VI*; but instead the exchange between Warwick and Edward finds a close parallel in the oath-taking of Othello and Iago. The movement and syntax of some of Warwick's lines are close to Othello's speech 'Never, Iago . . .'; and both men kneel, as they do in *Othello*. Further, although Warwick's speech has nothing exactly corresponding to

Octavius' 'Look' and Othello's 'Look here, Iago' (in each case followed by a physical action), it has instead a startlingly self-conscious and theatrical metaphor:

> And look upon, as if the tragedy
> Were play'd in jest by counterfeiting actors

which has, it may be felt, a comparable effect, as of an abrupt change of tempo. Lastly Edward's prayer to God ('Thou setter-up and plucker-down of kings') has an echo in the religious solemnity of Othello's 'Now, by yond marble heaven, / In the due reverence of a sacred vow . . .'. Even the final line of the temptation scene—Iago's 'I am your own for ever', which itself takes up Othello's earlier 'I am bound to thee for ever'—is anticipated in Edward's very differently intended 'And in this vow do chain my soul to thine!'.

What the two earlier of these three passages have in common is a civil war setting: friends and acquaintances are fighting each other. What all three have in common is the desire for revenge, solemnly sworn. This whole complex of action and feeling—the oath-taking, the soldierly profession or military activity of the men involved, above all the sense that an absolutely critical juncture has been reached which demands an act of solemn affirmation fortified by the highest religious sanctions—all this was recalled by Shakespeare when he devised the climax of the temptation scene. The moment is one of great splendour, but also one of shocking ferocity: for if *Othello* does not have the civil war setting of the two earlier passages, it has something even more barbarous—'domestic fury', in which a soldier is to murder his own wife.

Comparison of the three passages in their full contexts shows without much doubt that on this occasion at any rate Shakespeare improved on himself immeasurably. Probably few readers or play-goers remember the scene in *3 Henry VI*, or even the one in *Julius Caesar*. The solemn act of swearing is not particularly well placed in either play; if anything Shakespeare is being excessively profuse of scenic inventions and does not, in this case, do justice to his own idea. But in *Othello* the full possibilities of the form are realized. And moreover, so well integrated is the swearing, in the temptation scene and in the play as a whole, that one would hardly have guessed that it had a previous history in Shakespeare's own development. The impression it gives of inevitability within the context is one sign of Shakespeare's maturity as a dramatic artist.

II

The oath-taking scene in *Othello* is of course far from being an isolated case. While on the one hand Shakespeare was inventing new forms in every play he wrote, on the other he was continually adapting his own earlier forms to new contexts—and, no doubt, with little or no conscious effort. A good example is the one noticed by G. Wilson Knight: the death of Cardinal Beaufort (*2 Henry VI*, III. iii) and Lady Macbeth's sleepwalking scene.[1] In both scenes an accomplice to a murder betrays guilt while in a state of unconsciousness. In both the witnesses piously refrain from passing judgement (*King Henry*. 'Forbear to judge, for we are sinners all'; *Doctor*. 'God, God forgive us all . . . I think, but dare not speak'). Two other plays, *Richard II* and *All's Well that Ends Well*, belong to different genres and on the face of it have nothing in common; there is, nevertheless, one area of contact. In *Richard II* an odd scene occurs (v. iii) in which Aumerle begs pardon from Bolingbroke, now King, for his projected treason. Aumerle's plea is abetted by his aged mother the Duchess of York and opposed by his father York. The scene is tiresomely protracted and curiously uncertain in tone, but in the final scene (v. iii) of *All's Well that Ends Well* it seems to have been recalled and given a more vigorous and mordant life. The opening of this scene brings on stage a precisely similar group of characters: the King (corresponding to Bolingbroke), the Countess of Rousillon (the Duchess of York), and the loyal old courtier Lafeu (York), who are soon joined by Bertram who corresponds to Aumerle, another 'digressing son' (*Richard II*, v. iii. 66). The earlier scene had veered close to comedy, as Bolingbroke's ironical remark brings out:

> Our scene is alter'd from a serious thing,
> And now chang'd to 'The Beggar and the King'.
>
> (v. iii. 79–80)

This ballad title and something of its context of feeling and tone were carried over into the pardon scene of *All's Well*, in which the

---

[1] G. Wilson Knight, 'The Second Part of "King Henry VI" and "Macbeth"' (1927), reprinted in *The Sovereign Flower* (London, 1958).

King finally pardons Bertram and then in the Epilogue himself becomes a 'beggar' to the play's audience:

> The King's a beggar, now the play is done.

What had been peripheral and somewhat ineffectively serio-comic in the history play (the scene has often been cut altogether in performance) was thus used again in a much more strongly developed and closely integrated form in the tragicomedy.

A similar link relates the earliest of the history plays to what was possibly the last of the tragedies, for in *Timon of Athens* Shakespeare adapted a scenic arrangement first used in *Henry VI, Part One*. In the third act, Timon's servants go to three of his friends and beneficiaries to ask for help now that Timon is in need; they are all refused. In the fourth act of *1 Henry VI*, Sir William Lucy goes first to the Duke of York, then to the Earl of Somerset, requesting military aid on behalf of the distressed Talbot; in both cases he is refused. Here the scenic paradigm consists of a series of short parallel scenes; the dramatic interest lies in the variations on a given theme. When he came to write *Timon*, Shakespeare recalled the whole episode of Talbot and the way in which his fall illustrated his present subject, ingratitude. The scenes of Lucy begging for aid were then recast, but improved by increasing the number of interviews from two to three. It is significant that these three short scenes in *Timon* (III. i–iii) are probably the most theatrically compelling in this admittedly not very theatrical play. In performance they generate a keen, powerfully satirical interest as we wait to see how each of the false friends will excuse himself. (They are the closest things in Shakespeare to the bedside scenes in *Volpone*; but their prototypes in *1 Henry VI* show that Shakespeare was not necessarily indebted to Jonson.) This is a clear case in which the 'source' of one of Shakespeare's later plays is to be sought in his own earlier work; there is after all nothing corresponding to these begging scenes in the known classical and other sources of the play. When he came to plan *Timon*, Shakespeare's own gradually accumulated vocabulary of scenic forms helped to furnish not only structure but matter for this part of the play. So by learning how to write dramatically he learned not only how to say something but what to say.

In another late tragedy, *Coriolanus*, we can observe (or imagine we observe) Shakespeare laying out his narrative material in dramatic form, and, as he does so, his mind naturally reverting to something he had already written. In this instance the opening three scenes of the play are in question. The first presents the civic dissension of the Roman state and introduces the hero. The second brings on stage his antagonist, Aufidius, who eventually causes the hero's death. The third scene is domestic and feminine: we meet the hero's mother and wife. For this sequence, which is entirely expository, Shakespeare seems to have taken as a rough guide or model the first three scenes of *Romeo and Juliet* (the two plays, so different in essentials, have a point of contact in the theme of civic strife). In that play we are first shown the feud in operation, and we meet the hero Romeo. In the second scene Paris appears to make his suit to Capulet to marry Juliet. Only late in the play does Paris emerge as Romeo's rival and finally as the immediate cause of his and Juliet's death; in this respect he is comparable to Aufidius. Finally we are shown the Capulet women-folk at home: Juliet, her mother, and her nurse—the same number as in the third scene of *Coriolanus*. Of course the comparison be-tween these two opening sequences cannot be pushed very far; but it seems clear that the solution to the expository problem in the early play was tried out again in the later.

There is another place where *Romeo and Juliet* contributed to one of the mature tragedies. The scene in question is that in the second act of *Othello* (II. iii) where Othello quells the affray started by Cassio. Here again Shakespeare's mind slipped into an already existing pattern, which was then adapted to the new context. Cassio has been made drunk by Iago, has become quarrelsome, is provoked by Roderigo, and enters in pursuit of him with his sword drawn; he then attacks and wounds Montano. The garrison bell awakes Othello, who makes his appearance when the affray has reached its climax. Othello questions first Montano, then Iago, who gives a full account of what happened. As a result Cassio is cashiered. Othello appears for a comparatively short time (II. iii. 156–250), but the period he is on stage is the climax of Act Two: it sees the ruin of Cassio's fortunes, and concludes the first stage in Iago's schemes. The most crucial part of it is the speech of Iago's (212–38) in which he tells what happened. Here Shakespeare remembered the scene in *Romeo and Juliet* (III. i) where Tybalt starts an affray in the streets of Verona, kills Mer-cutio, and is killed by Romeo; Romeo makes his escape; and the

Prince of Verona enters full of anger that the feud has again broken out, this time with such loss of life. To his question, 'Where are the vile beginners of this fray?' Benvolio answers, and gives a full description of the sequence leading up to the deaths of the two young men. Lady Capulet cries out that Benvolio is palliating Romeo's guilt: 'Affection makes him false, he speaks not true'. Finally the Prince condemns Romeo to banishment. Shakespeare used this scene as a model for the one in *Othello*. Othello has the role of the angry Prince, Cassio that of the guilty Romeo— and honest Iago plays Benvolio. The kind of genuine loyalty to his friend that Benvolio candidly shows in his account of the fight, which Lady Capulet wrongly calls unfair partiality, is imitated by Iago in his well-acted grief and concern for Cassio:

> I had rather ha this tongue cut from my mouth
> Than it should do offence to Michael Cassio;
> Yet, I persuade myself, to speak the truth
> Shall nothing wrong him . . .

Othello's reply echoes, in milder and calmer tones, Lady Capulet's reproach of partiality:

> I know, Iago,
> Thy honesty and love doth mince this matter,
> Making it light to Cassio.

In the background of both scenes is a wedding: Cassio's brawl occurs on Othello's wedding night, Mercutio's and Tybalt's death on the day of Romeo's marriage to Juliet. It seems clear that, when planning this part of *Othello*, Shakespeare adapted some features of the earlier love tragedy.

III

I have so far discussed a few examples of the growth of scenes or parts of scenes, mere details in the complex structure which is an entire play. I now want to look at a related subject: the growth of entire plays from earlier plays, but still approaching it from the point of view of scenic contrivance. Any consideration of this matter is of course doomed to incompleteness, since we can never know all the plays Shakespeare was familiar with and used, and we can be certain that many of them no longer exist. But we are not condemned to complete ignorance either, and in what follows the stress will continue to fall on the extent to which Shakespeare made use of his own earlier work. I shall discuss, first, some aspects of *Hamlet*, and then, more extensively, the earliest of the mature tragedies, *Julius Caesar*.

The study of the structural sources of *Hamlet* is hampered by the loss of what was presumably the chief dramatic model: the older play of *Hamlet*, usually attributed to Kyd. Speculation is unavoidably hazardous; but if *The Spanish Tragedy* is anything to go by, the *ur-Hamlet* was probably fairly remote from the play Shakespeare based on it. What is reasonably certain is that much of the substance of *Hamlet* grew out of Shakespeare's earlier work, and in some cases the ideas for individual scenes probably came from his own earlier plays. Perhaps the best example of this is the closet scene (III. iv), in which Hamlet has his only private interview with his mother. Whether or not there was anything corresponding to this scene in the old *Hamlet*, when he came to write it Shakespeare seems to have recalled something from one of his earlier plays which furnished some curious parallels to Hamlet's present situation. This was the episode in the first act of *King John* in which the Bastard Faulconbridge questions his mother about his father. Faulconbridge's paternity has been the subject of the lawsuit which has filled most of Act One. Despite the fact that he is, as it seems, of legitimate birth according to the letter of the law, Faulconbridge chooses to give up his estate and throw in his lot with King John, accepting the stigma of bastardy.[1] For it is clear that he was in fact begotten not by Faulconbridge but by Richard Cœur-de-Lion, as the Queen Mother acknowledges. Near the end of the first act Lady Faulconbridge arrives, and the dialogue between mother and son opens as follows:

Lady Faulconbridge. Where is that slave, thy brother? Where is he
  That holds in chase mine honour up and down?
Bastard. My brother Robert, old Sir Robert's son?
  Colbrand the giant, that same mighty man?
  Is it Sir Robert's son that you seek so?
Lady Faulconbridge. Sir Robert's son! Ay, thou unreverend boy,
  Sir Robert's son! Why scorn'st thou at Sir Robert?
  He is Sir Robert's son, and so art thou.　　　　(I. i. 222–9)

[1] See J. W. Draper, 'Bastardy in Shakespeare's Plays', *Shakespeare Jahrbuch*, 74 (1938); and G. W. Keeton, 'The Bastardy of Falconbridge', in *Shakespeare's Legal and Political Background* (London, 1967), pp. 118–31.

The Bastard asks Lady Faulconbridge's servant to leave, and the conversation proceeds to more intimate matters.

> *Bastard.* Madam, I was not old Sir Robert's son;
>   Sir Robert might have eat his part in me
>   Upon Good Friday, and ne'er broke his fast.
>   Sir Robert could do: well—marry, to confess—
>   Could he get me? Sir Robert could not do it:
>   We know his handiwork. Therefore, good mother,
>   To whom am I beholding for these limbs?
>   Sir Robert never holp to make this leg.
> *Lady Faulconbridge.* Hast thou conspired with thy brother too,
>   That for thine own gain shouldst defend my honour?
>   What means this scorn, thou most untoward knave?
> *Bastard.* Knight, knight, good mother, Basilisco-like.
>   What! I am dubb'd; I have it on my shoulder.
>   But, mother, I am not Sir Robert's son:
>   I have disclaim'd Sir Robert and my land;
>   Legitimation, name, and all is gone.
>   Then, good my mother, let me know my father—
>   Some proper man, I hope. Who was it, mother?
> *Lady Faulconbridge.* Hast thou denied thyself a Faulconbridge?
> *Bastard.* As faithfully as I deny the devil.
> *Lady Faulconbridge.* King Richard Cœur-de-Lion was thy father.
>   By long and vehement suit was I seduc'd
>   To make room for him in my husband's bed.   (I. i. 233–55)

The Bastard is delighted by her confession—'With all my heart I thank thee for my father'—and takes her to meet his newly acquired kinsfolk.

For all its brevity, the scene makes a strong and curiously affecting impression. The genial insolence of the Bastard's opening attack, Lady Faulconbridge's shrill indignation, and the indelicacy of the whole situation do not conceal a current of real emotion which comes to the surface only towards the end of the scene when, his true identity discovered, the son can express frank affection for his dead father as well as his living mother. The familial intimacy of the dialogue is pointed by the Bastard's repeated use of 'mother' (six times in all; four times in one short speech, ll. 244–50). At the same time, for all his insistence on getting at the truth, he uses courteous forms of address: 'good lady', 'Madam', and 'lady', as well as the polite 'you', as opposed to his mother's unceremonious 'thou'.

The closet scene in *Hamlet* is much more fully developed and is placed at a position of climax. Nevertheless Shakespeare recalled the structure of emotion in the earlier scene and apparently used it as a basis. Hamlet is heard '*within*' calling 'Mother, mother, mother', and when he appears his first words are in a pugnaciously cool and impudent tone: 'Now, mother, what's the matter?' The exchange that follows, in which the Queen's indignation is promptly deflated by Hamlet, traces a course similar to that of the earlier scene:

> *Queen.* Hamlet, thou hast thy father much offended.
> *Hamlet.* Mother, you have my father much offended.
> *Queen.* Come, come, you answer with an idle tongue.
> *Hamlet.* Go, go, you question with a wicked tongue.
> *Queen.* Why, how now, Hamlet!
>
> (III. iv. 9–13)

The first movement comes to a sudden climax with Hamlet's killing of Polonius:

> *Queen.* O, what a rash and bloody deed is this!
> *Hamlet.* A bloody deed!—almost as bad, good mother,
>   As kill a king and marry with his brother.
> *Queen.* As kill a king!
> *Hamlet.*   Ay, lady, it was my word.
>
> (III. iv. 27–30)

Given the obvious differences in circumstance, the two scenes have in common a guilty mother's indignation, perhaps simulated, against her son, and the son's aggressive attitude towards his mother (although this is not at all incompatible with real affection). The Bastard's possibly ironical use of the phrase 'good mother' is repeated, with a more bitter edge, in Hamlet's 'almost as bad, good mother'. And Lady Faulconbridge's sudden confession of the Bastard's true paternity is echoed in the Queen's submission later in the scene to Hamlet's impassioned reproaches. The Bastard has of course nothing corresponding to Hamlet's long diatribes; but the general movement of feeling in the two scenes— the way they both work towards a position of mutual understanding and clarification between mother and son—is similar.

The argument for seeing a close relation between the two scenes may be strengthened if we consider one or two general affinities between *King John* and *Hamlet* as well as some resemblances between the Bastard and Hamlet himself. Two phrases can be taken as summing up the concerns of the two plays: 'the majesty, / The borrowed majesty, of England' (*King John*, I. i. 3–4), and 'the majesty of buried Denmark' (*Hamlet*, I. i. 48). The Bastard is the son of the heroic Richard Cœur-de-Lion, but the great hero-king is dead, and his uncle, the devious politician John, is on the throne. Moreover John's title is weak: the true heir is Arthur, the Bastard's cousin. As far as the Bastard is concerned, there are two 'father-figures' in the play: his true father, the dead King Richard, and the physically unheroic Sir Robert Faulconbridge; indeed to the extent that King John, also an unheroic man, has usurped the throne, he too may seem an unworthy father-substitute to the young Faulconbridge. A bastard may see himself as a disinherited son, and both the Bastard and Arthur are in different ways disinherited. Their similarity in situation is brought out in the second act, when, instinctively it seems, the Bastard sides with Constance and joins her in baiting Austria even though she is politically on the opposite side to his own. The Duke of Austria —an emblem of crass power and moral turpitude—incurs the Bastard's personal hatred because he had killed Richard Cœur-de-Lion and now presumes to wear his lion-skin. The Bastard's apparent inconsistency in siding with Constance against his own master (at least emotionally) is never settled, and later, after Arthur's death, the question of his divided allegiance becomes even more acute.

The world of *King John* looks forward to *Hamlet* in a number of respects. It is a world of two generations: the old are for the most part politic and corrupt; the young are appalled or disgusted by the world they inherit, but they have no power. If the Bastard himself anticipates some aspects of Hamlet, King John and the papal legate Pandulph are blended in Claudius, just as the Dauphin Lewis, who is corrupted by Pandulph, is in some ways taken up in Laertes. A few specific parallels may be mentioned. In III. iii John arranges for Arthur, who has just been captured in battle, to be sent to England where he is to be put to death; the scene ends with John telling Arthur, 'For England, cousin, go . . .'. In IV. iii of *Hamlet* an uncle similarly dispatches his nephew to England where he plans to have him put to death, and the phrase 'for England' is four times repeated. In the next scene in *King John* (III. iv) we see Constance in a frenzy of grief at the loss of her son Arthur, just as in *Hamlet* (iv. v), at a roughly similar point in the sequence, we see Ophelia '*distracted*' by the killing of her father. Later in the same scene in *King John* the worldly-wise churchman Pandulph prompts Lewis to take advantage of Arthur's coming death by invading England: 'How green you are and fresh in this old world!' (iii. iv. 145). The coldly politic tone of their dialogue is very close to that of *Hamlet* iv. vii, in which Claudius instructs Laertes:

> *Pandulph.* O, sir, when he shall hear of your approach,
>   If that young Arthur be not gone already,
>   Even at that news he dies . . .
>
> (iii. iv. 162–4)
>
> *Claudius.*   O, for two special reasons,
>   Which may to you, perhaps, seem much insinew'd,
>   But yet to me th'are strong.
>
> (iv. vii. 9–11)

The tone of gently condescending worldly prudence, cold and unscrupulous, but knowing, is very similar.[1]

No one would claim *King John* to be a very successful or satisfying play as a whole. Its various episodes and scenes do not cohere into an emotionally significant pattern. But some of these individual sequences are highly suggestive and charged with a richly potential life. Their full potential was realized only in the later tragedies—in *Hamlet, King Lear,* and *Macbeth*—where, unhampered by the recalcitrant facts of history, Shakespeare could pursue their suggestions into a more emotionally coherent mythical realm. In this way the later tragedies achieve a satisfying coherence that is lacking in such a history play as *King John.* In *King John,* we may feel, a personal drama of possibly great interest is struggling, but failing, to get out. Whenever the personal drama begins to be interesting—when it needs further development— it is dropped or shelved, and the play moves on to the next set of historical events which may have very little emotional connection with what went before. This impression—that it suffers a series of interruptions in the interests of a superficial historical sequence —is no doubt one of the reasons why *King John* (like most of the history plays) is less popular than most of the tragedies and comedies.

---

[1] Cf. also *King John,* iii. iii. 33 ff., and *Hamlet,* iii. ii. 378 ff., which are comparable in tone and imagery (churchyards at night figure in both).

Hamlet resumes certain elements in the structure of feeling of *King John* and clarifies what had there been only tentative or fragmentary. Like the Bastard, Hamlet can be said to have two fathers: the heroic elder Hamlet and the unheroic Claudius. As so often in folklore the dead parent is remembered with love, the living step-parent is hated. But what seems only incipient or fragmentary in the Bastard is more completely realized in Hamlet, for, different though they are, the Bastard probably helped Shakespeare to imagine Hamlet. Indeed Hamlet may be seen from one point of view as a kind of bastard—one who for a legal reason is debarred from inheriting his father's estate. Despite the fact that Claudius has declared him the heir to the throne, Hamlet's position at court is very much like that of a royal bastard, someone embarrassingly without a recognized role who has been passed over on his father's death. At one point in the play the notion of bastardy is brought into the dialogue: 'That drop of blood that's calm proclaims me bastard' (IV. v. 114). The speaker is Laertes, demanding satisfaction for his father's death. The implication of this might be that Hamlet *is* such a 'bastard'.

But *King John* was not the only history play to contribute to the dense tragic substance of *Hamlet*. Both *Richard III* and the two Parts of *Henry IV* were drawn on, consciously or otherwise, so that *Hamlet* would not be what it is if they had not been written. The use made of *Richard III* is mainly a matter of the development of the histrionic hero: not only the wit, the swagger and glamour of a brilliant personality—although this in itself is some achievement—but the illusion, successfully projected, of a thinking mind, a consciousness. A comparison between the characters of Richard III and Hamlet could certainly be made along these lines. In matters of scenic device, however, it may be enough to point out one specific similarity. In I. ii Richard conducts his outrageous wooing of the Lady Anne in front of the hearse of her father-in-law Henry VI. Before leaving him Anne has begun to relent, and when left alone Richard soliloquizes: 'Was ever woman in this humour woo'd?' This speech has one or two marked resemblances to Hamlet's 'O, what a rogue and peasant slave am I!' (II. ii. 543 ff.). Hamlet has welcomed the players to Elsinore. The First Player has just recited a speech describing the fall of Troy; he has shed tears in doing so, and his tears are the occasion for Hamlet's soliloquy. The similarities in the two soli-

loquies are of tone and movement, particularly in the opening
sections:

> What! I that kill'd her husband and his father—
> To take her in her heart's extremest hate,
> With curses in her mouth, tears in her eyes,
> The bleeding witness of my hatred by;
> Having God, her conscience, and these bars against me,
> And I no friends to back my suit at all
> But the plain devil and dissembling looks,
> And yet to win her, all the world to nothing!
> Ha!

> Is it not monstrous that this player here,
> But in a fiction, in a dream of passion,
> Could force his soul so to his own conceit
> That from her working all his visage wann'd;
> Tears in his eyes, distraction in's aspect,
> A broken voice, and his whole function suiting
> With forms to his conceit? And all for nothing!
> For Hecuba!

Each soliloquy comments, in a very personal way, on the scene
just past. They both have a tone of amazement or incredulity—
in Richard's case at the weak pliability of women, in Hamlet's at
the emotional volatility of actors—the amazement coloured by
a certain contempt. Both Richard and Hamlet express their feeling of wonder in a headlong agglomeration of phrases (with close
resemblances in phrasing: 'tears in her eyes', 'Tears in his eyes';
'all the world to nothing!', 'And all for nothing!'), which is
pulled up short by an exclamatory phrase ('Ha!', 'For Hecuba!')
followed by a histrionic pause. Hamlet's other long soliloquies
are more reflective and slow-moving, more in the style of Brutus,
but this most melodramatic of his soliloquies is a brilliant development of the earlier speeches of Richard Gloucester.

The affinities between *Hamlet* and the two Parts of *Henry IV*
are more comprehensive and elusive, as much thematic as structural. Both plays have a good deal to do with fathers and sons;
Hal and Hamlet are both unprincely princes and both have
'father trouble'; both are in a sense truants from their duty, for
both seem to delay in coming to terms with their situation. So in
both plays—and this is a major structural affinity—we are made

to wait for the moment when they will assume their appointed
roles: when Hal becomes Henry V, when Hamlet kills Claudius.
So the theme of 'death of fathers' (*Hamlet*, I. ii. 104) is common to
both, along with much else.[1] Their imaginative kinship—especially between the *Henry IV, Part Two* and *Hamlet*—could be
pursued further, but as it cannot be clearly demonstrated in
terms of scenic form it is not relevant here.

IV

In *Julius Caesar* Shakespeare's intention seems to have been to
achieve a work of greater literary dignity than any play he had
yet written: one that would unite the political and ethical seriousness of his history plays (or the graver parts of them) with the
grand and famous setting of republican Rome. It was to be a
classical tragedy of sorts, but the result was very different from
any other tragedy of the classicizing sixteenth century known
to us. He did not adopt the neo-classical plan, as exemplified in
Seneca's imitators (whether Italian, French, or English), which
opened the play shortly before the catastrophe; there was no
obeisance to the three unities. He instead ran together the events
of the Lupercalia (with the offers to Caesar of the crown), the
formation of Brutus' conspiracy and the assassination of Caesar,
the orations of Brutus and Antony in the Forum, the flight of
Brutus and Cassius, and finally the military campaigns which
culminated in Philippi. For his historical material he made the
unusual choice of Plutarch's *Lives* (Brutus, Julius Caesar, Antony),
as well as possibly some other sources for minor details.

It often seems to be assumed that Shakespeare's historical
sources somehow *dictated* the form the play he based on them
was going to take. But even a cursory reading of these biographies
will show that Shakespeare could not have derived from them
the form which *Julius Caesar* eventually acquired. The *Lives* of
Plutarch that he read were full of vivid detail of a kind which could
be used in a play, but as complete entities they were rambling and

---

[1] There is another scenic link between the two plays. Hamlet's scene with the
Ghost (I. v) has several correspondences with Prince Hal's final interview with his
father (2 *Henry IV*, IV. v). What Hal says to his father at the beginning of their
conversation, 'I never thought to hear you speak again', might equally well have
been spoken by Hamlet to his father's Ghost: both fathers have, in different senses,
returned from the dead.

shapeless. Shakespeare had to pick and choose what he was going to incorporate, and his choice was clearly governed by whether or not the Plutarchian material could be translated into his own dramatic system. It was further governed by the fundamental structural idea which Shakespeare must have had in his mind at the time he was reading Plutarch.

What Shakespeare did, apparently, was to take the *Henry VI, Part Two* as a fundamental structural model, a sort of rough guide, which could be used to accommodate the material taken from Plutarch.[1] With whatever degree of conscious awareness, he seems to have selected and arranged his source-material according to a preconceived idea of the kind of play he wanted to write —but the wholly new and original kind of play he now composed had nevertheless grown out of the plays which he had already written. It was at least to be a play laid out in two parts or stages, the first centring on an assassination, the second on civil war.

The first three acts of *2 Henry VI* include a good deal of miscellaneous material, but what unity they have derives mainly from their concern with the downfall and murder of Duke Humphrey. His murdered body is discovered in III. ii. The two chief agents of his downfall, apart from Queen Margaret, are Suffolk and Cardinal Beaufort, who both meet quick retribution: the Cardinal dies tormented by guilt in III. iii, and Suffolk is murdered by pirates in the following scene (IV. i). The rest of *2 Henry VI* (from IV. ii to the end) is concerned with, first, the Jack Cade rebellion, and then the outbreak of the Wars of the Roses following on York's return from Ireland. The play ends on an uneasy note: the Yorkists have won the first Battle of St. Albans; York and Warwick congratulate themselves and decide to march on London where, at the beginning of *Part Three*, York is to claim the crown.

It is remarkable how, given the totally different historical circumstances, Shakespeare managed to approximate to the pattern of *2 Henry VI* in *Julius Caesar*. But it is precisely his ability to see the possibilities of a narrative in already existing scenic forms that makes him the supremely resourceful dramatist he is. (Or, to put it differently, he no doubt tended to see, or look out

---

[1] A general thematic resemblance between *2 Henry VI* and *Julius Caesar* was noted by J. P. Brockbank in 'The Frame of Disorder: *Henry VI*' in *Early Shakespeare* (Stratford upon Avon Studies, 1961), ed. John Russell Brown and Bernard Harris.

for, things which were like, or potentially like, scenes or parts of scenes already in existence in earlier plays.) The tragedy, like the history play, divides into two clear parts. The first centres on the conspiracy against Caesar and his assassination; the second moves from Rome into the 'field' for the civil war. Caesar's assassination is placed in III. i; the elaborate *tableau* produced immediately after the killing recalls the dumb-show of Duke Humphrey's murder at the beginning of *2 Henry VI*, III. ii. The Jack Cade scenes, which fill most of Act Four of *2 Henry VI*, have some parallels in the riot scene which immediately follows the Forum scene of III. ii. In particular the killing of Cinna the Poet merely because his name is Cinna recalls the killing of a man who addresses Jack Cade by his true name instead of as 'Lord Mortimer'. In both plays the scenes of riot give way to a full-scale civil war. In *Julius Caesar* the war fills Act Five—just as it does in *2 Henry VI* (with the proviso that the Wars of the Roses continue for the entire length of *Part Three*). But the hostility of Antony and Octavius, although only incipient in *Julius Caesar*, was also of course to develop into the civil wars that ended at Actium. The endings of both plays, therefore, have a continuative aspect: *2 Henry VI* undoubtedly looks forward to its successor, while in *Julius Caesar* Shakespeare left it open to himself to write a sequel.

Of course the two plays differ markedly in certain details of structure. In the fourth act particularly they diverge: in *2 Henry VI* Shakespeare gives Jack Cade's rebellion very full (perhaps excessive) treatment, whereas in *Julius Caesar* he disposes of the mob's violence in one short scene in Act Three, and devotes his fourth act to developing the personal relationship of Brutus and Cassius. But in general terms the resemblances between the two plays seem indisputable.

But however important *2 Henry VI* was for the fundamental lay-out of *Julius Caesar*, other history plays also made their contributions, so that the final result was very different from any single previous play. (To say so much is to leave out of account the use Shakespeare may have made of plays other than his own. I have already mentioned, in Chapter I, his possible debt to Greene's *James IV*.) In the second act of *Julius Caesar* (the conspiratorial stage) the action takes something of its shape from the sequence in *Richard III* which leads up to the fall and execution of Hastings. This sequence (it is entirely contained in III. ii) takes place at Hastings's house during the small hours. There is a good deal of mysterious coming and going; the atmosphere is one of fear and menace. First a messenger rouses Hastings to tell him of Stanley's 'dream'—an oblique way of warning him to flee the path of the 'boar' Richard Gloucester. But Hastings, an example of impregnable 'security', refuses to listen. More visitors follow: Catesby tests Hastings's attitude to Richard; Stanley follows, then a Pursuivant, then a Priest, and finally, as if embodying his fate, arrives the sinister figure of Buckingham. In *Julius Caesar* the corresponding scene to this is set at Caesar's house (II. ii); the time is morning, following on from the previous night scene in Brutus' orchard. It resembles Hastings's scene in that it shows Caesar receiving a series of visitors, withstanding the pleas of Calphurnia that he should not go to the Capitol (Caesar, like Hastings, is an example of 'security'), and finally leaving for the Capitol, where he meets his death, just as Hastings finally leaves for the Tower of London, where he meets *his* death. Calphurnia's dream of the statue spouting blood corresponds to Stanley's dream of the murderous boar, although in the contrary interpretation given to her dream by Decius Shakespeare recalled the dream of Duke Humphrey and the contrary interpretation placed on it by his ambitious wife Eleanor (*2 Henry VI*, I. ii).[1] But the affinities between the two plays go further. The sequence of the following scenes in *Richard III* (III. iv to III. vii) bears a distinct structural resemblance to the first and second scenes of the third act of *Julius Caesar*. There are essentially two climaxes: first, a lesser climax in the sudden arrest and execution of Hastings (III. iv), followed by a more elaborately prepared movement in which Richard and Buckingham hoodwink the citizens and finally get the crown for Richard. The corresponding sequence in *Julius Caesar* shows, first, the killing of Caesar and the arrival of Antony (III. i; admittedly a more highly wrought scene than the downfall of Hastings), followed by the second, and greater, climax of the Forum scene (III. ii), in which Antony succeeds in winning over the sympathy and power of the people. These two major scenes of climax share one very important feature: both are primarily displays of formal rhetoric. The long speeches exchanged between Richard and Buckingham in front of the Lord Mayor, the

---

[1] Geoffrey Bullough points out the resemblance to the scene in *2 Henry VI* in *Narrative and Dramatic Sources of Shakespeare*, vol. v (1964), p. 42.

Aldermen, and the Citizens are of course quite different in tone and effect from the sustained formal orations of Brutus and Antony before the Roman populace, but in their position within the structure of the play as a whole, they exactly correspond to them.

Antony's great oration in the Forum scene (III. ii. 73–253) was one of the most ambitiously planned movements that Shakespeare had yet attempted, and nothing in the earlier plays clearly anticipates it. But in a number of scenes in *Richard III* Richard's ruthless drive and histrionic control are a match for Antony's, and one of his set-pieces may have been recalled by Shakespeare. This is the wooing of Lady Anne (I. ii), a prolonged exercise in willed persuasion played against the background of Henry VI's funeral hearse. This particular circumstance is matched in the Forum scene, for Antony's oration is also delivered in the presence of a blood-boltered corpse. Anne's curse on the murderer of Henry VI—

> Curs'd be the hand that made these fatal holes!
> Cursed the heart that had the heart to do it!
> Cursed the blood that let this blood from hence!
>
> (I. ii. 14–16)

—finds an echo in the previous scene of *Julius Caesar*, in the speech Antony speaks over Caesar's corpse when he is left alone:

> Woe to the hand that shed this costly blood!
>
> (III. i. 259)

(But otherwise this soliloquy, with its prophecy of 'Domestic fury and fierce civil strife', is in part modelled on the Bishop of Carlisle's similar prophecy in the deposition scene of *Richard II*, IV. i. 134–49.) The indebtedness of *Julius Caesar* to *Richard III* is pervasive, and it seems curiously fitting that Julius Caesar himself should at one point figure in a discussion in the earlier play (III. i. 68–88). Another scene which recalls *Richard III* is that of Brutus in his tent—or at least, the scene's second half, after the termination of the quarrel (IV. iii. 156 ff.); the corresponding tent scene takes place on the eve of Bosworth (V. iii). The occasion of both scenes is the eve of a decisive battle; both Richard and Brutus call for wine—as it happens, in identical words: 'Give me a bowl of wine' (V. iii. 72, IV. iii. 156); both men are emotionally disturbed and are visited by ghosts. Less important and more debatable is a link (or a possible link) between the second scene of *Julius Caesar* and the passage in *Richard III* where Buckingham tells Richard how the citizens of London received his oration which disparaged Edward IV's heirs and recommended Richard for the crown (III. vii. 1–55). Buckingham's account of the citizens' disappointing response is decidedly downright, and its tone is one of comic bathos:

> Now, by the holy Mother of our Lord,
> The citizens are mum, say not a word.
>
> (2–3)

He had duly delivered a skilful and rousing oration:

> And when mine oratory drew toward end
> I bid them that did love their country's good
> Cry 'God save Richard, England's royal King!'
> *Gloucester.* And did they so?
> *Buckingham.* No, so God help me, they spake not a word . . .
>
> (20–4)

Buckingham goes on to instruct Richard how to receive the Mayor and his party who are to offer him the crown: 'Play the maid's part: still answer nay, and take it' (51). And more sardonic comedy follows. In *Julius Caesar* after the return of Caesar's train, Casca gives Brutus and Cassius his 'blunt' account of what had happened (I. ii. 215–86). He relates how Antony three times offered Caesar a crown and how Caesar each time refused it, 'but for all that, to my thinking, he would fain have had it'. Common to both scenes is the way in which certain public events, which take place off stage, are narrated in a bluntly unceremonious manner; the public events themselves in both cases concern getting a crown while pretending not to want it.

The list of structural devices in *Julius Caesar* which seem to be derived from the English history plays can be extended further. The scene in which Portia asks to be admitted to Brutus' confidence (II. i. 233–309) is close to that in which Lady Percy makes a similar request of her husband Hotspur (*1 Henry IV*, II. iii); both husbands are about to join a fatal conspiracy. Indeed, for all their differences of personality and temperament, Brutus has a good deal in common with Hotspur. Both are men of honour who find themselves involved in conspiracy. It seems clear too that Brutus and Cassius' final leave-taking looks back to the leave-taking of Hotspur and his associates; the chivalrous epitaph spoken over Hotspur's corpse by Prince Hal (v. iv. 87–101) also has its counterpart in Antony's final tribute to the dead Brutus (v. v. 68–75). There can be little doubt that the Hotspur scenes of *1 Henry IV* influenced Shakespeare's portrayal of Brutus.

From all this it emerges that a large number of the scenic forms of *Julius Caesar* were adapted from others already in existence. There are some exceptions, notable among them the quarrel scene (iv. iii), which has no obvious forerunner in Shakespeare (although its position in the play and its dramatic function—it is an emotional *éclaircissement*—make it comparable with the final interview between Henry IV and the Prince in *2 Henry IV*).

Two conclusions may be drawn from what has been said so far in this chapter. The first is that early plays like the *Henry VI* trilogy, *Richard III*, and *King John* are of crucial importance for Shakespeare's development as a tragic dramatist. He never left them behind him; until the end of his career he continued to draw on them as sources of scenic form and contrivance, or in more elusive ways as guides or suggestions for dramatizing narrative materials. The same is true, if to a slightly lesser degree, of the two other early tragedies, *Titus Andronicus* and *Romeo and Juliet*. For Shakespeare's method reveals itself as one of accumulative accretion: by modifying or adapting forms in new combinations and new sequences he evolved an increasingly expressive dramatic language.

The second is that it is impossible to make any sweeping critical generalizations about his use of these forms. It is tempting to assert that when he adapts a form from an early play he always improves on himself. In many cases this is undoubtedly true; but in some others it is open to argument; in others it is not true. The scene I discussed earlier in this chapter from the second act of *Othello* is not obviously an improvement on its structural 'source' in *Romeo and Juliet*. That earlier scene, which shows the death of Mercutio and Romeo's brief agonizing conflict of allegiances, is an impressive one, perhaps more so than the one in *Othello*. But the scene of Cassio's disgrace is not a major climax in the larger economy of *Othello*; it would be wrong if it usurped the place reserved for the temptation scene in the next act. In this way a comparison between the use of scenic forms in early and later plays must be subject to larger considerations concerning their function within the play as a whole. Nevertheless, if we were to restrict the comparison to scenic forms occurring in two plays only—for example, *Richard III* and *Julius Caesar*—it might be possible to venture a generalization. It seems true that by the time he wrote the later play Shakespeare had gained decisively in economy. Many of the scenes of *Richard III* are quite simply too long. This is so, for example, of Richard's wooing of Lady Anne: the scene would be greatly improved if it were shorter. In *Julius Caesar*, on the other hand, the play as a whole makes an effect of formal clarity and unclogged freedom of movement. Not a single scene lapses into verbosity; every episode and minor scenic unit is cleanly and economically shaped. On the other hand, it could be argued that the sequence of Hastings's decision to go to the Tower and his unexpected fate there is quite as compelling as the corresponding part of *Julius Casesar*, and in some respects even more so. On the whole, it can be said that Shakespeare learned how to place his scenes to the best effect—a generalization which a comparison between *Richard III* and *Macbeth* would also bear out.

PART TWO

5. *Othello*

I

THERE has never been any doubt of *Othello*'s success on the stage. It was one of Shakespeare's most popular plays in the Jacobean period (to judge by the number of references that have survived and by the frequency of imitations),[1] and it has always kept the stage so long as there were actors who could meet the demands of its title role. Bradley found that of all Shakespeare's tragedies it was 'the most painfully exciting and most terrible'; it was also 'the most masterly of the tragedies in point of construction'.[2] And yet, while acknowledged as a masterpiece, it has often been felt to have certain limitations; it seems to be a common experience to find it less rewarding to read than *Hamlet*, *King Lear*, or *Macbeth*. The suggestion that it offers less to the mind than the three tragedies just mentioned is made by Bradley, who refers to 'the comparative confinement of the imaginative atmosphere', finds it 'less "symbolic"', and registers an impression 'that in *Othello* we are not in contact with the whole of Shakespeare'.[3]

These two aspects of *Othello*—its great theatrical power and what may seem, at least to a reader, a certain thinness in its imaginative substance—are not unrelated. The play is peculiarly of the stage, and interpretations of it which ignore or neglect its theatricality can be fatally out of focus. Whether or not we agree with Bradley in finding *Othello*, for all its power and beauty, deficient in some quality thought to be essential to Shakespeare at his greatest (something to be found in *Macbeth*, for example), it seems beyond dispute that the sustained element of intrigue—everything that is implied by the presence of the deceiver Iago (whose role is the longest in the play)—makes the plot of *Othello* very different from those of the other tragedies. Iago's sustained hypocrisy arouses nervous tension—it excites very successfully—

---

[1] For imitations of *Othello* see David L. Frost, *The School of Shakespeare* (Cambridge, 1968), pp. 110, 160.

[2] A. C. Bradley, *Shakespearean Tragedy*, pp. 176, 177.

[3] Ibid., pp. 185, 186.

but it may also cause a certain intellectual impatience: the play is so much more a theatrical contrivance than a dramatic poem. Of course to say so much is not to deny the power of *Othello* to move as well as to excite, or to ignore the true magnanimity of its vision of love. But the differences between it and the other tragedies written close to it in time are real, and it is legitimate to wonder why this should be so. Some part of an answer must lie in Shakespeare's choice of a source narrative and in the way he chose to translate it into dramatic form.

II

Brief though it is, Cinthio's story was of no use to Shakespeare in its opening and closing stages. Cinthio's Moor and Disdemona live together tranquilly in Venice after their marriage and before the move to Cyprus; and after Disdemona's death the story is carried forward an unspecified length of time until the Moor and the Ensign (Iago) also meet their deaths. Shakespeare takes up the sequence of Cinthio's plot at the point where the Ensign begins his designs against the Captain (Cassio), a point which corresponds to II. iii of *Othello*. In Cinthio's words:

And it happened not long afterwards that the Captain drew his sword on a soldier, when on guard, and wounded him, and so was deprived of his rank by the Moor. This was a cause of deep grief to Disdemona, and on many occasions she tried to reconcile her husband to him. The Moor told the wicked Ensign that his wife was worrying him so much about the Captain that he feared in the end he would be compelled to reinstate him.[1]

Thereafter, though of course with a number of departures and inventions of his own, Shakespeare follows Cinthio's sequence of events with reasonable faithfulness until the murder of Disdemona. The bulk, then, of Cinthio's story—omitting its opening and its ending—supplied Shakespeare with the main plot sequence of his last four acts (or, to be more precise, the last three and a half). This left the first act and half of the second to be wholly invented by himself.

Critics have often examined Cinthio's tale from the point of view of Shakespeare's use of it, and in the process have often un-

---

[1] The translation from Cinthio is by T. J. B. Spencer, in *Elizabethan Love Stories* (Penguin Books, 1968), p. 200.

fairly maligned it. The tale is in fact a competent piece of story-telling, clearly presented and swift in its development, and enlivened at key points by brief exchanges of dialogue.¹ One such passage of dialogue is important, since it gave Shakespeare the suggestion for his temptation scene (III. iii). Other details in Cinthio which were suitable to being worked up into stage scenes were the occasion when the Moor demands the handkerchief from Disdemona (Shakespeare's III. iv), the eavesdropping scene (IV. i), and the night attack on Cassio (V. i). Otherwise, for all the other scenes which comprise the play—for all the other scenic forms—Shakespeare was thrown back on his own resources. And of course even the temptation scene is utterly different from the brief passage of dialogue which we get in Cinthio. That is to say, Shakespeare was obliged to adapt scenic forms already in existence, either in earlier plays of his own or in plays known to him by other dramatists. No doubt many of the forms he used were very old—dramatic form is by its nature deeply traditional—and what their ultimate sources were, together with their intermediate stages, we can never know. Moreover many plays of Shakespeare's age have not survived, and we can be sure that some of them would have thrown light on Shakespeare's practice. Despite these necessary limitations to any inquiry of this sort, a good deal can be discovered about the ways in which *Othello* came into being by scrutinizing Shakespeare's earlier plays, for they (or those which are relevant) have as much right to be considered as 'sources' of *Othello* as Cinthio's tale itself.

It has often been noticed in a general sense that *Othello's* concern with love and jealousy links it with the comedies and that this is a major distinguishing mark of the play.² None of the other mature tragedies grows so completely out of the world of comedy and amatory romance. In structural terms the play's affinities with comedy reveal themselves in the prominent place taken by intrigue. Classical Roman comedy and the Italian *commedia erudita* of the sixteenth century were dominated by intrigue: wittily resourceful dissemblers improvised their way over every obstacle, and it was their schemes and practices which gave

¹ In this I agree with Ned Allen who, in his article 'The Two Parts of "Othello" ', *Shakespeare Survey*, vol. 21 (1968), defends Cinthio's *novella*.
² In her article ' "Othello": a Tragedy Built on a Comic Structure', *Shakespeare Survey*, vol. 21 (1908), Barbara Heliodora C. de Medonça argues for an influence on *Othello* of the *commedia dell'arte*.

momentum to the plot. In *Othello* Iago's schemes perform a similar function: once Othello has eloped with Desdemona (and that happens before the opening of the play), all the moving-power comes from Iago: he wakes Brabantio and fills him with alarm at the flight of his daughter, he tries to stir up an affray between Brabantio and Othello and later encourages Roderigo to follow Desdemona to Cyprus, and he it is who engineers Cassio's downfall before turning his full attention to Othello. When Iago's schemes are analysed, they can be seen to fall into three main stages. Two of the schemes have the aim of harming Othello; the other has Cassio as victim. (His treatment of Roderigo can be set aside for the moment.) The first scheme against Othello belongs to Act One. This is the attempt to destroy Othello's marriage by enraging Brabantio, an attempt which comes to nothing in the senate scene of I. iii. The disgracing of Cassio comes between this first scheme against Othello and the second, which begins in the third act and is completed only at the end of the play. If the plot against Cassio is also set aside for a moment, and Iago's two plots against Othello (one a failure, the other a success) are considered together as the basic plot device for the whole play, we are in a position to see where Shakespeare probably derived the shape of his main action from. By the time he was writing *Othello* he had already written *Much Ado About Nothing* a few years before. If we leave aside Beatrice and Benedick, the main action consists of Don John's villainous attempts to thwart Claudio's chances of married happiness. The first is a feeble failure; the second is, temporarily at least, wholly successful. Don John's first attempt exploits the power of hearsay. His servant Borachio has overheard Don Pedro talking with Claudio and offering to woo Hero for him. In the dance scene of II. i, in which the main characters are masked, Don John informs Claudio that Don Pedro intends to have Hero for himself; Claudio instantly believes him, not knowing who the speaker is, and is only undeceived by Benedick and by the Prince himself. The whole scheme of Don John's fizzles out quickly, and a little later in the same scene Claudio is happily betrothed to Hero. Don John's second scheme, the details of which are again furnished by Borachio, is conceived in the scene immediately following (II. ii): Borachio will speak with Margaret at Hero's window on the eve of her wedding, the whole transaction being witnessed by the two princes and Claudio. This culminates in the church scene of IV. i, with Claudio's public repudiation of Hero and her apparent death. It seems likely that this fundamental plot structure—a villain plotting against a marriage, the first time unsuccessfully, the second time more elaborately and cunningly and with success—came into Shakespeare's mind at an early stage of the composition of *Othello*. Don John gave way to Iago, Claudio to Othello, and Hero to Desdemona. The whole action was of course enlarged, filled out with further episodes (notably the plot against Cassio), and imagined afresh. But it none the less seems probable that the Don John–Claudio action provided the ground-plan for *Othello*. It should be noticed that in Cinthio there is nothing corresponding to Iago's first plot—small in scale and unsuccessful—which enlists Brabantio against Othello; Don John, on the other hand, does first fail before he succeeds.

But these two plays have more in common than their basic plot device. *Much Ado About Nothing* anticipates *Othello* in certain imaginative qualities and in some of its chief thematic preoccupations. Its main action concerns soldiers in peace-time: Claudio, like Othello a successful soldier, abandons 'war-thoughts' for thoughts of love which are wholly unfamiliar to him. Moreover, the society of Messina is talkative, suspicious, and volatile— qualities which reappear more sombrely in the implied social world of *Othello*. In *Othello* the strange detail about Cassio accompanying Othello in his wooing, which Iago uses to incriminate Cassio, may possibly have been suggested to Shakespeare by the early episode in *Much Ado* in which Don Pedro woos Hero for Claudio, a circumstance which, on Don John's prompting, instantly gives rise to jealousy on Claudio's part. And Othello's story of his wooing of Desdemona seems, at least in part, derived from Don Pedro's words in the same episode:

> And in her bosom I'll unclasp my heart,
> And take her hearing prisoner with the force
> And strong encounter of my amorous tale.

> (I. i. 285–7)

For Desdemona is similarly won by Othello's 'tale'. In other respects, of course, Claudio and Othello are quite unlike, especially in age and 'size' of personality; in general stature Claudio resembles Cassio, and both are said to be Florentines.

Both plays show man as a prey to illusion: he cannot trust his senses, not even his own eyes. They share too a concern with 'false report', and both show the disproportionate effect in terms of human suffering that words—mere malicious talk—can give rise to. The comedy is an affair of 'much ado about *nothing*', while in the tragedy a key property is a mere handkerchief. One striking feature brings the two plays close together: both Hero and Desdemona are 'undone' by a trusted female companion, yet neither Margaret nor Emilia is unsympathetically presented, probably because each is being unwittingly used by a villainous man. There is, further, something similar between Beatrice's indignation following on from her 'Kill Claudio' (IV. i. 287 ff.) and Emilia's great outburst after the discovery of Iago's villainy (V. ii. 221 ff.). In both passages a strong sense of the opposition between the sexes finds expression (Beatrice's 'O God, that I were a man!' and Gratiano's reproach to Iago who has tried to stab Emilia: 'Fie! Your sword upon a woman?' Desdemona had earlier exclaimed, 'O, these men, these men!' (IV. iii. 58).) And the loyalty, fiercely and bravely expressed, of Beatrice and Emilia for their accused friends (one apparently dead, the other actually dead) is similar in tone and in the pitch and volume of voice: Beatrice says, 'I will die a woman with grieving', and Emilia, 'I'll kill myself for grief'. But there are a number of further verbal correspondences between the two plays.[1] That Shakespeare's mind was running along lines already traced in the earlier play can be seen in the final episode of the last scene, where Lodovico appears in order to pass judgement on Othello; the comparable scene is that in which Leonato confronts Borachio, a short judgement episode which has something of the same tone and movement:

> *Re-enter Leonato and Antonio, with the Sexton.*
>
> *Leonato.* Which is the villain? Let me see his eyes,
>   That when I note another man like him
>   I may avoid him. Which of these is he?
> *Borachio.* If you would know your wronger, look on me.
>
>   (V. i. 245–8)

---

[1] Cf. *Much Ado*, IV. i. 86–93, with *Othello*, V. ii. 212–18, and V. i. 34–8 with III. iv. 141–51. Another possible scenic correspondence may be mentioned. The dialogue between the Duke and Senators about the movements of the Turkish fleet (*Othello*, I. iii. 1–46) forms a brief *exemplum* illustrating the working of false report. Shakespeare perhaps recalled the comparable short exchange between Leonato and

Lodovico. Where is this rash and most unfortunate man?
Othello. That's he that was Othello—here I am.
Lodovico. Where is the viper? Bring the villain forth.

(v. ii. 286–8)

In each of these passages the wrong-doer is made to identify himself—'look on me', 'here I am'—with an effect of a public admission of fault. In plays so much concerned with deception and mistaking, the self-proclamation comes as a welcome moment of truth.

So much for *Much Ado About Nothing* and its contribution to the making of *Othello*. Its importance for the structure of *Othello* is that it provided, in the two attempts of Don John against Claudio, a rough model for the development of Iago's schemes. I remarked earlier that Shakespeare's use of Cinthio begins in II. iii with Cassio's attack on Montano ('And it happened not long afterwards that the Captain drew his sword on a soldier when on guard, and wounded him, and so was deprived of his rank by the Moor'). I want now to consider the pre-Cinthio part of *Othello*: everything in the play that precedes the brawl of II. iii.

The plot for this part of the play, as invented by Shakespeare, runs as follows. Othello has just eloped with the daughter of Brabantio, a Venetian senator. The play opens with Iago explaining the situation to Roderigo, who has long been a suitor to her. The two men rudely awaken Brabantio to tell him the unwelcome news. Brabantio meets Othello in the streets and in his rage takes him before the Senate. But the Senate have already sent for Othello to order him to Cyprus to defend it against the Turkish attack; he is allowed to take Desdemona with him. The party arrive in Cyprus; a storm has dispersed the Turkish fleet, and celebrations are proclaimed. Iago plans, with the help of Roderigo, to get Cassio drunk and cashiered; the plan succeeds. At this point Shakespeare takes up Cinthio's narrative.

Shakespeare did not simply create these incidents out of nothing. Or rather, if we want to say he invented them, he did so in the sense of finding them ready-made in his own mind. What he

Antonio about Don Pedro's plan to 'woo' Hero, which has a similar function—to show men mistaking the truth through false report—and is also placed early in the play (*Much Ado*, I. ii). The Duke of Venice adopts a position of sceptical but sensible rationality, not unlike Leonato's sceptical reserve ('Hath the fellow any wit that told you this? . . . No, no; we will hold it as a dream . . .'. I. ii. 14–17).

seems in large part to have done is to adapt a few incidents from
a play he had written not many years before and which, like *Much
Ado About Nothing*, had some obvious affinities of subject with
Othello. The play was *The Merry Wives of Windsor*, one of whose
chief characters, Ford, is a jealous husband. But the parts of the
play levied on by Shakespeare for the opening scenes of *Othello*
do not concern Ford; they concern, in the first instance, Fenton
and Page, and in the second, Falstaff and Shallow.

Direct quotation will most easily indicate the nature of the self-
borrowing. Fenton loves and is loved by Anne Page, but her
parents have different intentions for her. Page favours Slender,
but his wife prefers Dr. Caius. In III. iv. the following exchange
occurs:

> *Page.* Now, Master Slender! Love him, daughter Anne—
> Why, how now, what does Master Fenton here?
> You wrong me, sir, thus still to haunt my house.
> I told you, sir, my daughter is dispos'd of.
> *Fenton.* Nay, Master Page, be not impatient.
> *Mrs. Page.* Good Master Fenton, come not to my child.
> *Page.* She is no match for you . . .
> Knowing my mind, you wrong me, Master Fenton.
>
> (III. iv. 66–75)

In the first scene of *Othello*, Brabantio tells Roderigo:

> I have charg'd thee not to haunt about my doors;
> In honest plainness thou hast heard me say
> My daughter is not for thee . . .
>
> (I. i. 97–9)

At the end of the final scene of *The Merry Wives*, it is revealed that
Fenton and Anne have eloped. Fenton is quite unrepentant, and
acknowledges no guilt in making a true-love marriage. He says
to Page:

> You would have married her most shamefully,
> Where there was no proportion held in love.
> The truth is, she and I, long since contracted,
> Are now so sure that nothing can dissolve us.
> Th' offence is holy that she hath committed;
> And this deceit loses the name of craft,
> Of disobedience, or unduteous title . . .

Ford offers Page conciliatory counsel:

> Stand not amaz'd; here is no remedy.
> In love, the heavens themselves do guide the state;
> Money buys land, and wives are sold by fate.

Page and his wife instantly relent, since this is, after all, the end of a comedy:

> *Page.* Well, what remedy? Fenton, heaven give thee joy!
> What cannot be eschew'd must be embrac'd.
>
> (v. v. 208–24)

In the council scene of *Othello* (i. iii), Brabantio again corresponds to Page, but this time Othello, not Roderigo, to Fenton. The Duke tries to persuade Brabantio to accept the match, just as Ford had done with Page:

> When remedies are past, the griefs are ended
> By seeing the worst, which late on hopes depended.
>
> (202–3)

However, this is not the ending of a comedy, but the beginning of a tragedy, and Brabantio, unlike Page, refuses to accept the situation.

The second area of *The Merry Wives* which Shakespeare drew on is located at the very beginning of the play. Justice Shallow is complaining that he has suffered an injury from Falstaff: 'The Council shall hear of it; it is a riot.' When Falstaff enters he is at once accused by Shallow. Their dialogue is as follows:

> *Falstaff.* Now, Master Shallow, you'll complain of me to the King?
> *Shallow.* Knight, you have beaten my men, kill'd my deer, and broke
> open my lodge.
> *Falstaff.* But not kiss'd your keeper's daughter.
> *Shallow.* Tut, a pin! this shall be answer'd.
> *Falstaff.* I will answer it straight: I have done all this. That is now
> answer'd.
> *Shallow.* The Council shall know this.
> *Falstaff.* 'Twere better for you if it were known in counsel: you'll
> be laugh'd at.
>
> (i. i. 98–108)

The constituents here are a quarrel between an elderly civilian and an imperturbable soldier; the civilian protests that he will take the soldier before 'the Council'. The dialogue continues with Slender taking up the quarrel with Falstaff and his men:

> *Slender.* Marry, sir, I have matter in my head against you; and against your cony-catching rascals, Bardolph, Nym, and Pistol. They carried me to the tavern, and made me drunk, and afterward pick'd my pockets.

Falstaff asks Pistol if this is true:

> *Evans.* No, it is false, if it is a pick-purse.
> *Pistol.* Ha, thou mountain-foreigner! Sir John, and master mine,
>   I combat challenge of this latten bilbo.
>   Word of denial in thy labras here!
>   Word of denial! Froth and scum, thou liest.
> *Slender.* By these gloves, then, 'twas he.
> *Nym.* Be advis'd sir, and pass good humours; I will say 'marry trap' with you, if you run the nuthook's humour on me; that is the very note of it.
> *Slender.* By this hat, then, he in the red face had it; for though I cannot remember what I did when you made me drunk, yet I am not altogether an ass.
> *Falstaff.* What say you, Scarlet and John?
> *Bardolph.* Why, sir, for my part, I say the gentleman had drunk himself out of his five sentences.
> *Evans.* It is his five senses; fie, what the ignorance is!
> *Bardolph.* And being fap, sir, was, as they say, cashier'd; and so conclusions passed the careers.
> *Slender.* Ay, you spake in Latin then too; but 'tis no matter; I'll ne'er be drunk whilst I live again, but in honest, civil, godly company, for this trick. If I be drunk, I'll be drunk with those that have the fear of God, and not with drunken knaves.
> *Evans.* So God udge me, that is a virtuous mind.

> (i. i. 143–67)

The whole of this opening situation in *The Merry Wives* seems to have contributed to the pre-Cinthio part of *Othello*. Slender corresponds to Cassio, in that both are made drunk and are then 'cashiered'—Bardolph's word-play gives the passage a slightly memorable quality—for Slender is robbed (relieved of his cash), while Cassio is 'cashiered' in the military sense (deprived of his officer's rank). (Shakespeare probably chose Cassio's name with a view to his cashiering: the phrase 'cashier'd Cassio' is used by Iago at ii. iii. 363.) Falstaff corresponds to Othello in that, first, he is accused by Shallow just as Othello is accused by Brabantio, and Shallow wants to bring him before 'the Council' just as Brabantio does in fact accuse Othello before the Senate (and the phrase 'the Duke's in council' occurs in *Othello* at I. iii. 92); secondly, Falstaff interrogates his men just as, in II. iii, Othello interrogates his juniors (Cassio, Montano, Iago).

This passage in *The Merry Wives* prompts one or two further remarks. Iago and Pistol share the rank of 'ancient' (i.e. ensign). Pistol is an obvious example of the braggart soldier; while in Cinthio's story the Ensign (Iago) is introduced thus: 'although he was a most detestable character, nevertheless with imposing words and his presence he concealed the malice he bore in his heart, in such a way that he showed himself outwardly like another Hector or Achilles'. In Cinthio, then, 'Iago' as well as being a hypocrite is something of a *miles gloriosus*, the very character he accuses Othello of being (I. i. 13–14, II. i. 216–17). There is one other point of contact between the two ancients: Pistol in the passage quoted above rejects Slender's accusation with the words 'froth and scum, thou liest'. In v. ii. of *Othello* Iago rejects Emilia's disclosure of the truth about the handkerchief in very similar terms: 'Filth, thou liest' (234). Finally, Slender's feebly moralistic words which round off the episode may find an echo in some of Cassio's maudlin remarks while he is drunk and even in some of his repentant speeches after his disgrace.[1]

To summarize: the various constituents of both the Fenton–Page and the Falstaff–Shallow–Slender situations were recalled during the composition of *Othello*, but were given an entirely new configuration; however, the basic elements of the elopement and the subsequent quarrel, and the 'cashiering' of a man who had been made drunk, were retained.

[1] Other stray details which suggest that *The Merry Wives* was in Shakespeare's mind at the time of *Othello* are the occurrence in both of the strange word (in slightly different forms) 'Anthropophaginian' (*Merry Wives*, IV. v. 8) and 'Anthrophagi' (*Othello*, I. iii. 144) and the following:

> *Mrs. Ford.* O that my husband saw this letter! It would give eternal food to his jealousy.
>
> *Mrs. Page.* Why, look where he comes . . .
> $\qquad\qquad\qquad\qquad\qquad\qquad\qquad\qquad\qquad\qquad\qquad$ (II. i. 88–90)
>
> *Iago.* Look where he comes! Not poppy, nor mandragora . . . $\qquad$ (III. iii. 334)

In both, the jealous husband is given an entrance which on Shakespeare's spacious stage would have made a striking effect (no doubt gesture and gait would have been made expressive).

Two other comedies relevant to *Othello* are *The Merchant of Venice* and *Twelfth Night*, of which the first is much the more important. It has, of course, the same Venetian setting, and turns, like *Othello*, on the poles of love and hate. Like Othello, Shylock is an 'alien' in Venice, and, as G. Wilson Knight pointed out, the Duke of Morocco, a Moor, speaks with something of the 'Othello music'.[1] But if his Jewish sense of apartness relates Shylock to Othello, his capacity for hatred—what he calls 'a lodg'd hate and a certain loathing' (IV. i. 60)—obviously anticipates Iago. In some imaginative qualities *The Merchant of Venice* is closest of all the comedies to *Othello*: in its poetic opulence, its picturesqueness, and its strong sense of the glamour of personality. But structurally *Othello* owes little to it, except for the council scene (I. iii) which, in a general way, recalls the trial of Antonio (IV. i), and the prose dialogue of IV. i. 165 ff., which echoes the fluctuating moods of Shylock's scene with Tubal (III. i. 66 ff.). From *Twelfth Night* Shakespeare remembered how Sir Toby 'uses Sir Andrew as his purse by promising to assist him in his wooing of Olivia';[2] in a similar way Iago makes use of Roderigo. I shall mention some further uses of *Twelfth Night* in a later section.[3]

These earlier comedies, then, supplied Shakespeare with a number of different kinds of suggestions for dramatizing Cinthio's tale; and one of them even gave him the main structure of Iago's intrigues. The comic provenance of this material explains why so much of *Othello* seems to take place in a comic setting, with its shrewd sanity and worldliness and its commonplace sense of actuality. (Even Othello can sink to the homely banality of ''twill do me good to walk', IV. iii. 2.) But of course this is not a true account of the play as a whole. The main omission is Othello himself, who endows his situation with a force of passion quite alien to comedy. The nature of his role, and the peculiar degree of sympathy he elicits from the theatre audience, call for separate attention.

III

Othello is one of Shakespeare's most profoundly dramatized plays; its realization in the dramatic medium is unusually complete.

[1] G. Wilson Knight, *The Wheel of Fire* (revised and enlarged edition, London, 1949), p. 119.

[2] Kenneth Muir, *Shakespeare's Sources*, vol. i (London, 1957), p. 131.

[3] See Appendix to Chapter 5 for Shakespeare's possible use in *Othello* of other plays than his own.

We can say of it that many of its constituent features clearly reflect certain fundamentals of the dramatic process, so that (more perhaps than for most of Shakespeare's plays) we need to remember that everything in it was designed with a view to its effect in theatrical performance. The character of Othello, for example, is structurally conditioned by the fact that a play is, among other things, a story cast in dialogue form, presented by living persons on a stage before an audience composed of persons arbitrarily assembled in the expectation of being excited, stimulated, or in some way entertained. In this section I want to consider the character of Othello from this point of view.

Othello is at first a man slow to anger, undemonstrative, apparently unpassionate. His first utterance in I. ii is of a flat, pacific nature: "'Tis better as it is'. Iago does his best to stage-manage a scuffle in the streets when Brabantio arrives, but Othello's serene refusal to be roused reduces the occasion to anticlimax. The Senate scene which follows might have grown into something like the trial scene of *The Merchant of Venice* if Iago and Brabantio had been granted their wish, but the Duke and Senators are friendly, and Othello's serenity is unviolated. The scene centres instead on Othello's story of his wooing and Desdemona's declaration of her love. There is of course no question of Shakespeare's success in holding our attention and exciting our concern throughout this long scene, but from another point of view it may be interpreted as a second calculated anticlimax. Othello for a second time refuses to 'make a scene': that is to say, he refuses to exhibit passion. Similarly with the more dangerous moment of his intervention in Cassio's brawl; this time passion threatens, but is controlled:

> Now, by heaven,
> My blood begins my safer guides to rule,
> And passion, having my best judgement collied,
> Assays to lead the way.
>
> (II. iii. 196–9)

Only one more brief appearance (III. ii), showing Othello calm and soldier-like and attentive to his administrative duties, comes before the temptation scene.

Now at a performance of the play, it may be suggested, in one part of our minds we strongly *desire* Othello to succumb to passion, terrible (in a sense) though the results are likely to be, and even though this desire is the one thing that certainly unites us with Iago. Such a desire does not rule out feelings of intense sympathy for Othello and hostility to Iago; nevertheless, there is an important sense in which we want Iago to succeed. One of our essential roles as members of the audience (as was remarked in Chapter 1) is merely to be in attendance, to *wait for* some notable event to take place. Our awareness of this role inevitably sets up a pressure in our minds, a desire for a certain outcome, which is independent of any moral considerations and may indeed run counter to them. Some critics quite ignore this aspect of the dramatic experience and in doing so falsify our response—our real response—to plays when they are acted.

But there is another consideration which also relates to the presence of the theatre audience. A solitary private reading of *Othello* may leave one feeling curiously unsure about Othello's reality as a person—he may seem less solidly realized than the heroes of some of the other tragedies. Bradley's comment on Othello is pertinent here: '. . . the hero himself strikes us as having, probably, less of the poet's personality in him than many characters far inferior both as dramatic creations and as men.'[1] To a reader it may seem that Othello has less 'mind', less interior life, certainly than Hamlet or Macbeth, but even less perhaps than Lear, Antony, or Coriolanus. But if he seems less solidly realized as a person, this is so only in reading; in performance he seems to acquire an intense reality, which is clearly in part due to the mere fact of embodiment in the actor, but also seems due to certain qualities latent in the text which acting serves to bring out. These qualities are affective ones: for Shakespeare makes Othello, the hero of his play (as he does pre-eminently with Hamlet), the focus for the readily available erotic feelings of the audience, its desire to bestow affection on one or more of the persons on stage. This means that, despite our recognition of Othello's enormous errors and folly, we are essentially *with* him in a way that could hardly be guessed from readings of the play which, like F. R. Leavis's, find in Othello someone unheroic and relatively unsympathetic. But more than that: in a performance we feel Othello's reality in the fact that it is he who at first provokingly resists our wishes and then indulges them, for no one else on

[1] A. C. Bradley, op. cit., p. 186.

stage has the power, as he has, to give this specifically dramatic pleasure.

It is in the temptation scene that we can see most clearly that aspect of Othello's character which can be called structurally functional. The temptation itself (the 'trying' of Othello by Iago) is set out in two phases. The first phase (III. iii. 91–261) ends with Iago taking his leave; a bridge passage follows during which Desdemona and Emilia enter, the handkerchief is dropped just before Othello leaves with Desdemona and is then passed from Emilia to Iago; the second phase of the temptation is then resumed with the re-entry of Othello (333–483). These two phases which make up the entire temptation are carefully planned as a complete strategy by Shakespeare/Iago. In the first phase Iago sows doubt and suspicion in Othello's mind by indirectly bringing him to contemplate the fact, possibly never considered by him before, that no man can ever know for certain what another man is thinking. This whole movement—whose tempo is controlled by Iago—is distressingly gradual: an irritatingly slow-paced shuffle towards a disclosure which is never made; a sequence of question and half-answer, challenge and evasion, earnest entreaty and hesitant admission. In performance, from an audience's point of view, it is the studied slowness of tempo that is so agitating: we are made, with Othello, to wait upon Iago's apparently artless pauses, his cleverly manufactured reluctance. But after Othello has left the stage and returned for what is the second phase of the temptation, the pace is very different. Now Othello sets the tempo, and Iago is no longer fully master of the situation. This final movement falls into three stages: first, a burst of passion; then a brief lull; thirdly, a wave of even greater passion. In the first outburst Othello bids farewell to the 'tranquil mind' and the life of war, and then makes a physical attack on Iago which Iago seems wholly unprepared for. The lull follows when Iago regains his composure and tells Othello of Cassio's dream, and only after that has had its effect mentions the handkerchief. The mention of the handkerchief prompts the second and even greater wave of passion which culminates in the swearing of revenge. It is notable how carefully prepared for and how relatively brief are Othello's exhibitions of passion; their effect is accordingly very great.

In the first of his two passionate outbursts Othello gives expression to his complete bewilderment:

> I think my wife be honest, and think she is not;
> I think that thou are just, and think thou art not.
> I'll have some proof.

(III. iii. 388–90)

In these words he recalls what he had said earlier in the scene:

> No, to be once in doubt
> Is once to be resolv'd . . . No, Iago,
> I'll see before I doubt; when I doubt, prove;
> And on the proof, there is no more but this:
> Away at once with love or jealousy!

(III. iii. 183–96)

The first phase of the temptation had left Othello in a lingering state of doubt, but it is precisely being in doubt that he cannot endure. If he does not love his wife he must find relief in loathing her. He must go to an extreme; and it is his inability to tolerate the middle way that ensures the scene's final grand climax. But Othello's desire for an extreme position is tacitly endorsed by the audience: like Othello we are in acute discomfort till he has gone one or the other way. So the solemn ritual of the oath-taking commits Othello to a course of murder, but for us it brings an effect of fulfilment, almost of relaxation. The scene finishes with an exchange magnificent in its economy and point:

> *Othello.* Now art thou my Lieutenant.
> *Iago.* I am your own for ever.

Othello's decision to invest Iago with Cassio's rank harks back to the opening of the play with Iago's account of his failure to get the Lieutenancy. The sudden, unprepared-for recall here of this theme, together with Iago's mocking reply, contributes to the effect of finality as the two men leave the stage. 'Now' and 'for ever': we have reached a state gratifying in its absoluteness.

I have been arguing that Othello as a character acquires full reality only in the presence of a theatre audience. Another way of putting it would be to say that it is the audience that endows Othello with his frightening power. And Othello in his turn provides what an audience will always take intense pleasure in: an exhibition of elementally simple passion. That is to say, the relationship between Othello and the audience is an unusually close and reciprocal one. The matter may be illuminated by referring to a study well known to readers of Freud: Gustave le Bon's *The Psychology of Crowds* (1895). Le Bon is concerned not with theatre audiences as such, but with crowds and mobs. A few of his statements will suggest his thesis:

. . . by the mere fact that he forms part of an organised crowd, a man descends several rungs in the ladder of civilisation. Isolated, he may be a cultivated individual; in a crowd he resembles a barbarian—that is, a creature acting by instinct. . . . A crowd is extraordinarily credulous and open to influence; it has small critical faculty. Its feelings are always very simple and very exaggerated. It knows neither doubt nor uncertainty, but goes at once to extremes. If a suspicion is expressed, it is instantly changed into incontrovertible certainty; a trace of antipathy is turned into furious hatred . . .[1]

I quote this passage because some of its statements seem surprisingly applicable to Othello. Like le Bon's 'crowd' he too is 'extraordinarily credulous and open to influence'; his feelings too are strong and simple (if not 'exaggerated') and, as I have already remarked, he cannot tolerate doubt and uncertainty and finds satisfaction only in simple absolutes. Of course a theatre audience (certainly a Shakespearian audience) is not the same thing as a mob. But any assembly of people, including a theatre audience, will have something in common with le Bon's hypothetical 'crowd'; and when an audience watches *Othello*, part of its imaginative experience will be analogous to the simple, even crude, emotions which le Bon ascribes to crowds. It is hardly necessary to add that this simple response is only a part of the whole artistic experience, and that it will coexist with other responses more critically discriminating and self-aware.

I shall return to the temptation scene in the final section of this chapter, in which I comment on some of *Othello's* individual scenes.

IV

Modern editions follow the Folio in dividing *Othello* into five acts, and it seems reasonably clear that Shakespeare did in fact work to a five-act scheme. Act One (Cyprus) and Act Two (the arrival at Cyprus and Cassio's brawl) are clearly defined units, and are marked as such by the Folio. But the Folio's divisions

[1] Quoted by S. Freud, *Group Psychology and the Analysis of the Ego*, tr. J. Strachey (London, 1959), pp. 9–10.

between Acts Three and Four and Acts Four and Five are more open to dispute, and in what follows I shall argue that preferable places for marking the acts would be after III. iii and IV. ii. This arrangement would help to clarify (at least for the reader) Shakespeare's disposition of his material.

The first three acts, ending with III. iii, may be taken together first. There is obviously a clear division after I. iii, with the move to Cyprus, but there would seem to be no more need for an interval at this point in the performance than there would be after the comparable division at the end of the first act of *Hamlet*. The long dialogue between Iago and Roderigo at the end of I. iii, followed by the opening speeches of II. i spoken by Montano and the two Gentlemen on the shore at Cyprus, serve in performance as a perfectly adequate link between the scenes. When Desdemona enters (II. i. 82), and much later, Othello (II. i. 179), it seems as if enough time has elapsed since their exit at I. iii. 300 for the voyage to Cyprus to have taken place. It is, as always in Shakespeare, a matter of rhythm—*felt* time—rather than any merely measurable lapse of minutes. From here the action proceeds continuously, through the drunken brawl, Othello's reappearance, the dismissal of Cassio, and so to the end of the act. But there is, on the face of it, no place for an interval after II. iii. Act Three opens with Cassio and the musicians: it is now only a little later on the same morning that Cassio took his leave from Iago in II. iii and he has not been to bed (III. i. 30); in a few moments Iago reappears. From here again the action is continuous, until the end of III. iii. And here, it seems to me, we have the main interval. It could be argued, in fact, that at this point the performance *must* stop—and certainly in most modern stage productions the producer arranges an interval here. But in order to see why this should be so it is first necessary to recall the dramatic shape of the action up to this point.

During the first two acts of *Othello* Shakespeare plays a waiting game with his audience. By means of a number of devices he arouses a strong sense of anxiety, which at times seems to merge into something rather different: a keen interested desire for something to happen, at times even an appetite for violence—but an appetite which is so far frustrated. In the first act the conflict is felt to be not so much averted as postponed. In Act Two the cashiering of Cassio goes so entirely according to Iago's plan that, despite its involvement and occasional excitement, the audience is still in a position of waiting—for what is now felt to be the long-promised face-to-face struggle between Iago and Othello. The temptation scene of III. iii is the occasion it has been waiting for, only, so skilfully is it wrought, so convincingly is it protracted, through several stages of sustained suspense, that it surpasses expectation and finally (as I have already suggested) leads up to a climax certainly as great as any which Shakespeare had yet fashioned. At this point of fulfilment, I suggest, Shakespeare intended the performance to be discontinued, or rather, to put it so as to imply a design fully realized, the first part of *Othello* comes to an end.

It is important to note that Shakespeare has not provided a link between the end of III. iii and the beginning of III. iv, whereas he does so between the end of III. iv and the beginning of IV. i. For at III. iv. 135 Iago says (he is talking to Desdemona and Emilia of Othello's recent fit of rage):

> Can he be angry? I have seen the cannon
> When it hath blown his ranks into the air,
> And, like the devil, from his very arm
> Puff'd his own brother—and is he angry?
> Something of moment then. I will go meet him,
> There's matter in't indeed, if he be angry.

Iago leaves to meet Othello; Desdemona and Emilia exchange some further words with Cassio before they too leave; finally Cassio is accosted by Bianca and their dialogue concludes the scene. The next scene (IV. i) opens with Othello and Iago in the middle of a conversation:

> *Iago.* Will you think so?
> *Othello.* Think so, Iago . . .

Shakespeare's characteristic technique of scenic continuativeness shown here is not found at the end of III. iii; its absence may be taken as a further reason for seeing a deliberate pause at this point.

If we now consider *Othello* as a whole and compare the first part (up to III. iii) with the second, something of Shakespeare's larger design emerges. The first part presents the preparation of Othello's jealousy. Only in the second part, after the interval, are we shown Othello acting as a jealous man. This second part is made up of six scenes, which fall into two groups of three: the first three exhibit Othello's frenzied behaviour, while the last three show the violence which it leads to. If this analysis of the play into two parts is accepted, it can be seen to be organized in Shakespeare's usual way; its construction is not as anomalous as Bradley believed. Just as Richard Gloucester, for example, is markedly different as a character in the second part of his play, so is Othello too in some ways a different man. Emilia's comment, 'Is not this man jealous?' (III. iv. 100), after witnessing Othello's repeated demands for the handkerchief, would sound with a more significant emphasis if this scene were the first after an interval to show Othello and Desdemona together.[1]

There is, finally, the question of the 'time-scheme' of the play. Kenneth Muir observes that 'a week could elapse between III. 3 and III. 4. This, however, would conflict with Othello's demand at the end of III. 3 that Cassio should be killed within three days and with the natural assumption that Othello would demand the handkerchief at the first opportunity.'[2] The suggestion that a passage of time could elapse after III. iii is a fair one, but (as I argued in Chapter 2) the time concerned is unspecified and to try to limit it to a period as precise as a week seems untrue to Shakespeare's dramatic method. It seems truer to say that, if there were an interval after III. iii, one of its effects would be to disorientate us even further in our sense of the time sequence. (As I argued earlier, in these middle scenes we are aware of sequence, but not of duration.) Muir's remark about the three days Othello gives Iago within which he must kill Cassio fails to come to terms with the experience of an audience at a performance of *Othello*: once the remark is made we are never allowed to recall it—the opportunity for asking 'Where are we now in the time sequence with respect to III. iii?' never arrives. My main point here is that an interval has a disorientating effect: when the play is resumed after the interval we know that quite literally some time has elapsed, but how much exactly in terms of the play's

---

[1] I am aware that it could be argued that an interval might be in place at the end of Act Two. There is a sense of demarcation there, after Cassio's disgrace and before Iago starts to work on Othello. Conceivably *Othello* follows *3 Henry VI* and such comedies as *As You Like It* which apparently have a break after the second act. My reasons for choosing III. iii as the likeliest place have been given, and they seem to me to make it preferable.

[2] New Penguin *Othello*, p. 207.

action we are not told, and at a performance we would never ask the question anyway.

V

The first two acts can be passed over briefly, since they have already been discussed from various points of view. The Council scene (I. iii) is the climax of the first preliminary movement, and of great importance for the establishment of Othello's nobility and his habitual (or what has been his habitual) imperturbability. We are led to expect a clash of angry antagonists, but the centre of the scene is Othello's calm narrative of his wooing. For all its avoidance of conflict, the scene surprises and gives a different kind of pleasure, for after Iago's slanders and Brabantio's angrily prejudiced aspersions we now have a revelation of the individuality of the newly married pair—they are not types but persons. In the first two scenes of the play Othello is never named: he is simply referred to as 'he', 'his Moorship', 'the Moor', and so on, whereas on his first entry to the Council the Duke publicly greets him by using his proper name:

> Valiant Othello, we must straight employ you
> Against the general enemy Ottoman.
>
> (I. iii. 48–9)

For this is the main business of the scene: to establish what he is really like. In the midst of the restless, Iago-dominated sequence of the first two acts, this calm, almost still passage—the story of the wooing—stands out: we will refer back to it for our estimate of Othello throughout the rest of the play.

In II. i. 100 ff., while Desdemona and the others wait for the arrival of Othello's ship, Iago entertains them with cynical reflections on women: his 'praise' of women takes the form of a set of rhyming couplets (129 ff.). Desdemona is privately anxious for Othello's safety but pretends to be amused by Iago's laboured versifying. She says:

> I am not merry; but I do beguile
> The thing I am by seeming otherwise.
>
> (122–3)

In II. ii. of *All's Well that Ends Well* the Countess of Rousillon passes time by listening to the Clown. She too is conscious of more important matters:

> I play the noble housewife with the time,
> To entertain it so merrily with a fool

(II. ii. 54–5)

A comparison between the two scenes helps to bring out that Iago is very deliberately playing the fool. The occasion, with Iago already plotting to implicate Cassio with Desdemona, is really a sinister parody of the true fooling which we find in the comedies.

The long scene of Cassio's drunkenness and disgrace (II. iii) has already been discussed for its handling of time in Chapter 2, and in Chapter 4 the brief episode of Othello's appearance and the cashiering of Cassio was shown to have grown out of the scene in *Romeo and Juliet* in which the Duke banishes Romeo. However, the essential structural idea for this whole sequence apparently derives from *Twelfth Night*. The occasion of II. iii is one of nocturnal merry-making, with wine-drinking and singing. The scene in *Twelfth Night* which supplied a model for it is the roistering scene (II. iii), in which Sir Toby, Sir Andrew, and Feste make merry until they are interrupted by Malvolio. Here too the participants drink and sing. It ends with Sir Toby saying, ''tis too late to go to bed now', just as the scene in *Othello* ends with Iago saying:

> By th' mass, 'tis morning!
> Pleasure and action make the hours seem short.

(II. iii. 366–7)

(and a little later, III. i. 31, Cassio admits that he has not been to bed). Iago's geniality of tone is again part of the over-all tendency of *Othello* to parody or twist to a tragic issue the forms usually associated with comedy.

But the influence of *Twelfth Night* in this sequence goes further. The following scene in *Twelfth Night* (II. iv) begins with the entry of Orsino, Viola, Curio, and others. Orsino says:

> Give me some music. Now, good morrow, friends.

He asks for a song, and a little later the Clown Feste enters to sing it. In the corresponding scene in *Othello* (III. i), Cassio enters with Musicians; he says:

Masters, play here; I will content your pains.
Something that's brief; and bid 'Good morrow, General'.

Immediately after, the Clown enters. Of course the Clown in
Othello is miserably lacking in entertainment value, and his role
is restricted to a bare minimum; but by following the sequence of
scenes in *Twelfth Night* Shakespeare shows that he is keeping up
his point-by-point allusion to the world of comedy.

The next movement (III. i. to III. iii) consists of two brief
exchanges which prepare for the major action of the temptation
scene. For this scene of passion Shakespeare abandons the use of
forms derived from comedy. I remarked earlier that the temptation falls into two phases which are separated by a bridge passage
during which, first Iago, then Othello, leave the stage. Although
the whole of the temptation scene is acted continuously and is
therefore received as a single scene by the audience, the first
phase of the temptation (91–261), from Desdemona's first exit to
Iago's first exit, can be taken as a single scenic unit. The most
obvious earlier example of a 'temptation', in which one man deliberately works on another with a view to implanting thoughts
in his mind, is the second scene of *Julius Caesar*, in which Cassius
conveys to Brutus something of his own discontent. I have already discussed the form of this scene in Chapter 1 and drew
attention to the striking use made of Caesar's train, which shortly
after its first appearance leaves the stage, only to return and depart
a second time. There is nothing as spectacular as Caesar's train in
the present scene of *Othello*, but Desdemona and Emilia fulfil
something of its punctuating function. The scene opens with the
two women and Cassio; Cassio leaves before Othello and Iago
enter; a little later (90) the women leave for the first time. After the
first phase of the temptation they return, and leave again shortly
after, Desdemona first with Othello, Emilia a little later. It seems
possible that the general shape of the Roman temptation scene
was in this way remembered and adapted for a new purpose. But
there is more to be said, and a few qualifications to be made. The
first phase of the temptation scene in *Othello*, which is much more
tentative, hesitant, and low-keyed than the second, seems to be
modelled in a very general way on the first colloquy of Brutus
and Cassius (I. ii. 25–177) before the return of Caesar's train.
(Desdemona is made the subject of Iago's hostile insinuations,

just as Caesar was of Cassius'.) But the latter part of this scene in
Julius Caesar offered nothing which Shakespeare could follow:
it showed Casca relating how Caesar had been offered a crown.
Its blunt, off-hand, almost comic, tone was very remote from what
Shakespeare wanted for the second phase of his temptation scene
in *Othello*. What he seems to have done here is to take a later scene
in *Julius Caesar* which could give him a more suitable model for
the way Iago deliberately stimulates Othello into a raging passion.
This was the Forum scene (III. ii), in which Antony works upon
the feelings of the plebeians in such a way as to convert them into
a raging mob capable of nothing but acts of wild destruction.
In this second phase of the temptation, therefore, Iago corresponds to Antony while Othello corresponds to the plebeians. The
circumstances of both scenes are so different that close comparison is impossible. But Antony, like Iago, is a consummate but
unscrupulous rhetorician. His victims, the crowd of commoners,
are gullible but at the same time wield great power; the same could
be said of Othello. For the second half of his oration Antony
descends from the rostrum in order to exhibit Caesar's corpse,
and before he does so emotionally exploits the torn and blood-
stained mantle; his use of anecdote ('I remember / The first time
ever Caesar put it on') has a similar emotional pull. Iago's invention of Cassio's dream (417–30) works on Othello in a comparable
way, for like Antony, Iago makes telling use of circumstantial or
anecdotal detail to guarantee the truth of what he is saying. Finally, just as the plebeians are reduced to shouting 'Revenge!
About! Seek! Burn! Fire! Kill! Slay! Let not a traitor live!'
(204–5), so Othello cries 'O, blood, blood, blood!' (455). It is *as if*
he has become a barbarously violent member of an enraged mob.
And in each case the hypocritical efforts of Antony and Iago to
counsel moderation ('Good friends, sweet friends, let me not
stir you up . . .'; 'Patience, I say; your mind perhaps may change')
have the effect of increasing the frenzy of the other party.

   A few verbal details help to establish that there was indeed a
link in Shakespeare's mind between the two scenes. Antony says
at one point:

> It is not meet you know how Caesar lov'd you.
> You are not wood, you are not stones, but men;
> And being men, hearing the will of Caesar,

> It will enflame you, it will make you mad.
> 'Tis good you know not that you are his heirs.
>
> $(141-5)$

Iago says in a precisely similar tone (this is during the first phase of the temptation):

> It were not for your quiet nor your good,
> Nor for my manhood, honesty, or wisdom,
> To let you know my thoughts.
>
> $(156-8)$

After he has finished his oration and the mob has rushed away from the Forum, Antony, left alone, cynically remarks:

> Now let it work. Mischief, thou art afoot,
> Take thou what course thou wilt.
>
> $(261-2)$

Iago has no remark corresponding to this at the end of his scene, since he is of course still in Othello's presence; however, there is a kind of displaced echo of Antony's remark in a later scene. This is when Othello has fallen down unconscious in an epileptic fit, and Iago standing over him says:

> Work on,
> My medicine, work. Thus credulous fools are caught . . .
>
> (IV. i. $44-5$)

From this comparison between the two scenes we can see that the magnificent strategy of the temptation scene is a development of the extended use of formal suasive rhetoric in *Julius Caesar*. Moreover, the fact that Othello's role corresponds to that of the crowd-mob helps to corroborate the suggestion I made earlier that there is a striking similarity between Othello in this and some later scenes of the play and the typical crowd as described by le Bon. What Shakespeare has done in the temptation scene is to informalize, almost domesticate, Antony's public rhetoric, with the result that an audience can attend to Iago's and Othello's exchanges without noticing the rhetorical foundations of the whole scene. (This is a far cry from such an earlier example of the persuasion scene as Richard Gloucester's wooing of Lady Anne, which is in some ways brilliantly clever but is also inflexible and monotonous and suffers from the obtrusiveness of its rhetorical means.)

I have already (in Chapter 4) discussed the oath-swearing at the
end of III. iii; I now resume the commentary on the remaining
scenes, the second movement of the play. The following three
scenes (III. iv, IV. i, IV. ii) ought probably to be seen as a group,
a series of episodes each presenting a stage in Othello's jealousy.
They are skilfully varied in shape and weight so that there is no
sense of monotony or repetition; at the same time there is, very
economically suggested, an atmosphere of intense oppressive-
ness. Each of the three scenes confronts Othello and Desdemona,
the behaviour of Othello following an ascending order of out-
rageousness. In the first he demands the handkerchief; in the
second he strikes her in front of Lodovico; in the third he treats
her as a prostitute. The sequence is brought to an end with the
entry of Roderigo (IV. ii. 172) for the last of his colloquies with
Iago. Roderigo's impatience with Iago is the first unmistakable sign we have that we are now entering the final phase of the
action.[1]

These three scenes, which correspond to a presumptive fourth act
in Shakespeare's plan, establish a pace and rhythm which is very
hard on the nerves of the audience. In performance we probably
do not in fact notice that they are three distinct scenes: what we
actually experience is a series of numerous short episodes in
which the main characters—Othello, Desdemona, Iago, Emilia,
Cassio, and Bianca—come in and go out with something of the
stylized timing and economy of farce. This is so especially in the
scene in which Othello eavesdrops on Cassio and Bianca (IV. i)—
the moment of Othello's greatest humiliation. Here the scenic
structure obviously resembles that of comedy, and the stage *tableau*
formed by the actors at this point is potentially risible. Indeed it
is precisely the tension set up between two possible ways of responding to this scene—either with detached amusement, or the
way in which we do see it, from the point of view of the fiercely
unhumorous dupe—that gives it its dry nervous intensity. What
is true of this episode in an extreme form is true also to a lesser
degree of the others in this sequence: the scenic forms are often
comic. There is a good deal of angry or incredulous iteration
(e.g. the thrice repeated 'The handkerchief!' in III. iv, and 'What
committed!' in IV. ii; and finally Emilia's 'My husband?' in V. ii,
which prompts Othello's explicit reference to the device: 'What

[1] Cf. Chapter 2, pp. 61–2, for a comparison of this effect with one in *As You Like It*.

needs this iterance, woman?'), and an atmosphere of exaspera-
tion and bewilderment is worked up, of a kind associated more
with comedy than tragedy. The whole of this movement recalls,
in a painfully distorted way, the later climactic scenes of confusion
and mistaken identity in *The Comedy of Errors*; here, Othello's
persistent 'mistaking' of Desdemona—his treatment of her, in IV.
ii, as if she were no other than Bianca, the true prostitute—echoes
the traditional preoccupation of farce with mistaken identity. The
decorum of *Othello* is therefore one which results from an audacious mingling of comic forms with tragic issues. The first scene
in this movement (III. iv) signalizes this 'comi-tragic' decorum by
opening with a dialogue between Desdemona and the Clown. If
we want a precise model for it, the scene in *Twelfth Night* between Viola and Feste (III. i) fits perfectly, and it shows, moreover, that Shakespeare's mind is still recalling the sequence of
scenes in that part of *Twelfth Night* which he had already been
following. (The Clown's previous appearance in *Othello*, at III. i,
corresponded to II. iv of *Twelfth Night*; the intermediate scene is,
in one case, Malvolio's letter scene, in the other, the temptation
scene, both scenes exhibiting a spectacular conversion of attitude
in their main character.) At the end of this phase in the action (IV.
ii. 170–2), Iago's cruelly hypocritical benediction sounds for a
moment with the authentic note of comedy, as if to prepare us
for a denouement in which (as in *The Comedy of Errors*) the discovery of the truth and the achievement of harmony will be the
work of an inspired moment:

> Hark how these instruments summon you to supper.
> The messengers of Venice stay the meat.
> Go in, and weep not; all things shall be well.

(The Duke in *Measure for Measure* speaks with sincerity at a
similar point in the play: 'Look, th' unfolding star calls up the
shepherd. Put not yourself into amazement how these things
should be: all difficulties are but easy when they are known . . .
Come away; it is almost clear dawn'. IV. ii. 195–203.)

The next three scenes (IV. iii, V. i, V. ii) form the final phase
or fifth act of Shakespeare's scheme, since they all take place on
the evening and night of the same day. The scene of Roderigo's
attack on Cassio (V. i) is partly concurrent with the 'willow' scene
(IV. iii), and V. ii follows on immediately.

The 'willow' scene is quite different in mood and tempo from anything that has gone before (it is, as it happens, the only scene in which Iago does not appear). Though relatively brief, it is highly concentrated and oblique in its expression. This dialogue between Desdemona and Emilia serves to express, though only indirectly, certain feelings which at this stage of the play need to be given scope. These feelings are self-assertiveness and reproachfulness on Desdemona's part, as well as the more amorphous but still powerful feelings which are elicited by the action as a whole and which the song serves to focus. In the brief compass of the scene a number of topics are touched on. Emilia criticizes Othello; Desdemona defends him. She asks to be shrouded in one of her wedding sheets if she should die; she speaks of Barbary, whose lover went mad and forsook her; she mentions Lodovico, 'a proper man'. The 'willow' song follows, and she sings a wrong line: 'Let nobody blame him; his scorn I approve'. Her exclamation 'O, these men, these men!' introduces the subject of husbands and wives, in which Emilia first jocularly defends adultery and then, with complete seriousness, speaks of what husbands owe their wives.

The whole scene is rich in unspoken thought and pervasive feeling. It derives power from the fact that the great subject is not mentioned, although both women are thinking of nothing else: Othello's terrifying disease of mind. Nor is Othello himself mentioned by name ('He looks gentler than he did'; 'he'll come anon'). The pressure of emotion is felt in the rapidity with which Desdemona jumps from subject to subject, but never to the subject which most occupies her, or if she does it is only involuntarily, as in the mistake she makes in the song. The dialogue has a powerfully implicit quality: there seem to be large gaps between the speeches which the audience is required to supply. So, for example, the brief reference to Lodovico—'This Lodovico is a proper man'— is made by Desdemona in an entirely impassive way as she tries to make conversation with Emilia: she has not the slightest sexual interest in him—that is left to Emilia to take up—but views him as if from a great distance, noting his good looks but finding them irrelevant to her present concerns. (At the same time there is the possibility that the thought of a more conventional suitor passes across her mind; the tone of her remark remains a little ambiguous.)

The provenance of this style of dialogue, with its abrupt transitions from topic to topic, is hinted at in Desdemona's remark: 'Good faith, how foolish are our minds!' (22). For what Shakespeare is doing here, it seems, is adapting the mode of talk associated with Fools. A Fool's talk (like a madman's) was characteristically without logical order and clearly marked connectives; it jumped unpredictably from one subject to the next, so seeming to be made up of discrete odds and ends. (This is how Hamlet talks when he is playing the fool, as in some of his exchanges with Polonius: e.g. III. ii. 364 ff.)

The second scene of this group, v. i, may seem a curiously long-spun-out intrusion into the sequence. As a scene it is taken up with messily violent or fussily repetitive action: Cassio is attacked by Roderigo, and Roderigo by Iago, who later returns under cover of darkness to finish off the job; then there are a number of tentatively polite exchanges between Iago, Lodovico, and Gratiano, and later a quarrel—a brush between Iago, Emilia, and Bianca—none of which amounts to very much. But the sordid violence and ineffectuality of the scene are probably the main effects Shakespeare is trying to make. Something is needed to set off by contrast the solemn stillness and attempted ceremoniousness of Othello's entry in the following scene, but at the same time to bring out Othello's own violence, his own connection with those who 'kill men i' th' dark'. And to make the connection unmistakable, Shakespeare brings Othello on stage for a few moments (probably 'above' at a balcony or window) for no other purpose than to demonstrate visually Othello's implication in the mean and savage deeds being undertaken or supervised by Iago.

The long final scene is really a series of brief episodes or actions which are carefully spaced out so as to make the greatest effect.[1] These individual units include the murder of Desdemona, Emilia's discovery of the crime and of Iago's villainy, her death, Othello's full realization of what he has done, and finally his death in the presence of Lodovico, the representative of the Venetian Senate. I shall comment on the first and last of these actions.

The episode of Desdemona's murder (1–92), for all the calm solemnity of Othello's opening soliloquy, marks an extreme

---

[1] Granville-Barker has some good comments on this scene in his *Preface to Othello*.

point in the action of brutality and cruelty. Too often the element of atrocity in *Othello* is glossed over by critics of the play. However, in writing this scene, Shakespeare's mind went back, significantly, to the most savage of all the killings which he had dramatized in the *Henry VI* plays: Clifford's murder of the child Rutland. This is an act of gratuitous brutality which we are not allowed to forget throughout *Henry VI, Part Three* and *Richard III*. There are several verbal reminiscences: Rutland pleads with his killer:

> O, let me pray before I take my death!
>
>   (*3 Henry VI*, I. iii. 35)

just as Desdemona does:

> Kill me to-morrow; let me live to-night . . .
> But half an hour! . . .
> But while I say one prayer!
>
>   (v. ii. 84–6)

Clifford's protestation of his insatiable lust for revenge

> Had I thy brethren here, their lives and thine
> Were not revenge sufficient for me;
> No, if I digg'd up thy forefathers' graves,
> And hung their rotten coffins up in chains,
> It could not slake mine ire nor ease mine heart . . .
>
>   (*3 Henry VI*, I. iii. 25–9)

is echoed by Othello:

> Had all his hairs been lives, my great revenge
> Had stomach for them all
>
>   (v. ii. 78–9)

(and also in his earlier speech, 'O that the slave had forty thousand lives! / One is too poor, too weak for my revenge', III. iii. 446–7). Both men, when they are about to kill, assume frightening facial expressions. Rutland says,

> Ah, gentle Clifford, kill me with thy sword,
> And not with such a cruel threat'ning look!
>
>   (*3 Henry VI*, I. iii. 16–17)

and Desdemona:

> And yet I fear you; for you're fatal then
> When your eyes roll so.
>
>   (v. ii. 40–1)

All these details link Othello with 'bloody Clifford' (who at one point, *Richard III*, I. ii. 158, is referred to as 'black-fac'd Clifford'). This strain of violent and bloody vengefulness relates Othello to the most barbarous incidents in the civil war Shakespeare had already dramatized. Indeed Othello's attack on Desdemona (a soldier's attack on a woman, something which is to be repeated later in the scene with Iago's attack on Emilia) is in fact a kind of 'civil' war, as its resemblances to Clifford's attack on the child Rutland bring out.[1] Another atrocious crime which Shakespeare remembered in this scene is the murder of the Princes in the Tower, for Othello's 'beautiful' opening soliloquy has a few details in common with Tyrrel's description of the double murder (*Richard III*, IV. iii. 1–22: Tyrrel's soliloquy is exactly the same length as Othello's). Tyrrel mentions 'alabaster', compares the lips of the sleeping princes to 'roses on a stalk', and states how they were murdered: 'smothered'. In Cinthio's tale Disdemona is not suffocated; this detail may have come to Shakespeare from *Richard III*. It seems clear, then, that when the action of *Othello* erupts into a realm of savage violence, Shakespeare's mind went back to the early history plays, and in particular to the killing of children.

I now turn to the final action of the scene (286 ff.). Lodovico is kept off stage until this point, so that when he enters he carries with him the authority of the Venetian Senate; this last episode takes on the nature of a judgement scene. But it is also the kind of scene which conventionally occurs at the end of tragedies and history plays, in which the future of the State, here Cyprus, is settled, and wrongdoers are handed over to punishment. Shakespeare seems to be adopting this form, but then introduces a complication. Lodovico enters upon what sounds as if it is going to be the concluding speech of the play (333–40), relieving Othello of his command in Cyprus, transferring his authority to Cassio, promising dire punishment to Iago, and ordering Othello back to Cyprus under close arrest. But the orderly *exeunt omnes* which seems due at this point is interrupted by Othello, who asks to speak 'a word or two'. In this way Othello's last speech and suicide interrupt the decorous state proceedings, leaving the final moments of the play free to be given to the personal side of the

[1] Cf. what Antony prophesies will come to Italy: 'Domestic fury and fierce civil strife' (*Julius Caesar*, III. i. 264); the first phrase is relevant to *Othello*, the second to *3 Henry VI*.

tragedy: the punishment of Iago and the contemplation of 'This heavy act'. The conventional speech of formal conclusion, with its assurance that social order is restored and its summary distribution of rewards and punishments, is thus placed a little before the actual ending of the play. This modification in the usual order of things is repeated at the end of *King Lear*, probably the next tragedy to be written after *Othello*.[1]

The care with which Shakespeare shaped the ending of the play is shown in the form of Othello's last speech (to which, of course, everything in this final episode leads). This speech, an indirect last address to the Senate, is exactly the same length (eighteen and a half lines) as Othello's *first* address to the Senate in the first act (i. iii. 76–94). The exact symmetry is perfectly expressive of his sense of service to the State: it announces the return to himself of the old Othello, with his self-control, temperance, and firm adherence to an even-handed justice.

---

[1] Cf. my note on the ending of *King Lear*, in *Critical Quarterly*, 3 (1961), 72–5.

APPENDIX TO CHAPTER 5

THERE is one other comedy belonging to the years immediately preceding the probable date of *Othello* which has a bearing on its composition: Ben Jonson's *Every Man in his Humour*, which appeared in quarto in 1601. This was the first version of the play, with the Italian setting. In this version the jealous husband, later called Kitely, is called Thorello. Since Shakespeare apparently invented the name of Othello, it seems possible that the name was partly modelled on Jonson's Thorello. (The change to Othello would perhaps evoke Othoman and the Othomites. This possible derivation of Othello's name was suggested by F. N. Lees in *Notes and Queries*, N.S., viii (1961), 139–41.)

In Jonson's play the following exchange occurs between Thorello and his wife Biancha (a name also used by Shakespeare, neatly transferred to Cassio's prostitute friend):

> *Biancha.* Sweete hart will you come in to breakfast?
> *Thorello.* And she have over-heard me now?
> *Biancha.* I pray thee (good *Musse*) we stay for you.
> *Thorello.* By Christ I would not for a thousand crownes.
> *Biancha.* What ayle you sweete hart, are you not well, speake good *Musse.*
> *Thorello.* Troth my head akes extreamely on a suddaine.
> *Biancha.* Oh Jesu!
> *Thorello.* How now? what?
> *Biancha.* Good Lord how it burnes? *Musse* keepe you warme, good truth it is this new disease, there's a number are troubled withall: for Gods sake sweete heart, come in out of the ayre.
> *Thorello.* How simple, and how subtill are her answeres?
> A new disease, and many troubled with it.
> Why true, she heard me, all the world to nothing.
>
> (I. iv. 184–200; ed. Herford and Simpson)

This passage seems to have been recalled by Shakespeare in the following:

> *Desdemona.* How now, my dear Othello?
> Your dinner, and the generous islanders
> By you invited, do attend your presence.
> *Othello.* I am to blame.
> *Desdemona.*   Why do you speak so faintly?
> Are you not well?
> *Othello.* I have a pain upon my forehead here.
> *Desdemona.* Faith, that's with watching; 'twill away again.
> Let me but bind it hard, within this hour
> It will be well.

(*He puts the handkerchief from him, and she drops it.*
Othello. Your napkin is too little.

(III. iii. 283–91)

The two passages have obvious resemblances and one identical sentence ('Are you not well?'), but it should also be noted that Biancha's phrase 'keepe you warme' is used by Desdemona earlier in the same scene:

> 'Tis as I should entreat you wear your gloves,
> Or feed on nourishing dishes, or keep you warm . . .

(III. iii. 78–9)

When Biancha leaves, Thorello soliloquizes:

> A new disease? I know not, new or old,
> But it may well be call'd poore mortals Plague;
> For like a pestilence it doth infect
> The houses of the braine: first it begins
> Solely to worke upon the fantasie,
> Filling her seat with such pestiferous aire,
> As soone corrupts the judgement, and from thence,
> Sends like contagion to the memorie,
> Still each of other catching the infection,
> Which as a searching vapor spreads it selfe
> Confusedly through every sensive part,
> Till not a thought or motion in the mind
> Be free from the black poison of suspect.

(I. iv. 205–17)

Othello, on the other hand, soliloquizes before, not after, Desdemona's appearance:

> . . . I had rather be a toad,
> And live upon the vapour of a dungeon,
> Than keep a corner in the thing I love
> For others' uses. Yet 'tis the plague of great ones;
> Prerogativ'd are they less than the base;
> 'Tis destiny unshunnable, like death:
> Even then this forked plague is fated to us
> When we do quicken.

(III. iii. 274–81)

Common to both speeches is the idea of jealousy as a 'plague' incident to all men, and both use the image of 'vapour'.

Earlier in the same scene Othello asks himself, 'Why did I marry?' (III. iii. 246); in a later scene Thorello too asks: 'Bane to my fortunes: what meant I to marrie?' (III. iii. 15). There seems nothing unlikely in Shakespeare's taking a few hints from Jonson's comedy; Thorello is a brilliant portrait, and Shakespeare could not have escaped knowing the play, since he probably acted in it. In another scene of *Every Man in his Humour*, Prospero (another Shakespearian name; indeed another *Tempest* name, Stephano, occurs in this play) pacifies the foolish Stephano, who is in a rage at discovering he has been gulled into buying a sword under the impression that it is a Toledo blade: 'It's better as 'tis: come gentlemen shall we goe?' (II. iii. 166). It may be a mere coincidence that Othello's first remark is one made in a similarly pacific tone: ''Tis better as it is' (I. ii. 6). It would be interesting to know if this was a common phrase for cooling hot tempers.

Another play which may have left its mark on *Othello* is the anonymous *The Weakest Goeth to the Wall*, which was printed in 1600. One of its characters is the Duke of Brabant, whose daughter elopes with a young man, Ferdinand, who has been brought up by the Duke as a foundling. The Duke is unforgiving and angrily pursues the pair until, in the last scene of the play, he sees to it that Ferdinand is brought to trial. It then comes to light that Ferdinand is in fact Frederick, son of Lodowick, Duke of Bulloigne. Brabant's paternal bitterness, his repeated cries for 'justice and the law', and his sense of outrage at being deceived by a man whom he had admitted to his own household, all seem recalled—together with his name—in Shakespeare's Brabantio. (Lodowick is similarly Italianized in Lodovico, another character in *Othello*.)

6. *King Lear*

I

As a stage play *King Lear*, unlike *Othello*, has often been subjected to adverse criticism. The clearest testimony to this is the fact that Nahum Tate's version, with its 'romantic interest' between Cordelia and Edgar and its happy ending, held the stage for over a hundred and fifty years, to the exclusion of Shakespeare's own text. The Romantic critics, led by Charles Lamb, were the first to exalt the play as the high point of Shakespeare's genius,[1] but at the same time serious reservations were voiced, also by Lamb, as to its suitability for the stage; and whatever allowances must be made for the theatrical traditions of Lamb's time, it should not be overlooked that Bradley to some extent upheld Lamb's point of view:

> The stage is the test of strictly dramatic quality, and *King Lear* is too huge for the stage.
>
> ... *King Lear*, as a whole, is imperfectly dramatic, and there is something in its very essence which is at war with the senses, and demands a purely imaginative realisation.[2]

Since Bradley wrote, the play's critical reputation has, if anything, continued to climb, so that for a number of critics it is self-evidently the greatest of Shakespeare's tragedies. A good deal of criticism, since Bradley, has been addressed to interpreting the play's substance, its 'doctrine of Nature', its quasi-religious affirmations, or (conversely) its 'pessimism'. But not very much has set out to meet Bradley's specifically dramatic criticisms. It is true that *King Lear* has become much less of a rarity on the stage than it apparently was in the late nineteenth century, and a few actors have positively succeeded in the title role. But whether the play is more genuinely liked by playgoers is a different question—liked, that is, as a whole rather than for a few scenes. Bradley goes on, after the sentence last quoted:

---

[1] See Alfred Harbage, *Conceptions of Shakespeare* (Cambridge, Mass., 1966), p. 87.
[2] A. C. Bradley, *Shakespearean Tragedy*, pp. 247, 248.

It is therefore Shakespeare's greatest work, but it is not what Hazlitt called it, the best of his plays; and its comparative unpopularity is due, not merely to the extreme painfulness of the catastrophe, but in part to its dramatic defects . . .[1]

Some of the 'defects' which Bradley went on to specify may no longer seem defects: increased knowledge of the Elizabethan stage has made them imaginatively accessible and acceptable. But others are more substantial and less easily disposed of: in particular those which, as Bradley argues, arise from the double action, and which are felt, he says, especially in the fourth act and in long passages of the fifth:

The number of essential characters is so large, their actions and movements are so complicated, and events towards the close crowd one on another so thickly, that the reader's attention, rapidly transferred from one centre of interest to another, is overstrained. . . . A comparison of the last two Acts of *Othello* with the last two Acts of *King Lear* would show how unfavourable to dramatic clearness is a multiplicity of figures.[2]

No doubt many readers and playgoers would concede this, or much of it, although there is more to be said in defence of Shakespeare. But what Bradley neglects to bring out (he could undoubtedly have done so) is the high degree of artistry in the play's over-all design, not only in 'the gradual interweaving of the two plots', which he admits,[3] but in the management of the entire action from first scene to last. For despite the immediate impression it makes of huge scale, unwieldy massiveness, even clumsiness, *King Lear* is not by any means shapeless or unformed; indeed, the author's shaping presence can be found even in those places, or many of them, which at first seem merely disproportionate, artless, and ill-judged.

II

If the main action of *King Lear* is compared with that of the other so-called great tragedies, a peculiarity emerges. At the beginning of *Hamlet* the hero is given a task which he must eventually discharge. His foreordained role as killer of Claudius

[1] Ibid., p. 248.　　[2] Ibid., p. 255.
[3] Ibid., p. 247.

creates suspense, so that the entire play derives tension from it. *Othello* is of course structurally different from *Hamlet* in its gradual accumulation of momentum, but the plot is similar in that it too moves forward to a last-act crisis. *Macbeth* is obviously fashioned so as to arouse anxiety and excitement. The criminality of Macbeth, his duplicity not only to others but to himself, and the counteraction against him which his crimes provoke, all work to prepare us long in advance for the denouement, so that the entire play is unremittingly tense.

King Lear is certainly not without its scenes of tension: the scene before Gloucester's castle (ii. iv) is one of the greatest of its kind in Shakespeare. But there is nothing corresponding to Hamlet's duty to revenge his father's murder, no malevolent Iago plotting against an unsuspecting victim: in short, no grandly comprehensive structural device of a kind which will ensure tension until the end of the play. It has often been noticed that, once Lear has divided his kingdom and banished Cordelia and Kent, he becomes very largely a passive figure whose power to initiate action becomes progressively reduced. He certainly dominates the play during the first two acts, but from the third to the beginning of the last he is more of a talker than a doer, and becomes more and more enfeebled. It has also been noticed that, to a great extent, the characters of the Gloucester sub-plot, and especially Edmund, supply the driving-power which in the middle and later scenes Lear fails to give. But it would be an exaggeration to say that Edmund is a hero, even a secondary one. After his lively second appearance (i. ii), his role is usually unstressed: in one scene he plays a supporting role to Cornwall, in another to Goneril, and so on; but, except for his soliloquy of triumph, carefully placed shortly before his downfall (v. i), he never dominates the stage in the way we should expect of a 'hero', at any rate of one who is supplying the energizing forward-looking function of a protagonist. In the last two acts it would be truer to say that this function is shared by several characters—Goneril, Regan, Oswald, Edgar, even Cordelia for a brief period. But to say that it is shared between so many characters is to concede that there is in fact no alternative hero and that what keeps the action moving is some force other than the will of a single strong personage. What we are given is a sense of widening circles, ramifying side-lines of interest, even as late in the action as

Edmund's soliloquy in v. i a promise of yet further intrigues—all merging with the spectacle of things simply running down, a progressive randomness. There is nothing corresponding, in these last two acts, to the strong counteraction supplied by Macduff and Malcolm in *Macbeth*; nor, of course, is there intended to be; and it is in keeping with this comparative lack of stress on individual parts that the battle is so quickly disposed of. In the play's last episode after Cordelia's death, Lear's heroic, dominating energy briefly returns; but the energy is uncontrolled and spasmodic, of the kind associated with death throes,[1] and with Lear's death the play sinks into its final lethargy.

If the plot of *King Lear* is without that kind of single comprehensive structural device which works to arouse suspense, it should at once be said in qualification that some parts of the play are in fact constructed in this more usual fashion. When Goneril instructs Oswald to provoke her father so as to bring about a clash of wills between herself and him (I. iii), it is no surprise to find that the scene which follows is one which a number of critics have singled out as one of the most dramatically successful (Bradley, for example, follows Hazlitt in doing this). In a similar way the stages leading to Lear's departure into the storm (II. iv) and to Gloucester's blinding (III. vii) are marked by very firm structural lines. These are undoubtedly the most exciting parts of the play. However, apart from these episodes, we do not have any *ultimate* aim in view—anything like, for example, the *final* confrontation of Hamlet and Claudius, or Othello's *final* discovery of the truth concerning Desdemona. We seem to move from episode to episode without much sense of what the final destination is to be. We do of course want Lear to redress the wrong he did Cordelia, and this is the final business of the fourth act. But it is not the end of the play (much as many critics would apparently like it to have been). Indeed the play's true ending has

[1] With the spasmodic energy of this, cf. Northumberland's lines:

> And as the wretch whose fever-weak'ned joints,
> Like strengthless hinges, buckle under life,
> Impatient of his fit, breaks like a fire
> Out of his keeper's arms, even so my limbs,
> Weak'ned with grief, being now enrag'd with grief,
> Are thrice themselves . . .   (*2 Henry IV*, I. i. 140–5)

and also Pope's line, 'As fits give vigour just when they destroy' (*Epistle to Cobham*, 223).

become a critical problem precisely because it has seemed to
many readers, including Bradley, not properly prepared for, an
inartistic surprise. This uncertainty about the final destination of
the action, about where we are going, is accompanied by another
characteristic feature of *King Lear*. This is the recurrence of scenes
of a curiously static nature, scenes of brooding, reflection, or, in
a more impassioned style, of declamation. These include the
early scenes with the Fool (I. IV, I. v, and parts of II. ii), the
storm and heath scenes (III. ii, iv, vi) and the Dover Cliff scene
between Lear and Gloucester (IV. vi). These scenes, rich in interest though they are from one point of view, from another can
be seen as working to clog the onward movement of the action;
they differ from some comparable passages in *Hamlet* in being
far less imbued with the personality of the hero; in this they are
more like the later scenes of *Timon of Athens* (with which Bradley
was inclined to associate *King Lear*'s 'structural defects').

   If all these features of the play are taken together, they amount
to so many reasons why *King Lear* should be comparatively
unpopular as a stage play. It is as a whole less exciting, certainly
less *entertaining*, than *Hamlet* or *Othello*; it has less than either of the
element of melodrama. One might put this another way by say-
ing that *King Lear* is more exacting, more painful and exhausting
to experience; it gives less immediate pleasure. And this can in
part be explained in terms of structure: for despite its scenes of
episodic heightening, the over-all action lacks, or appears to lack,
a clear *terminus ad quem*—we are given nothing specific to *wait for*.
Nothing, that is, except perhaps something which cannot be
brought about by any foreseeable move in the plot: the death of
the old man who is the hero. In his first speech Lear declares that

> 'tis our fast intent
> To shake all cares and burdens from our age,
> Conferring them on younger strengths, while we
> Unburden'd crawl toward death.
>
> (I. i. 37–40)

And 'crawl toward death' is, in a sense, what the play does. Its
movement of sinking spasmodically into a final lethargy and
dissolution is what can make it seem, to reader and playgoer, so
powerfully oppressive: powerful, it goes without saying, but
also laying a burdensome weight on the feelings.

Freud's comment on *King Lear* is well known: he has been
discussing the myth of the three caskets and has argued that the
story of King Lear as Shakespeare dramatized it is an application
of this myth. What we have at the end of the play, with Lear
carrying Cordelia dead in his arms, is a representation of Lear's
death, for Cordelia *is* Death, according to Freud: 'Eternal wis-
dom, in the garb of the primitive myth, bids the old man renounce
love, choose death and make friends with the necessity of dying.'[1]
Freud's mythical interpretation undoubtedly violates the fabric
of Shakespeare's play: this is simply not, on the face of it, what is
happening in this final scene; the particular circumstances which
create the situation are quite other than those that Freud suggests. Nevertheless it has been felt, and rightly, that his remark
embodies an insight into an obscure but central region of *King
Lear*. The difficulty arises only when we try to develop his insight
in a way consistent with the obvious and acknowledged nature
of the play's action.

There is, however, a way of reconciling Freud's remark with an
approach more historically orientated, one which takes account
of the dramatic traditions which were available to Shakespeare.
For it seems likely that Shakespeare had in mind an earlier dramatic form which traditionally incorporated precisely the subject
which Freud saw as inhering in the story of the old man and his
three daughters. This form was the late medieval morality play,
as we find it in *The Castell of Perseverance*, *The Pride of Life*, and
Everyman. It has often been pointed out that some of the incidents
and episodes of *King Lear* derive from traditional materials in the
moralities: Kent in the stocks is a conspicuous example.[2] The
relatively simple characterization of the play, with a clear division into good and bad, is another feature which recalls the method
of the moralities. But it seems not to have been noticed that one
subject, which was given powerful treatment by the moralities,
has a special relevance to Shakespeare's conception of Lear: the
coming of death.[3] This motif not only links *King Lear* with

[1] S. Freud, 'The Theme of the Three Caskets' (1913), in *Collected Papers*, vol. iv
(London, 1956), p. 256.
[2] e.g. T. W. Craik, *The Tudor Interlude* (London, 1958), p. 95; and Maynard Mack,
'King Lear' in Our Time (London, 1966), pp. 56 ff.
[3] Maynard Mack (op. cit., p. 59) mentions 'the old theme of Death's Summons',
but only in connection with Kent's last speech: 'I have a journey, sir, shortly to go.
/ My master calls me . . .' (v. iii. 321–2). Mack also illuminatingly compares the

these earlier native plays but may have been the reason why Shakespeare originally chose to treat his new tragic subject in what must have seemed a pointedly archaic style. The coming of death makes an impressive episode towards the end of *The Castell of Perseverance* and forms the entire subject of the late fifteenth-century morality *Everyman*. *The Pride of Life* (which exists only in fragmentary form) anticipates *Lear* in some particular details, since the hero is a king and is accompanied by his knights (Strength and Health). The way in which Lear is deprived of his hundred knights is especially interesting in this context.[1] In all these morality plays a simple lesson is powerfully inculcated : the hero is humbled and made to recognize his own weakness and vulnerability, which are the necessary conditions of his existence. *King Lear* is of course not so directly homiletic, but the downward curve of the typical morality play plot, which brings the hero to his knees and finally prostrates him in death, possibly accounts for a similar movement clearly discernible at the centre of the tragedy despite its great profusion of character and episode.

In a certain obvious sense the play I have been describing so far—a primitive or archaic history of a man's decline—is something to be discerned *within King Lear* rather than constituting the whole of *King Lear* as we know it. For a special characteristic of Shakespeare's play is something that has nothing to do with primitiveness or archaic simplicity : *King Lear* is a capacious, perhaps over-weighted, play, containing a mass of heterogeneous and sometimes sophisticated detail, all of which works together to evoke not only the career of a single man but an entire social order, even a world. I have already remarked that the hero is at the centre of the play and yet often curiously limited in function, or even passive, within it. For what Shakespeare means to present, it seems, is not only the personal story of one man's decline and death; he also gives us the closing stages of the history of a whole society, even a whole world's destruction—as imminent

story of King Robert of Sicily (the proud king who was transformed by an angel into a beggar) and refers to the medieval romance on the subject (pp. 49–51). He does not mention, however, the relevant fact that a play on this subject is known to have been acted at Chester in 1529 and that, as Chambers noted, 'a still earlier *ludus de Kyng Robert of Cesill* is recorded in the Lincoln *Annales* under the year 1453'. See Chambers, *Mediaeval Stage*, vol. 2, p. 151.

[1] The best text of *The Pride of Life* is Norman Davis's, in his E.E.T.S. edition of *Non-Cycle Plays and Fragments* (1970). Professor Davis kindly allowed me to see his edition in proof.

as was that ending of the real world which many of Shakespeare's
contemporaries anxiously anticipated:

> This great world
> Shall so wear out to nought.
>
> (IV. vi. 134–5)

So the personal theme of the coming of death is set within another
larger theme of the ending of the world: both are epitomized in
Albany's phrase 'this great decay' (v. iii. 297).[1] The impression
we have in the later scenes of *King Lear* of increasing randomness
and inertia—'The centre cannot hold'—is part of Shakespeare's
governing artistic idea; unless we recognize this we shall merely
find the play 'structurally defective'. The truth is that the work of
organizing and making significant the play's unusually diverse
source-materials by means of a strikingly simple device was one
showing remarkable ambition and resourcefulness. The processes
involved are particularly rewarding to study.

III

The morality play tradition accounts for only some elements
in the complex form of *King Lear*. Lear is himself a British king as
well as a representative of *Humanum Genus*, and behind the play
(although a long way behind it) is the earliest of Elizabethan
tragedies, *Gorboduc*, which has a British setting and, like *Lear*,
is concerned with a weak or delinquent king. But it can hardly be
considered an important formative influence on Shakespeare's
play. The accepted 'sources' of *Lear*—the old play of *Leir*, the
episode of the Paphlagonian king in Sidney's *Arcadia*, and the
various historical accounts of Lear (such as Holinshed's)—have
been frequently studied, but, as usual, they are not of a kind which
would allow us to predict the form of the play which Shakespeare
was to build on them, and indeed they are all so remote from the
finished tragedy as to throw little light on the process of its composition. In this section I shall approach *Lear* from the direction
of Shakespeare's earlier plays in an attempt to show how some of
its more salient features came into being. But it is first necessary
to have a clear idea of the fundamental design of the play.

[1] Cf. John Holloway, *The Story of the Night* (London, 1961), pp. 76 ff., and Jan
Kott, *Shakespeare Our Contemporary* (London, 1965): 'The theme of *King Lear* is the
decay and fall of the world' (p. 120).

King Lear makes use of the two basic principles of dramatic organization which Shakespeare seems to have inherited: the division into five acts and into two parts. The act-division is quite clear, and the Folio numbering can be accepted. Each of the first three acts opens on a similar note: division in the realm of Britain. So Kent and Gloucester open the play with a reference to the coming 'division of the kingdom' (i. i. 4). The second act has Curan asking Edmund whether he has not heard of 'likely wars toward 'twixt the Dukes of Cornwall and Albany' (ii. i. 9–11), and the third act has Kent reverting somewhat improbably to the same topic in his dialogue with the Gentleman: 'There is division . . . 'twixt Albany and Cornwall' (iii. i. 19–21). The fourth act opens differently, with Edgar soliloquizing; the fifth resumes the theme of division, but in a different way from formerly, since Cornwall is now dead: we are shown, in the scene before the battle, Goneril and Regan mauœuvring for Edmund's affections. Each of the acts seems to have been conceived as a structural unit (unless we except the first, which is essentially two units). No matter how many individual scenes it may contain, the act itself is planned as a composite whole, with its own rhythm and tempo and its own final objective. (This will emerge in the later analysis.)

But Shakespeare also makes use of the other basic principle of organization: the two-part structure. Whatever brief pauses may have been thought desirable between the first and second and between the second and third acts, it seems clear that these three acts form a single dramatic movement which should not be interrupted by an interval. The place for an interval is—where, in modern productions, it usually occurs—after the third act. Thus the blinding of Gloucester brings the first part of *King Lear* to a close, and it is with a sense of initiating a fresh movement that the fourth act opens with Gloucester, led by Poor Tom, setting out for Dover. The 'pilgrimage' (v. iii. 196) begins here.

Despite the clearly articulated stages marked by each act-division, the first three acts are planned as a continuous action, as can be seen if we examine the separate yet related progresses of Lear and Gloucester. The first two scenes of the play serve as prologues, the first highly formal and weightily dramatized, the second designedly more perfunctory and 'stagey'. In the first

scene Lear speaks from the throne; he still has the autocrat's
capacity for arbitrary and self-indulgent wilfulness. Since he is
still at this point a king in the full sense, he has the *power* to enforce
his will no matter how irrationally misguided it is. This is the only
time we see Lear as he was before he relinquished power. *That*
is how he *was*; we are now to see him in circumstances created
by himself but different from what he expected. The play's main
action gets under way in the third and fourth scenes. In the first
Goneril briefly instructs Oswald to provoke Lear, and in the second
the clash between Lear and herself comes about. Despite Lear's
curses, Goneril achieves what she wants, since in effect she drives
him from her house. In the second act the situation is repeated
on a larger scale: Lear is rejected by Regan, who is then joined
by Goneril, and again Lear is deprived of his will; he leaves the
castle for the heath and storm. In the third act Lear delivers himself up to all the force of his rage, but he has no antagonist except
the wind and the rain. For all his threats of revenge he can accomplish nothing; all he *can* do is to change, to abandon pride for
humility, force for weakness. At this stage he acquires the beginnings of self-knowledge, but only at the cost of having his autocrat's will broken. The three scenes in which he appears in Act
Three (ii, iv, vi) show Lear descending from a pitch of impotent
rage through increasing exhaustion and feebleness to final unconsciousness. At the end of his third scene (III. vi) he falls asleep,
and is carried away. What Lear undergoes in these three acts,
from I. iv. to III. vi, is a progress in weakness; his rages may increase in force and wildness, but they are quite ineffectual, and
are no different in nature from gigantic tantrums. They merely
exhaust him, and so the movement of these three acts ends appropriately, as far as Lear is concerned, with exhausted sleep. He
becomes a spectacle of perfect weakness and vulnerability. For
Gloucester it is quite otherwise. He develops from being Edmund's
dupe in I. ii, through a distracted recognition of the King's
plight and his own duty to him in Act Two, to a decision in Act
Three to put his duty as a human being before his own safety.
As G. F. Kernodle has noted, the scenes of Act Three are
arranged contrapuntally: Lear's scenes descend from the rage of
his first storm speech ('Blow, winds, and crack your cheeks . . .')
to his last drowsy words in III. vi ('Make no noise, make
no noise; draw the curtains. So, so. We'll go to supper i' th'

morning').[1] The scenes concerning Gloucester, on the other hand, mount from a comparatively quiet beginning to the terrible violence of the blinding scene.

The first three acts form a massive single movement that is different in a number of ways from the second movement, which fills the fourth and fifth acts. Lear's dealings with Goneril and Regan, for example, are entirely confined to the first movement: indeed after Act Two he sees neither of them again (their dead bodies are brought on stage in the final scene, but only Edmund makes any response to them). Nor does Gloucester meet Edmund after the third act. Furthermore, in a way common with Shakespeare, certain characters drop out of the action for the second part of the play. Cornwall receives his death-wound at the close of Act Three; we see no more of him. And Lear's Fool, for an undisclosed reason, never appears in the last two acts. But there are also other, less tangible ways in which the second part of *King Lear* differs from the first. With the exception of Lear's final scene, the second part is far less painful to the feelings than the first. It is altogether less violently passionate, and, as far as the good characters are concerned, more reflective, more philosophical, even more retrospective (it occasionally looks back to events in the first part, such as Lear's night in the storm); and for all these reasons it can be said to be lighter, less dense, in substance. Another reason for this impression of comparative lightness of texture is the prominence of intrigue. A good deal of these last two acts is taken up with the comings and goings of Goneril, Regan, Edmund, and Oswald; their doings, like the characters themselves, are small in scale, and none of them excites any depth of feeling. The same, of course, is not true of the scenes in which Lear appears: his reconciliation with Cordelia is the supreme occasion in the play for the expression of purely natural feeling, and it gives a profound sense of relief—although it is part of Shakespeare's purpose that Lear's joy is to be only short-lived. But Lear's appearances in these last two acts are few and relatively brief: the scene on Dover Cliff with Gloucester, the reunion with Cordelia, the brief scene with her after the battle, and finally his death. His appearances have almost the nature of intrusions, as if he were surviving into someone else's play. For

---

[1] G. F. Kernodle, 'The Symphonic Form of "King Lear" ', in *Elizabethan Studies presented to George F. Reynolds* (Boulder, Colo., 1945), p. 189.

most of the time we are taken up with the other characters, with each of whom we are less deeply involved. The second part, in short, may be said to be far closer to romance or tragicomedy than the first: the journeyings and changing relationships of the characters, the strong element of intrigue, and Shakespeare's technique of short scenes or, in the final scene, of multiple discoveries, make it—despite the violent deaths to which a number of the characters are brought—curiously akin to such a romantic tragicomedy as *Cymbeline*. (Indeed this affinity with a lighter genre may be why Bradley felt the unrelieved desolation of Lear's last scene to be something of an artistic mistake and found himself hankering after a 'happy ending': 'If I read *King Lear* simply as a drama, I find that my feelings call for this "happy ending". I do not mean the human, the philanthrophic, feelings, but the dramatic sense.')[1] A tentative distinction might be risked: what we have in the first three acts is the mingling of comic with tragic forms; in the last two acts we have the mingling of tragicomic with tragic forms. Such a distinction may help to account for the very elusive tone of some of the writing in these later scenes. It should be noticed, for example, that Lear's reconciliation with Cordelia is a recognition scene, and recognition scenes are a not uncommon feature of romantic tragicomedies (such as *Pericles*, *Cymbeline*, and *The Winter's Tale*).

If we now ask how Shakespeare devised the ground-plan, so to speak, for the work which was to become *King Lear*, with its double plot, and its five act and two-part structure, we must look among some of his earlier plays, since, consciously or not, this is what Shakespeare must have done himself. *King Lear* is a tragedy at least peripherally concerned with a divided kingdom; it shows the British realm given over to the rule of selfish will and impulse, and makes clear that there is no possibility of amity between two equally powerful groups of unprincipled rulers (hence the repeated rumours of 'division' between the two dukes). This is the basic political situation of the play; and it seems likely that at an early stage of working it out, Shakespeare's mind went back to the *Henry VI* plays which are also concerned, not peripherally this time but centrally, with division in the kingdom. *Parts Two* and *Three* are more relevant than *Part One*, since in them the Wars of the Roses take place. I would tentatively suggest that what

---

[1] A. C. Bradley, op. cit., p. 252.

Shakespeare did was to take the first movement of *Henry VI,
Part Two* (Acts One to Three) as a very general model for the
first movement of *King Lear* and the second movement of *Part
Three* (Acts Three to Five) as a very general model for his second
movement. (I shall make some qualifications later.) The first three
acts of *Henry VI, Part Two* are largely concerned with the fall
and death of Duke Humphrey of Gloucester. There is a good deal
of subsidiary episode and a wealth of characters; but what gives
this first movement of the play its unity is the fall of Duke Humphrey, which forms a small tragedy in itself. The last two acts of
Part Two and the first two acts of *Part Three* are largely given
to Jack Cade's rebellion and the course of the civil war; they were
of no use to Shakespeare in *King Lear*. But Act Four of *Part Three*
had something more to his purpose. It is made up of a long series
of short scenes showing the state of England under the simultaneous rule of two kings, Henry VI and Edward IV. Fortune's
wheel spins dizzily; Warwick has crossed over to Henry's side,
abandoning Edward; he then captures Edward, who is later released by his brother Richard. Later (v. i), Clarence betrays Warwick and crosses over to Edward. What this long sequence
demonstrates is the lack of principle of all the personages, with
the exception of Henry, and the impossibility of any stability in
the land while there are two claimants to the throne. The question is finally settled at the battle of Tewkesbury, when Edward
and his brothers defeat Margaret's army. Immediately after the
battle her son, Prince Edward, is stabbed to death before her eyes.
Although these historical circumstances are of course very different from those of the second part of *King Lear*, it is possible to
discern a large structural resemblance between them, and even
some thematic affinities. In general, both plays have a sequence of
short scenes showing power-seeking characters getting into position for a final decisive conflict; after the battle a parent on the
losing side witnesses the killing of a beloved child. So, for all the
obvious differences of character and situation, Margaret after
the battle is momentarily in a position like Lear's. *Henry VI,
Part Three* was not the only play remembered by Shakespeare for
the ending of *King Lear*, and it is not suggested that Shakespeare
recalled it in any very clear detail. But it seems not unlikely that it
contributed something—and something essential—to the shaping
of the last two acts.

One scene in particular suggests that Shakespeare associated Henry VI and Lear as kings. In *Part Three* (IV. vi) Warwick releases Henry from prison. Henry thanks his keeper in the following speech:

> Nay, be thou sure I'll well requite thy kindness,
> For that it made my imprisonment a pleasure;
> Ay, such a pleasure as incaged birds
> Conceive when, after many moody thoughts,
> At last by notes of household harmony
> They quite forget their loss of liberty.

He then asks Warwick to rule England for him:

> Warwick, although my head still wear the crown,
> I here resign my government to thee,
> For thou art fortunate in all thy deeds.

Warwick protests that Clarence has a prior claim, but Henry makes them *both* rulers:

> Now join your hands, and with your hands your hearts,
> That no dissension hinder government.
> I make you both Protectors of this land,
> While I myself will lead a private life
> And in devotion spend my latter days,
> To sin's rebuke and my Creator's praise.

Warwick quickly agrees:

> We'll yoke together, like a double shadow
> To Henry's body, and supply his place;
> I mean, in bearing weight of government,
> While he enjoys the honour and his ease.
>
> (IV. vi. 10–52)

This short scene contains in little a good deal of *King Lear*, and points forward to two scenes in particular. Henry's desire to surrender the duties of kingship—'government'—while keeping the title clearly anticipates Lear's initial decision. (It should be noted that this stipulation is not found in the more obvious 'sources' of *King Lear* such as the old play of *Leir*, Holinshed, Spenser, etc. It may be that this speech of Henry's furnished this detail.) Henry's other remarks anticipate the beginning of v. iii,

where Lear and Cordelia enter as prisoners after the battle and
Lear hopes for an undisturbed life in prison with his daughter:

> Come, let's away to prison,
> We two alone will sing like birds i' th 'cage . . .

Henry's reference to 'incaged birds' comes close to this; his
desire for a private life, his hopeless political irresponsibility
and ignorance of public affairs were all recalled by Shakespeare
when portraying Lear. And like Lear, Henry hands over power
to not one substitute, but two. His tragic folly is underlined by the
way that, shortly afterwards, Clarence betrays Warwick. In a
similar way Lear delivers the kingdom over to a divided rule.

There may be a further link between *3 Henry VI* and *King Lear*.
There is a well-attested tradition that at the second battle of St.
Albans (1461) Henry VI was left in the care of two guards under
an oak tree and that during the battle he laughed and sang.[1]
Neither Hall nor Holinshed mentions the incident, but it seems
possible that Shakespeare knew of it. Although he did not
dramatize it directly in *3 Henry VI*, it may well have suggested
the scene (II. v) in which Henry meditates alone, sitting on a mole-
hill, during the battle of Towton. In *King Lear*, v. ii, however,
the detail of the tree seems directly recalled when, during the
battle, Edgar leaves the blind Gloucester alone on stage under
'the shadow of this tree'. (In Peter Brook's 1962 production of
Lear, this moment—Gloucester sitting alone during the off-stage
battle—was very strikingly realized.)

I have so far been considering the political ground-plan of
King Lear, what it has discernibly in common with the design of
the last two of the *Henry VI* plays. I want next to focus on the
tragic course of Lear as a man, rather than on his political errors
as king. I want to suggest that Shakespeare's conception of Lear as
a tragic figure is to some extent a combination or re-configuration
of two or three tragic figures in his early plays (we can say, if
we wish, that the conception of Lear transcends and eclipses
those earlier attempts). The first character to serve as a partial
model for Lear was Duke Humphrey, in *Henry VI, Part Two*.
There are two scenes in particular which help to establish this
relation. These are I. iii and III. i. Both are scenes in which
Humphrey is 'baited' by his enemies, and both can be interpreted

---

[1] See J. R. Lander, *The Wars of the Roses* (London, 1965), p. 120.

as exhibiting the tragic hero's passion. The first is very brief, but in it Humphrey, usually so self-controlled, is so overcome by passion that he leaves the stage without any warning. He returns a little later, saying:

> Now, lords, my choler being overblown
> With walking once about the quadrangle,
> I come to talk of commonwealth affairs.

> (I. iii. 150–2)

The sudden exit and re-entry are visible signs of lack of self-control. The first of the two scenes in which Lear is 'baited' (I. iv) contains exactly the same stage effect: Lear exits (289) and abruptly re-enters, so making a similar impression of uncontrollable passion.[1] The other scene in *2 Henry VI* shows a massed effort on the part of Humphrey's enemies to overthrow him. Although he defends himself against the taunting accusations of the court party led by the Queen, Suffolk, and Beaufort, he is led off under arrest on a charge of treason; he is murdered shortly after. The corresponding scene in *King Lear* is II. iv, in which Lear's enemies similarly mass themselves against him in a successful effort to break him down. This design—having the hero 'baited'—is alike in both plays in being set out in two stages: first, a relatively short scene which works as a kind of dress rehearsal for, second, the big ensemble scene which, with protracted ritualistic deliberateness, isolates and breaks down the hero.

Another early tragic figure to serve as a partial model for Lear was Constance in *King John* (which I take to be an early play). Constance was probably more important for the conception of Lear than Duke Humphrey, although she is never 'baited' as the two men are. What Constance does present, in the three scenes in which she appears, is a descending arc of increasing weakness and helplessness in face of the strong and purposeful wills of other people. She finally loses everything: her hopes for Arthur, and also Arthur himself. She dies, we are told, 'in a frenzy'. Her scene of inconsolable grief (III. iv) anticipates the single-mindedness of Lear's grief for Cordelia more than anything else in Shakespeare. She stands, in fact, as a figure of abject weakness, with nothing but her rage, her scorn, and her power of words to

---

1 Cf. the way Hieronimo 'goeth in at one door and comes out at another' in the first of his mad scenes (*The Spanish Tragedy*, III. xi. 8).

fall back on, and in all these things she comes close to some essential qualities of Lear as a tragic protagonist.

But Constance's kinship to Lear as a tragic figure can be taken further. She commands a remarkable personal rhetoric, a power of expressing passion, which Shakespeare remembered and adapted to Lear's circumstances. When driven to a point of desperation, both Constance and Lear plead with their adversaries by appealing to the concept of *need*. So, just before leaving Gloucester's castle for the heath, Lear picks up Regan's 'What need one?' to exclaim 'O, reason not the need!' and goes on to play desperately with the term: 'You heavens, give me that patience, patience I need' (II. iv. 263–70). Constance too rings changes on the word:

> O, if thou grant my need,
> Which only lives but by the death of faith,
> That need must needs infer this principle—
> That faith would live again by death of need.
> O then, tread down my need, and faith mounts up:
> Keep my need up, and faith is trodden down!
>
> (*King John,* III. i. 211–16)

Her earlier frenzied invocations to heaven are close to the style of Lear's speeches in the storm:

> Arm, arm, you heavens, against these perjur'd kings!
> A widow cries: Be husband to me heavens! . . .
> Hear me, O, hear me!
>
> (III. i. 107–12)

Later, in her scene of distraction, she has something very like Lear's majestic egoism:

> O that my tongue were in the thunder's mouth!
> Then with a passion would I shake the world . . .
>
> (III. iv. 38–9)

And in the same scene she anticipates Lear's final grief for Cordelia, and in particular his 'Thou'lt come no more', followed by the five-times repeated 'never', in her own grief for a beloved lost child:

And so he'll die; and, rising so again,
When I shall meet him in the court of heaven,
I shall not know him. Therefore never, never,
Must I behold my pretty Arthur more.

(III. iv. 86-9)

If these parallels are accepted, it can be seen that Constance's great speech, 'Gone to be married! Gone to swear a peace!' (III. i. 1-26), probably formed the model for Lear's own outburst of outraged incredulity, beginning 'Deny to speak with me! They are sick! They are weary!' (II. iv. 86-117).

Quite apart from Constance and Lear, memories of *King John* show themselves at several points in *King Lear*, especially in the third and fifth acts. (They will be specified in the next section.) Here the relation between the two plays can be clarified by focusing on the Bastard Faulconbridge. Faulconbridge is not in the strict legal sense a bastard at all, since he could legally have inherited Sir Robert Faulconbridge's estate. But he chose bastardy in order to follow his fortunes with the King. He therefore does not have the moral and personal qualities with which bastards, in literature and drama, were conventionally endowed: he is not basely disloyal, nor is his primary object the acquisition of land.[1] On the contrary, he remains the King's most loyal supporter, and speaks increasingly with the voice of moral authority. He is important for *King Lear*, since his qualities are refracted into two of its characters: his bastardy and perhaps his engaging manner are given to Edmund, his loyalty and honest bluntness to Kent. In his book on *King Lear* Maynard Mack remarks: '. . . almost every character in the play, including such humble figures as Cornwall's servant and the old tenant who befriends Gloucester, is impelled soon or late to make some sort of stand—to show, in Oswald's words, "what party I do follow". One cannot but be struck by how much positioning and repositioning of this kind the play contains.'[2] In saying this, he might also have had *King John* in mind, since questions of legality, allegiance, and loyalty are especially important to it, and are focused in the person of the Bastard, who is himself a loyal illegitimate. The rising progress of Edmund through the entire length of *King Lear*—from a position

[1] See J. W. Draper, 'Bastardy in Shakespeare's Plays', *Shakespeare Jahrbuch*, 74 (1938).
[2] Maynard Mack, op. cit., p. 90.

of dependence and subordination to one at the centre of power, with Goneril and Regan competing for his favour and with the King of Britain and the Queen of France at his mercy—may have been adapted, in its general conception, from the rising progress of the Bastard Faulconbridge, who becomes the King's most loyal and disinterested right-hand man. The likenesses in their progress are as interesting as the differences.

I have so far been considering the ways in which four of the early history plays were turned to further account in the making of *King Lear*. The relation to it of another early play, the tragedy *Titus Andronicus*, has often been noticed; but since it has been made the subject of a special study, it need not be gone into here in any detail.[1] It may be enough to recall that the character of Titus provided Shakespeare with a few points for Lear's own character. Both Titus and Lear are ageing fathers, at first passionate in wrath, later passionate in grief; both commit initial acts of folly, and suffer agonizing grief for it; and both go mad. But here their paths sharply diverge: Titus achieves a horrifying revenge on his enemies, while Lear, when he has recovered from his madness, forgets his earlier thoughts of revenge and is concerned only to live with Cordelia (his final killing of the soldier is of course a spontaneous act of rage). One phrase is common to them: Titus' 'I am not mad, I know thee well enough' (v. ii. 21) survived in Lear's 'I know thee well enough; thy name is Gloucester' (IV. vi. 178), and, as Kenneth Muir suggests, 'Shakespeare may have taken some hints for his portrait of Edmund from the character of Aaron, and the idea of the intrigue with Goneril from the Aaron-Tamora-Saturninus triangle.'[2] Structurally, the part of *Titus Andronicus* which comes closest to *King Lear* is its first three acts, where Titus suffers a fall which might be compared with Lear's. But the influence here, if it exists, seems to have merged with that of *2 Henry VI*, where the fall of Duke Humphrey occupies a similar position in the play. Otherwise, the only scene which distinctly anticipates one in *King Lear* is the mad scene (IV. iii), which has a few things comparable to Lear's speeches on Dover Cliff.

[1] Thomas P. Harrison, ' "Titus Andronicus" and "King Lear": A Study in Continuity', in *Shakespearean Essays* (Knoxville, Tenn., 1964), ed. Alwin Thaler and Norman Sanders. The resemblances are for the most part verbal and thematic, not scenic.
[2] Kenneth Muir, *Shakespeare's Sources*, vol. i, p. 161.

One major structural arrangement in *King Lear* has not yet been accounted for. This is the double plot: the way in which Shakespeare reinforced the story of Lear and his three daughters with that of Gloucester and his two sons. Of course Shakespeare based this sub-plot on Sidney's tale of the blind Paphlagonian king. But the idea of blending two parallel stories for their mutual dramatic benefit seems to have come from *As You Like It*, a play whose affinities with parts of *King Lear* have often been noted, although their extent has perhaps not been fully explored. G. F. Kernodle noticed that in *King Lear* Shakespeare took over an arrangement he had already used in *As You Like It*: the double exposition, in which first the Orlando plot, and then the Rosalind plot, are expounded in successive scenes (I. i, ii).[1] But this correspondence goes much further than Kernodle suggested; and in fact the parallel between the Orlando and Rosalind plots is misleading, from the point of view of *King Lear*. If we omit Rosalind and Celia as being from this viewpoint irrelevant, we are left with, first, Orlando and his unnatural brother Oliver, and, secondly, Duke Senior and *his* unnatural brother Frederick. That is to say, we have two sets of good and bad brothers, just as in *King Lear* we have two sets of fathers with good and bad offspring. The influence of *As You Like It* on the structure of *King Lear* is strongest in Acts Three and Four, where the action moves, first to the heath, and then to Dover Cliff. Duke Frederick foreshadows Cornwall, Oliver Edmund, and Orlando Edgar. Indeed Orlando's journey with the aged Adam (II. vi) comes remarkably close in feeling to Edgar's more extended journey with the blind Gloucester. The subsidiary figure of Adam seems to have made a strong impression on Shakespeare: in *King Lear* his qualities are distributed among three characters. He is like Gloucester in his quasi-paternal relationship to Orlando, while his extreme old age (he is 'now almost fourscore', 'at fourscore', II. iii. 71, 74) he shares with Lear as well as with the Old Man who gives help to the blind Gloucester (IV. i. 14). Further, the servant who stands up to Cornwall and Regan in the blinding scene is called 'dog' by Regan (III. vii. 74), while in the first scene of *As You Like It* Oliver similarly addresses Adam: 'Get you with him, you old dog', to which Adam replies: 'Is "old dog" my reward? Most true, I have lost my teeth in your service' (I. i. 73–5). Both Adam and Cornwall's servant are,

---

[1] G. F. Kernodle, op. cit., p. 187.

apparently, peasant servitors of long standing: the one loses his
'teeth' in his master's service, the other his life. The loyal and
selfless behaviour of Gloucester (also in the third act of *King
Lear*), who risks, and eventually suffers, Cornwall's anger in
order to serve Lear, possibly takes its germ too from another
early scene in *As You Like It*. The courtier Le Beau goes out of his
way to warn Orlando to leave the court so as to escape the Duke's
anger (i. ii. 240 ff.). He does it 'in friendship' (240), and his parting
words are:

> Hereafter, in a better world than this,
> I shall desire more love and knowledge of you.
>
> (263–4)

These small touches in the opening scenes of *As You Like It* are
all adapted with immeasurably greater effect; in their new contexts
they are placed in positions of greater saliency, and the moral
issues involved have been more carefully expounded.

The most important, perhaps, of the scenes in *King Lear* which
seem to derive from something already dramatized in *As You
Like It*, remains to be mentioned. Duke Senior has been driven
from his dukedom to the Forest of Arden. Orlando too sets out
for the same Forest, where, in the company of Adam and almost
starving, he eventually meets with the Duke and his followers.
The scene in which they confront each other (ii. vii) is written
with elaborate formality. Orlando appeals for charity in simple
but plangent rhetoric:

> If ever you have look'd on better days,
> If ever been where bells have toll'd to church . . .

and the Duke replies, chiming line for line to Orlando's appeal:

> True is it that we have seen better days,
> And have with holy bell been knoll'd to church . . .

This rhetorical device, whereby the Duke echoes Orlando,
serves to bring out that each mirrors the other's state of human
misfortune—as the Duke comments when Orlando leaves to
bring Adam:

> Thou seest we are not all alone unhappy:
> This wide and universal theatre
> Presents more woeful pageants than the scene
> Wherein we play in.
>
> (ii. vii. 136–9)

Jaques proceeds to speak of the Seven Ages of Man; a speech whose cynicism is challenged by the *tableau* of quasi-filial piety presented by Orlando carrying on his shoulders the exhausted old man Adam. The Duke's words, 'Welcome. Set down your venerable burden' suggest how the *tableau* should be interpreted: the phrase 'venerable burden' (Ovid's 'venerabile onus') described Æneas' flight from Troy carrying his father Anchises on his shoulders. The whole moving and even solemn occasion is now further heightened by the song sung by Amiens, 'Blow, blow, thou winter wind', whose words ('man's ingratitude', 'benefits forgot') anticipate the concerns of *King Lear*, as many critics have noted. This scene as a whole, however, in which Orlando meets Duke Senior, mirrors him and is mirrored by him, marks the point where the two plots converge, and in this function it seems to have formed the model of the great scene on Dover Cliff (IV. vi) in which Lear confronts Gloucester, and speaks of the 'great stage of fools' in a way recalling Jaques's 'All the world's a stage'. Both scenes contain passages of still contemplation: we listen to the reflections—'matter and impertinency mix'd', for Lear combines the Duke's 'philosophy' with Jaques's partial satire—but we also look at the *tableaux* visually formed on the stage. In *As You Like It* this scene is the last which deals with the themes of nature, nurture, and need (it feels almost like the end of a play; perhaps an interval was meant to follow it). The parallelism between the Duke and Orlando is not given a very extended treatment, for the remaining three acts are largely devoted to love. In *King Lear* the parallel between the two plots is extended much further, so that the two protagonists do not confront each other in their sufferings until late in the fourth act; as a result the scene itself gains greater weight and emphasis.

The ways in which Shakespeare drew on his own earlier work can now be briefly summarized. From among his early plays the three Parts of *Henry VI*, *King John*, and *Titus Andronicus* he took essential suggestions for the design of *King Lear* as a whole and for its tragic treatment. But the peculiarly comprehensive range of *King Lear* can be indicated by the fact that Shakespeare drew on romantic comedy as well as tragedy and the history play. Not only *As You Like It* but *Twelfth Night* and *All's Well that Ends Well* contributed to the fabric of the play. What these comedies have in common with each other as well as with *King Lear* is that they each contain a professional Fool and, in their different ways, are much concerned with the topic of folly.

If we look for a principle of unity in these very diverse 'source' plays, we may perhaps find one in the inclusive notions of Law and Right. This is in keeping with the generally admitted 'philosophical' nature of *King Lear*, its tendency to raise fundamental questions about man and his nature. Among the history plays the *Henry VI, Part Two* and *King John* are specially concerned with law and justice, and both have scenes showing justice being administered. Similarly, although one must not make too much of the distinction, the three 'Fool' comedies just mentioned make us reflect, however momentarily, about 'this great stage of fools'. A contrast may be drawn between *King Lear* and *Othello*. *Othello* is a relatively unphilosophical and un-abstract tragedy, whose links with the comedies include *The Merry Wives of Windsor* and *Much Ado About Nothing*, both of which are set in a firmly realized society and neither of which is particularly speculative (although this is not to say that *Much Ado* at least does not embody a view of human nature: 'man', Benedick concludes, 'is a giddy thing', a statement which the whole comedy has dramatized). It is, on the other hand, entirely characteristic of *King Lear*'s tendency to draw on passages relevant to its philosophical interests that an exchange as brief as the following in a comedy otherwise concerned with love and friendship should have been remembered and put to use (and, as it happens, in a much more emphatically telling position than in the original). The exchange occurs in the last act of *The Two Gentlemen of Verona*, where Silvia is captured by the forest outlaws:

> *Outlaw.* Come, come,
>   Be patient; we must bring you to our captain.
> *Silvia.* A thousand more mischances than this one
>   Have learn'd me how to brook this patiently.
>
> (v. iii. 1–4)

This passage was recalled at the beginning of the last scene of *King Lear*, where Lear and Cordelia are about to be led away to prison. Silvia's exemplification of the uses of adversity looks forward to Cordelia's tougher stoicism—

> For thee, oppressed King, am I cast down;
> Myself could else out-frown false Fortune's frown

—while Cordelia's captor, Edmund, is also a kind of outlaw: a lawless illegitimate.

IV

In this section I shall make a selective commentary on the scenes of *King Lear*, bearing in mind the contours of the dramatic experience as they are perceived in a performance of the play. The act-divisions, as I have remarked already, quite adequately account for the major units, except that the first act really comprises two units, or even three. For the first two scenes serve as separate expositions to the two plots, and there is little sense of liaison between the first and second scenes, and none at all between the second and third. This slightly halting sequence helps to account for the feeling that the play is a ponderous, even clumsy, machine which gets into motion only slowly and effortfully.

The play opens with the long scene of the dividing of the kingdom, the banishment of Kent, and France's offer of marriage to Cordelia. The informality of the brief opening dialogue between Gloucester, Kent, and Edmund helps to throw into relief the solemn public formality of the court scene which follows; but, more subtly, it also prompts us to notice the dangerous instability of Lear's ceremonious manner, with its oscillations between public and private, king and old father, royal 'we' and private 'I'. And the entire scene is concluded with the private conversation of Goneril and Regan, which balances the private conversation that opened it. The main effect produced by the court scene itself is one of studied anticlimax, since its purpose is to show the thwarting of Lear's tyrannically arbitrary will. Everything seems set for an occasion of pre-arranged ceremony. The three daughters are required to play their parts like marionettes; and everything does go according to plan until Cordelia shatters the monstrous game with her 'Nothing'. Dramatically, therefore, the scene is a version of the 'violated ceremony' formula described by Hereward T. Price,[1] and it is of course precisely the violation that gives the scene its dramatic life. Yet Cordelia's 'Nothing' comes early on, well within the first third of the scene. Tension is maintained by the summary rapidity with which the two remaining items of business are dealt with: the futures of

[1] See Hereward T. Price, *Construction in Shakespeare* (University of Michigan, 1951).

Kent and Cordelia. Kent's outburst is promptly followed by his
banishment; the two suitors for Cordelia appear, and France
offers her his hand. Both these short episodes have the effect of
showing the limitations of Lear's power, so that when Lear leaves
the stage on the arm of the mercenary Burgundy, he is, despite his
apparent authority, thwarted of everything he wants, powerless
in everything that matters. Although so much happens in it, this
first scene has something of the summary nature of a preliminary
dumb-show: the pace is brisk, one has almost the sense of hurry-
ing through it in order that the real play can begin. We are, after
all, plunged into this scene with no preparation other than the
opening prose dialogue; it is as if the play opened on a high climax, but since we have had no time to become deeply involved
with any of the characters we necessarily watch it with a certain
detachment.

'No other of Shakespeare's great tragedies opens with a great
set scene', comments Dame Helen Gardner.[1] Among the early
plays, however, *Titus Andronicus* opens with an exceptionally long
and full opening scene, and is followed by a soliloquy from the
villainous Aaron the Moor, just as here the scene is followed by a
soliloquy from Edmund. There is probably some carry-over from
the earlier tragedy, but otherwise this opening scene seems more
decisively modelled on the 'suitors' scene' in *All's Well that Ends
Well* (II. iii)—if the usual assumption is right that that is an
earlier play than *King Lear*.[2] That scene, like this, opens with a
prose dialogue between courtiers, Lafeu and Parolles; the King of
France, now cured of his disease, enters with Helena, summons
the young lords, and offers Helena her choice of a husband from
any one of them. The King is like Lear in expecting the persons
involved to behave like puppets; he says of the young men:

> . . . O'er whom both sovereign power and father's voice
> I have to use. Thy frank election make;
> Thou hast power to choose, and they none to forsake.
>
> (*All's Well*, 52–5)

Just as Cordelia rebels against her father's unreasonable demands,
so here does the very different Bertram, so that both scenes are

---

[1] Helen Gardner, *King Lear* (John Coffin Memorial Lecture, London, 1966), p. 4.
[2] I owe this observation to my wife Barbara Everett, who compares Cordelia with
Bertram in her New Penguin edition of *All's Well that Ends Well* (1970), p. 34.

alike in showing a king's arbitrary will being thwarted: on both
occasions the set ceremony is violated. And there are other affinities between the two scenes. In each a young girl is offered in
marriage, but whereas Lear strips Cordelia of all her worldly
advantages, yet even so France chooses to marry her, in *All's
Well* the King offers to make up Helena's worldly standing, yet
even so Bertram *refuses* to have her. (Later in the scene, of course,
he complies, and takes her on sufferance.) The King says of
Helena:

> Virtue and she
> Is her own dower; honour and wealth from me.
>
> (ii. iii. 141–2)

Of Cordelia the King (also of France) says to Burgundy:

> Will you have her?
> She is herself a dowry.
>
> (i. i. 240–1)

In *All's Well* the scene concludes with the departure of everyone
'but Lafeu and Parolles who stay behind, commenting of this wedding'
(S.D. 181); similarly this scene concludes with Goneril and
Regan commenting on the events they have just witnessed. There
are a number of other thematic points of contact between the two
plays. In this same scene Lafeu tells Parolles: 'I have a desire to
hold my acquaintance with thee, or rather my knowledge, that
I may say in the default "He is a man I know"' (ii. iii. 222–4).
Similarly, and in a similar position in the scene, Cordelia tells her
sisters: 'I know you what you are' (269). Later in the scene Parolles, left alone after being insulted by Lafeu and spluttering with
rage, says: 'Well, I must be patient; there is no fettering of
authority. I'll beat him, by my life, if I can meet him with any
convenience, an he were double and double a lord. I'll have no
more pity of his age than I would have of—I'll beat him, an if I
could but meet him again.' (228–35.) At this point Lafeu re-enters
and Parolles becomes all politeness. This is a comic version of
Lear's comparably helpless rage, especially later in ii. iv:

> I will have such revenges on you both
> That all the world shall—I will do such things—
> What they are yet I know not; but they shall be
> The terrors of the earth.
>
> (278–81)

As in the speech just quoted of Parolles, Lear's impotence here is focused in the use of anacoluthon. Like Parolles also, Lear sees the need for patience; and just as Parolles is reduced to acknowledging 'the thing I am' (IV. iii. 310), so Lear is later brought to see 'the thing itself' (III. iv. 106). I will return to the affinities between Lear and Parolles a little later.

Adhering to his usual principle of contrast, Shakespeare makes the second scene of the play as different as possible from the first. Edmund's opening soliloquy establishes once and for all his humorously ruthless energy, and for the rest of the scene he is allowed to hustle his father and brother as if they were the mutely unprotesting dupes in an Italian farce.[1] Shakespeare disposes of the Gloucester and Edgar business with almost indecent haste; he seems, as any audience will be, impatient for the main action to be got under way.

A pause follows, and it begins. The next three scenes (I. iii, iv, v) form a single movement, with prologue (iii), the play itself (iv), and epilogue (v). Goneril and Oswald first set the scene and arrange their roles: Oswald is to provoke Lear, while Goneril herself will put in a later appearance to finish off the job. She will goad Lear into a rage: 'I would breed from hence occasions, and I shall, / That I may speak'. Everything goes according to plan: Goneril's stratagem succeeds perfectly, and Lear and his knights are induced to go. Surprisingly, this scene (I. iv) is the longest in the play—surprisingly, because in performance, perhaps, its earlier stages will come across more as a succession of short episodes than as a continuous action. Certainly, it is a crucially important scene, which powerfully draws us into the real world of the play (particularly in the speeches of the Fool) as the opening scene designedly has not done. Kent first appears alone in disguise, and presents himself to Lear; Oswald makes his two brief provocative appearances, and is beaten by Kent; the Fool appears, talks, and sings, until the entertainment (such as it is) is interrupted by

[1] In his essay 'Repeated Situations in Shakespeare's Plays' (in *Essays on Shakespeare and Elizabethan Drama* in honour of Hardin Craig, ed. R. Hosley, London, 1963), Matthew Black compares Edmund's pretended concealment of the letter from Gloucester with the situation in *Richard II*, V. ii, in which Aumerle similarly, but genuinely, tries to conceal a letter from his father York and is similarly made to surrender it. (Behind this scene, as Black observes, is I. iii of *The Two Gentlemen of Verona*, involving Proteus and his father Antonio.) *Richard II* and *King Lear* have some obvious thematic affinities (both show a king in different ways 'unkinged'), but structurally they seem to have little in common.

Goneril; she remonstrates with Lear, who responds by laying on her his solemn curse; left alone with Albany, Goneril comments, and, for a third time, Oswald briefly appears. The scene's climax is clearly the curse on Goneril (275–89), but the scene's true form as a whole may be clarified by considering its models. Shakespeare has here made use of more than one scene in *Twelfth Night*, another of the comedies which contributed to the form and substance of *King Lear*. Three scenes seem to have coalesced in his mind: Feste's first conversation with Olivia (I. v), the roistering scene, in which Sir Toby, Sir Andrew, and Feste are interrupted and silenced by Malvolio (II. iii), and the final scene in which Malvolio demands restitution from Olivia (v. i. 314–64). In the earliest of these scenes Feste makes his first appearance and shows off his skills: he 'proves' Olivia a fool, just as here the Fool 'proves' Kent and Lear to be fools. Both scenes have a household atmosphere, with comfort and hospitality within and a cheerless repressiveness outside,[1] while Malvolio's dislike of Feste is recalled in Goneril's hostility to Lear's Fool. When Goneril appears she aims her protest against Lear's knights:

> Men so disorder'd, so debosh'd and bold,
> That this our court, infected with their manners,
> Shows like a riotous inn. Epicurism and lust
> Makes it more like a tavern or a brothel
> Than a grac'd palace.
>
> (241–5)

This recalls the roistering scene in *Twelfth Night*, in which Malvolio's role corresponds to Goneril's here, while Sir Toby and Sir Andrew *are* 'riotous knights' (the phrase used by Regan of Lear's followers at II. i. 94). When Malvolio appears he cries: 'Have you no wit, manners, nor honesty, but to gabble like tinkers at this time of the night? Do ye make an ale-house of my lady's house . . .? My lady bade me tell you that, though she harbours you as her kinsman, she's nothing allied to your disorders. If you can separate yourself and your misdemeanours, you are welcome to the house; if not, and it would please you to take leave of her, she is very willing to bid you farewell' (II. iii. 84–96). Shakespeare puts these potentially painful rebukes into Malvolio's

---

[1] William Elton notes a connection between *Twelfth Night* and *King Lear* in this respect; see '*King Lear' and the Gods* (Huntington Library, San Marino, Calif., 1966), pp. 309–10.

mouth, not Olivia's own, so that the effect is softened, suitably to
a comedy; in *King Lear* the harshness of the daughter's rebuke
to her own father, and king, carries the situation to a tragic extremity. Until Lear by cursing her cuts off all hope of reconciliation, the scene can therefore be regarded as a bitterly distorted
echo of the earlier revelling scene with the 'riotous knights'
and the household Fool. Immediately after the curse Lear leaves
the stage, only to make an abrupt re-entry and to embark on a new
flood of mingled remonstrance and threat. The rapid exit and
re-entry are themselves clear signs of a helpless lack of self-control
(I have earlier related them to Duke Humphrey's similarly passionate behaviour); the form of the speech which follows, however, curiously corresponds exactly to Malvolio's remonstrations
in the last scene of *Twelfth Night* (v. i. 315–31). Malvolio is pro-
testing to Olivia against his ill-treatment:

> *Malvolio.* Madam, you have done me wrong,
>   Notorious wrong.
> *Olivia.*   Have I, Malvolio? No.

He replies with a fifteen-line speech, ending

> . . . And made the most notorious geck and gull
> That e'er invention play'd on? Tell me why.

Lear too begins with a one-and-a-half-line speech, separated by a
brief interruption from a speech of fifteen (or rather fourteen and
a half) lines:

> *Lear.* What, fifty of my followers at a clap!
>   Within a fortnight!
> *Albany.*   What's the matter, sir?

And Lear's reply ends with something of the same ineffectual
anticlimax as Malvolio's:

> Thou shalt find
> That I'll resume the shape which thou dost think
> I have cast off for ever.
>
>   (I. iv. 293–310)

It seems clear that something in Malvolio's situation, probably
his feeling of impotent rage, was recalled by Shakespeare when
giving shape to Lear's behaviour here. Malvolio's final outburst
immediately before his exit, 'I'll be reveng'd on the whole pack

of you' (v. i. 364), corresponds to Lear's curse: but it comes after his remonstrance, whereas Lear's comes before it. Of course Malvolio is to be 'entreated to a peace', whereas Goneril is far from placating her father. In II. iv he is to be goaded even further, into the storm, whereas at the end of *Twelfth Night* the 'wind and the rain' are present only in the Fool's song.

One thing that emerges from this investigation into the comic provenance of the scenic forms in the first act of *Lear* is that Shakespeare sometimes closely associates Lear with Malvolio and Parolles at their moments of sharpest humiliation. Such a link gives support to Charles Lamb's remark that 'Malvolio is not essentially ludicrous', as well as to G. Wilson Knight's penetrating essay '"King Lear" and the Comedy of the Grotesque'.[1] Malvolio and even Parolles have a tragic potentiality, just as Lear comes perilously close at times to the comic.

In modern editions of *King Lear* Act Two is divided into four scenes. In performance, however, we experience it as, first, one fairly short scene in the nature of a prologue, given to forwarding the Gloucester plot and to the arrival of Regan and Cornwall at Gloucester's castle, and secondly, one very long scene which fills the entire act, except for the soliloquy of Edgar (II. iii), which interrupts it and allows for the passage of night; during Edgar's speech Kent in the stocks is visible on the stage, so that our impression of the essential continuity is not violated. This long, massive, and tremendously powerful movement is the chief scene of passion in the play, and is undoubtedly one of the grandest pieces of continuous dramatic writing in the whole of Shakespeare. The first scene (II. i) takes up the sequence from I. ii: Edmund is still plotting to get Edgar out of the way, and in a brief passage of highly stylized serious farce almost pushes him off stage before Gloucester arrives. The rest of the scene is taken up with Edmund's Iago-like improvisations, Gloucester's grief and sense of outrage, and then the arrival of Regan and her husband. Everything is set for the remainder of the act, which takes its sense of place from an imaginatively realized castle off stage.

The second scene opens with the quarrel and fight between Kent and Oswald; Cornwall and Regan appear; after further

---

[1] Charles Lamb, 'On Some of the Old Actors'; G. Wilson Knight, *The Wheel of Fire*. Lamb says later in the same essay: 'I confess that I never saw the catastrophe of this character, while Bensley played it, without a kind of tragic interest.'

exchanges, Kent is put in the stocks. The opening quarrel between the blunt 'plain' Kent and the time-serving Oswald is
very like that between Lafeu and Parolles (*All's Well that Ends
Well*, II. iii. 182–258), as Maynard Mack has observed.[1] With the
appearance of Cornwall and Regan, however, it develops into a
kind of judgement scene, with Cornwall as judge. The scene seems
intended as an example of unwarrantably harsh justice, as Gloucester's comment (153–4) makes clear. *King Lear* is of course
throughout concerned with justice, and there are other judgement or trial scenes elsewhere in the play. In this scene of Kent's
'trial' there are signs that *Henry VI, Part Two* furnished
some substantial hints. In its first and second acts there are two
trial scenes, in the second of which Duke Humphrey is involved
as judge. One of them is about the quarrel between 'Horner the
Armourer and his man Peter', the other about the impostors
Simpcox and his wife, who claim that Simpcox's sight has been
cured by a miracle. The second (II. i) is particularly relevant for
this scene of Kent's 'trial', since it has something of the same
harsh and coarse rural atmosphere, as well as a similar suggestion
of legalized cruelty. Simpcox claims to be lame, whereupon Duke
Humphrey sends for beadles with whips as a means of exposing
the imposture: 'Now, sirrah, if you mean to save yourself from
whipping, leap me over this stool and run away. . . . Well, sirrah,
we must have you find your legs. Sirrah beadle, whip him till he
leap over that same stool.' (II. i. 139–45.) After a stroke of the
whip Simpcox runs away. Queen Margaret's response is

> It made me laugh to see the villain run.
>
> (II. i. 151)

There is an unpleasantly sadistic quality in this scene which
recurs in Cornwall's trial of Kent. Again there is a woman
present who takes pleasure in the infliction of punishment:
Regan's rawly physical 'Put in his legs' (145) recalls Humphrey's
'we must have you find your legs', and her earlier remark, 'Till
noon! Till night, my lord; and all night too' (130) has something
of the gloating amusement of Margaret's speech just quoted.
Later in the play, in his scene on Dover Cliff, Lear is to speak of
the close association of lust and cruelty in the administration of
legal punishment.

[1] Maynard Mack, op. cit., pp. 54–5.

The action pauses to allow for the passing of night: Kent
sleeps; Edgar announces his plan of disguise; and then Lear
appears, accompanied by a Fool and a Gentleman. From here
until Lear's departure into the storm, the effect is one of accumu-
lating momentum. The long scene develops in careful stages:
Lear remonstrates with Kent on his shameful punishment, then
goes to demand an explanation; a brief interval lapses for the
Fool to taunt Kent; Lear returns with Gloucester, and finds the
Duke's refusal to speak with him impossible to credit; Cornwall
and Regan appear, fetched by Gloucester, and Lear begins his
ineffectual attempt to win Regan over to his side; the arrival of
Goneril and Oswald announces the final phase of the scene,
since all Lear's enemies are now ranged against him. He now
wanders from one daughter to the other, while they systematic-
ally reduce the number of his train, leaving him—breathtakingly
—with *nothing*. Lear's final response is as bewildered and confused
as it is throughout the scene: a mixture of abject entreaty, rage,
grief, fear; while Goneril, Regan, and Cornwall are left at the end
still speaking with their habitual fiercely demure restraint.

What marks the scene structurally is its increasingly tight control, which in the final phase becomes focused in the consciousness of the audience through the use of numbers: *hundred, fifty,
five and twenty, ten, five, one*. As it develops the scene acquires a
frightening ritualistic deliberateness, as if Lear were being ceremoniously baited, plucked of his feathers, stripped, ostracized.
And as always in this kind of prolonged set scene, the action
acquires rhythm through the use of repeated phrases, so that we
move through several carefully gradated series, each of which has
its precise quasi-musical rigour and, in performance, considerable
power to agitate. Lear's rising passion, for example, is signalized
by the emphatic and, as it goes on, obsessively random use of
iteration, such as 'Who put my man i' th' stocks?', 'Who stock'd
my servant?', 'How came my man i'th' stocks?' When at last
Cornwall condescends to answer him,

> I set him there, sir; but his own disorders
> Deserv'd much less advancement

Lear's only reply is the pathetic and ludicrous 'You! did you?',
upon which Regan cruelly spells out the reality of the situation:
'I pray you, father, being weak, seem so.' So this particular series

of repetitions—'Who put my man i'th' stocks?'—collapses in Lear's complete inability to do anything about it when he is given an answer. Regan next introduces the topic which is to carry the scene to its climax: the number of knights Lear is to be allowed to keep. The topic is well chosen since it allows of a descending arithmetical progress to a fixed terminus: nought. In dramatic terms the descending numbers symbolize the iron necessity against which Lear's will is to be broken, and when, with accelerating speed, we are carried through the final stages of the descent,

> *Goneril.*   Hear me, my lord:
> What need you five and twenty, ten, or five,
> To follow in a house where twice so many
> Have a command to tend you?
> *Regan.*   What need one?

there seems to be no possibility for Lear to do anything but what he does: after a final frenzied expostulation, take his leave of them for ever.

I have already suggested that this scene of Lear's baiting seems in some ways modelled on the scene in *2 Henry VI* (III. i) in which Duke Humphrey is similarly baited by his enemies. But in other respects a parallel is provided by the two scenes in *King John* which take place before the walls of Angiers and in the French camp (II. i, III. i). Both scenes form a long continuous sequence (except for one brief interruption), and since seven or eight important characters are on stage, they share with II. iv of *King Lear* some obvious features of duration in playing-time and massiveness of effect. These two scenes concern the policy-making—governed by considerations of 'Commodity'—of unprincipled potentates. Their chief victim is Constance, whose cause is betrayed by her champion the King of France when he agrees to marry the Dauphin to John's niece. Her helplessness and desperation make her role in these scenes correspond exactly to Lear's in this, and (as I have already suggested) some of Lear's speeches seem to be modelled closely on hers. But there is also one other small detail in the Angiers scenes which relates them to the present one. King John and King Philip have joined hands as a seal of their amity, when Pandulph the Papal Legate appears, denounces John, and orders Philip to 'Let go the hand of that arch-heretic' (III. i. 192). A conflict ensues in Philip's mind as to whether or not he

should obey; at length he does. The visual effect here of the prolonged holding of hands is a striking one. When, similarly, in the
present scene Goneril arrives, Regan takes her hand, an action
which Lear is quick to interpret:

> *Lear.* O Regan, will you take her by the hand?
> *Goneril.* Why not by th' hand, sir? How have I offended?
>
> (ii. iv. 193–4)

The expressive physical action may have been prompted by the
scene in *King John*.

We have already noted, following Kernodle, that the seven
scenes of Act Three form a composite movement, arranged
contrapuntally, on a descending scale for Lear, and an ascending
scale for Gloucester. One reason for this arrangement is that the
Cornwall and Gloucester scenes are made to provide structural
bracing for Lear's three scenes of rage and madness: brief though
they are, iii. iii and iii. v (Gloucester and Edmund; Cornwall and
Edmund) give the audience a respite from the heath scenes and
at the same time allow Shakespeare to articulate more clearly the
stages of Lear's distraction. They serve as 'containers' for the
heath scenes, which might easily become shapeless if they were
not kept short.

Kent's opening dialogue with the Gentleman (iii. i) acts as
prologue to the new movement and prepares us for the spectacle
of Lear 'Contending with the fretful elements'. (The second part
of this dialogue, about the growing division between the Dukes
and the arrival of the French 'power', is very clumsily inserted.)
As Lear sinks further into distraction and exhaustion, so his three
scenes become more elaborate in action. The first (iii. ii) is vir-
tually a monologue, interrupted by the Fool, and later by Kent.
The second (iii. iv) moves to the entrance of a hovel; its main
event is the discovery of Poor Tom, who adds to the hubbub of
voices. The third and last heath scene (vi) takes place inside the
hovel; its main action is Lear's 'arraignment' of Goneril and
Regan: he makes his accusation and, overcome, subsides into
sleep. These three scenes, particularly the second and third, are in
terms of form potentially deliquescent; they move sluggishly,
by fits and starts, under the eddying impulse of Lear's distracted
consciousness or Poor Tom's ravings. After the disciplined pur-
posiveness of the scene before Gloucester's castle they may, in

performance, seem flaccid. But a sense of direction and purpose is supplied by the Cornwall and Gloucester scenes, the first two of which are reduced to the utmost brevity, and which mount to a climax with the 'trial' and blinding of Gloucester. Cornwall, abetted by Regan, is all will and purpose; and, horrifying though the blinding scene is, its fast tempo—marked by the use of repetitions ('Wherefore to Dover?')—and even the violence of the atrocity itself may be felt to come almost as a relief.

The parallelism of the two plots in this act was probably derived, as I suggested earlier, from the first two acts of *As You Like It*, but is used here with a more obtrusive symmetry. *King John* is the other play which seems to have contributed most to the shaping of Act Three. Apart from the likeness of Constance's rhetoric to Lear's, there is a more intangible relationship between the general development of the two plays at this stage (that is, in their third acts). A stray verbal resemblance hints at a larger affinity: near the end of III. vi Gloucester urges Kent to remove the sleeping Lear from the danger of a 'plot of death':

> Good friend, I prithee, take him in thy arms . . .
> . . . Take up thy master . . . Take up, take up . . .
>
> (88–95)

The finest passage in *King John* is probably the speech spoken by the Bastard to Hubert over the body of Prince Arthur:

> Go, bear him in thy arms . . .
> I am amaz'd, methinks, and lose my way
> Among the thorns and dangers of this world.
> How easy dost thou take all England up!
>
> (IV. iii. 139–42)

(And later in this same speech the Bastard says: 'Now happy he whose cloak and cincture can / Hold out this tempest'—lines which have already been related to *King Lear* by John Danby.)[1] The act of lifting the unconscious king in one context probably recalled lifting the dead prince in the other. That this is probable rather than merely possible is borne out by the sequence of scenes at this point in *King Lear*: in the next scene (III. vi) Gloucester is blinded, while at a point roughly corresponding to it in *King John* (IV. i) occurs the scene of the intended blinding of Arthur.

---

[1] John F. Danby, *Shakespeare's Doctrine of Nature* (London, 1949), p. 68.

From the editorial point of view, the fourth act is made up of seven distinct scenes, with, as usual, the passages of climax being reserved for a position late in the act. The different structural principle which operates in the second movement of the play can be suggested by considering the implied time sequence. The second and third acts of *King Lear* are closely continuative: Kent is put in the stocks on one day and stays there during the following night; next day Lear arrives, goes out into the storm, and spends the following night in the hovel. In the fourth act, however, there is a good deal of travelling, of moving to and fro over unspecified distances, and this contributes to the lighter, less dense, effect which was referred to earlier. The dramatization is sometimes highly allusive and elliptical: for example, the growth in intimacy between Edmund and Goneril and Regan has to be inferred—it is something which has developed since the end of Act Three. The spare yet musical economy of the fourth act can be seen in the fact that Edmund makes only one appearance (IV. ii) in the company of Goneril and Oswald, and is given only half a line to speak ('Yours in the ranks of death', 25); yet at intervals throughout the act we are made aware of his rising fortunes, so that when, at the end of it, we are informed that he is 'conductor' of Cornwall's 'people' (IV. vii. 88) and so more or less the equal of Albany, it seems perfectly acceptable. He is within reach of absolute power by the beginning of the fifth act.

It no longer makes sense to speak of a 'double plot', since what we now have is essentially three distinct interests, all interacting at some point and all set within the larger action of the French invasion of Britain, but perceived as separate from each other within the dramatic sequence. In Act Four these three interests are taken in turn, not in a mechanically rotatory order, but with as much counterpointing as the relatively brief sequence will allow, and with the place of climax being reserved for the reunion of Lear and Cordelia. So the first scene resumes the Gloucester–Edgar action; the following scene (IV. ii) initiates the triangular Goneril–Edmund–Regan intrigue, with Oswald acting as go-between; next, Kent and a Gentleman (IV. iii) prepare for the re-entry of Cordelia into the play, since her reconciliation with Lear is to form the third action. These first three scenes can be taken as the first cycle. The second cycle takes the three interests in reverse order: Cordelia herself appears in the next scene (IV. iv),

Regan and Oswald in the scene following (IV. v), while Gloucester and Edgar complete the cycle by reappearing at the beginning of IV. vi for the scene of Gloucester's suicide attempt on
Dover Cliff. But this last scene initiates a longer connected sequence
of episodes, which constitutes the third cycle. In this way variety
and some degree of formal complexity make the whole sequence,
with its complicated and disparate materials, more easily receptible
in performance. At IV. vi Lear enters '*fantastically dressed with flowers*',
and his colloquy with Gloucester follows; shortly after Lear's
exit, Oswald appears, and the following rapidly taken business—
the fight with Edgar, Oswald's death, and the discovery of the
letter from Goneril to Edmund inviting him to murder Albany—
represents the other main interest in this act. In this long scene,
in fact, all three interests have been merged together, since
Gloucester and Edgar have been on stage continuously. The final
scene (vii) is given to Lear, Cordelia, and Kent. It is of course the
most emotionally charged and the most firmly shaped of the entire
act; it resolves tension, provides relief, and fittingly closes the
sequence.

This sequence of seven distinct scenes is a good example of
Shakespeare's habitual skill in finding different *occasions* on which
to mould each dramatized episode. We never get the impression
of a merely repetitive series; there is always an element of unpredictability in what comes next and the form in which it comes.
The profoundest 'occasion' is undoubtedly that of the last scene:
the reunion of Lear and Cordelia. It possibly derives its essential
form from the remote past of the English dramatic tradition. In
the early morality play *Mankind*, a dialogue occurs which momentarily foreshadows this of Lear and Cordelia:

> MERCY. A-ryse, my precyose redempt son! ye be to me full dere.
> he ys so tymerouse; me semyth hys vytall spryt doth expyre.
> MANKIND. Alasse! I have be so bestyally dysposyde, I dare not
> a-pere.
> To se yowur solaycyose face, I am not worthy to dysyer.
> MERCY. Yowur crymynose compleynt wondyth my hert as a
> lance . . .[1]

Cordelia, though Lear's youngest daughter, has something of
Mercy's maternal tenderness, while Lear's 'burning shame' which

---

[1] *Mankind*, ll. 804–8, in *The Macro Plays*, ed. F. J. Furnivall and Alfred Pollard
(E.E.T.S., London, 1904).

'Detains him from Cordelia' (IV. iii. 46–7) is not unlike Mankind's here ('I dare not a-pere. . . . I am not worthy').

The very general resemblance between this sequence and that in the fourth act of *3 Henry VI* has already been mentioned, as well as that between the meeting at Dover Cliff of Lear and Gloucester and the meeting of Orlando and Duke Senior in *As You Like It*. Two other small details may be added. Goneril's gift of a 'favour' to Edmund ('Wear this; spare speech. / Decline your head', IV. ii. 21–2) recalls the much more romantically innocent occasion when Rosalind gave Orlando a chain ('Gentleman, / Wear this for me', *As You Like It*, I. ii. 224–5). Secondly, Oswald's death at the hands (as he thinks) of a peasant resembles, in this respect, the death of the proud courtier Suffolk at the base hands of Walter Whiter the pirate (*2 Henry VI*, IV. i).

In editorial terms the fifth act consists of three scenes, but essentially it is one long intricate movement, a denouement significantly more like those of tragicomedy than of most of Shakespeare's other tragedies. The first scene is an adaptation of the usual exchange before battle; the keynote here is, as usual, division: there are two armies, and every character is in isolation from the others. Edmund's concluding soliloquy is discordantly flippant, more like something in the middle stages of a comedy than the last act of a tragedy. The battle remains entirely theoretical, as far as the drama is concerned; Edgar hurries Gloucester from the stage for the last time, and Lear and Cordelia enter as prisoners to Edmund. This last scene has been so often criticized for being (with the obvious exceptions of the moments when Lear is on stage) poorly written and overweighted with uninteresting and perfunctorily dramatized business that it needs to be looked at afresh and with a sympathetic open mind. It may be that it is in fact a serious lapse of art on Shakespeare's part.[1] But he may, on the other hand, be attempting something so unusual that it requires from the audience a correspondingly unusual degree of tolerance in its earlier stages if it is to make its effect.

However, before the structure of the last scene is described, it is first desirable to suggest an interpretation, in however general terms, of the action that has led up to it; only if we are in some such way prepared for it will the expressive force of the structural

[1] See H. A. Mason's partly adverse critique of the play, in *Cambridge Quarterly*, vol. 2 (1966–7), pp. 23–48, 148–66, and 212–35.

arrangement become apparent. At the beginning of the play Lear
handed over power to those who were unworthy of it. The folly
of this act—not only dividing the kingdom, but handing it over
to wickedly unprincipled rulers—is not explicitly condemned in
the text of the play, and for that reason many critics have ignored
the question of Lear's folly altogether or considered it irrelevant.
But contemporaries of Shakespeare would hardly have needed
prompting on this matter (to judge merely from the passages
from the *Henry VI* plays which I have already quoted), and it
seems on this occasion that Shakespeare has chosen to leave the
matter to speak for itself. A king was theoretically expected to
embody justice and to guarantee law and order; but what Lear
ensures is the reverse of this: he hands over the kingdom to the
rule of persons who despise law and whose chief concern is not
the welfare of the State but the satisfaction of their own appetites.
The play sees a reign not of justice but of justice's opposites,
arbitrariness and impulsiveness—since the workings of appetite
necessarily are anarchic, governed by capricious chance, not by
steady principle. This is what we are shown in the treatment Lear
receives from his daughters, in the stocking of Kent, the blinding
of Gloucester and the killing of the servant, the plots against the
lives of Lear and Gloucester, and the rival loves of Goneril and
Regan for Edmund. At the beginning of the last scene, Lear and
Cordelia enter as Edmund's prisoners: 'captive good attending
captain ill'. They form what is in effect a *tableau* (for Shakespeare
is careful to keep the other characters off stage until a later point
in the scene). A king and a queen are in the hands of a bastard—
that is what the *tableau* informs us. And it is at this point too that
Lear looks forward to a life in prison of privacy, peace, and
mutual love with his daughter. But Edmund has already determined—in his soliloquy of v. i—that he will not spare the lives of
Lear and Cordelia if they lose the battle, and Lear's words to
Cordelia are cut short: father and daughter are hurried to prison,
and Edmund gives orders for their killing. What we are shown,
then, in the *tableau* at the beginning of the scene is the Bastard at
the high point of his fortunes: unprincipled illegality in power.

   As soon as the other characters appear—Albany, Goneril, and
Regan—they start squabbling: first, over matters of precedence.
Then Albany accuses Edmund of treason; then the duel takes
place between Edmund and Edgar, and is followed by Edgar's

account of Gloucester's death, which moves Edmund; the death
of the sisters is announced; Kent appears, looking for Lear; and at
last, mention of the King arouses Albany:

> Great thing of us forgot!
> Speak Edmund, where's the King? and where's Cordelia?
>
> (236–7)

The embarrassing melodramatic scuffle to get Edmund's reprieve
to the prison in time is cut short by Lear's appearance; everything
was too late.

What is so painful, and what has seemed so offensive to so many
readers in the past, is the fact that Cordelia dies not only an unjust
death, but a death which is so ostentatiously accidental—it could
so easily have been averted. But the effect of painful suspense and
cruel disappointment, stressed by the narrowly unsuccessful
attempt to save her life, is one which is clearly worked out by
Shakespeare with some deliberateness. The effect is one of art, not
oversight or deficiency, and the artistic motivation behind it
must be sought not only in the shaping of this last scene, but in the
context given it by the play as a whole.

The immediate agent of Cordelia's death is of course Edmund,
who had given the orders for her execution. When Edgar relates
the circumstances of Gloucester's death, Edmund is emotionally
affected by it:

> This speech of yours hath mov'd me,
> And shall perchance do good . . .
>
> (199–200)

The qualification here—*perchance*—should not be overlooked;
and in fact Edmund does nothing further in the way of goodness
until the bodies of Goneril and Regan are produced, and he is
once again emotionally moved. But his tardy impulse does no
good; Cordelia is hanged. The painful element of chance in
Cordelia's death, therefore, is largely due to the moral nature of
Edmund, which seems capable only of unpredictable impulses of
humanity and benevolence, but is unsustained by principle. However, if Edmund was the immediate agent of Cordelia's death,
the person ultimately responsible for it must be judged to be Lear
himself. It is this that brings about the tough irony of the final
scene: that Lear, who had handed over his kingdom to a reign of
arbitrary impulse and blind chance, should lose, also through

impulse and chance, the person most dear to him. Certainly her death was unjust; but it was also, from one point of view, not inappropriately unjust; it was even justly unjust. Justice is an aesthetic as well as an ethical matter; and from the dramatic point of view the irruption of what seems to be mere chance into this crucial area of the drama must be finally comprehensible in artistic terms: the element of randomness must be under control, as it is here.

If this is accepted, the final scene becomes comprehensible as a means of dramatizing this idea. The long middle part of the scene (41–256), with the heterogeneous business of the other characters, serves an obvious function in tying up the loose ends of the plot; but in its manner of presentation—one thing leading on to another, in a whole concatenation of by-issues—it dramatizes the play's over-all tendency to disproportion, the tendency to run down, get lost in clogging detail. Lear and Cordelia are squeezed out— such is the impression we get—by the other characters. They are pushed aside and forgotten while subordinate issues take the centre, and only Kent, with his single-minded devotion to the King, jolts their attention to where it should have been all along. Moreover, the writing here is sometimes very oddly mannered, at times awkwardly or violently so:

> This would have seem'd a period
> To such as love not sorrow; but another,
> To amplify too much, would make much more,
> And top extremity.
> Whilst I was big in clamour . . .
>
> (204–8)

> O, is this he?
> The time will not allow the compliment
> Which very manners urges.   (232–4)

There is in much of it a kind of calculated perfunctoriness or triviality; everyone is frantically, or at least busily (even fussily), self-preoccupied; certainly Shakespeare is withholding something from the writing. With the appearance of Kent the whole solemn charade is exploded, but even here Albany—and, at this point, Edgar too—are touched by a hint of the absurdly ineffectual:

> *Albany.* Great thing of us forgot!
>   Speak, Edmund, where's the King? and where's Cordelia? . . .
>   Run, run, O, run!
> *Edgar.* To who, my lord?   (236–48)

But with Lear's re-entry, the full power of Shakespeare's language returns : a naked force and natural simplicity.

It may of course be objected that a scene which, even if deliberately, is so extensively concerned with material of the second order is seriously flawed; fault may be found with the fundamental conception. But it should at least not be dismissed as a dully incompetent winding-up scene with a fine beginning and a great ending; the entire formal conception has an expressive value which ought to be acknowledged. As I suggested earlier, the scene has a significant resemblance to such final scenes of multiple discovery as we get at the end of *Cymbeline*. Chance plays its part in both : fortunate chance in tragicomedy, unfortunate chance here. Kent, for example, has been hoping for a moment—of a kind which occurs in *Cymbeline*—when he can throw off his disguise and be formally recognized and reinstated by his king. But, as it happens, such a moment never comes : Lear is too confused and exhausted to play the role Kent so pathetically requires of him. As Albany says :

> He knows not what he says; and vain is it
> That we present us to him.
>
> (293–4)

Near the end of the scene, Albany's attempt to restore order in the way conventional at the close of plays is similarly frustrated by Lear's anguished death; so that the end of the entire scene is as far removed as possible from the note of joy sounded at the end of *Cymbeline*: the note here is one of unrelieved desolation. And yet the subdued echo of the joyously harmonious endings of romance, with all their reconciliations and pardons, remains to sharpen the bitterness of this close, so *in*harmonious and bleak.

No one has quarrelled with the magnificent conception of Lear's death itself. As earlier in the play, a powerful formative influence comes from *King John*; in this case the death of John himself (v. vii). In both scenes the King's death occurs as the aftermath of a battle in which a French invasion has been defeated. In both, the King's death has something of violence in it : John has been poisoned and is delirious, while Lear is beside himself with grief. Both lapse into unconsciousness, and their death is noted by bystanders. Moreover, Kent's role here is very similar to the Bastard's, whose phrase 'my faithful services' (v. vii. 104) is entirely applicable to Kent. Both men expect to die themselves and to follow their masters. In character Lear and John have nothing in common; in his capacity for passionate grief Lear is matched by Constance, not John, and her grief, like Lear's, is caused by the death of a beloved child. Formally, therefore, what we have in Lear's death scene is a reconfiguration of some of the most highly charged moments of *King John*: the grief of Constance, which came near the end of the first movement of the play, and the death of John, which concluded the second. It seems likely that the presence of a formal model for Lear's death scene in an earlier play helped to make possible its effect of unwavering economy and intensity. Shakespeare was improving on—surpassing—his own earlier self.

7. *Macbeth*

I

MACBETH is an exceptionally short play whose scenic forms are marked by an extreme economy. There are very few elaborate ensemble scenes; duologues abound, some of them of great tension; and in the first act the use of soliloquy and aside reaches its furthest point of development in Shakespeare's hands. In the early scenes we are probably on more intimate terms with Macbeth than we are with any other of Shakespeare's characters (not excluding Hamlet), and from the presentation of the hero the whole play takes its mood, one of profound inwardness. From the start Shakespeare locates the action in a region deep in our minds. The play opens with masterful abruptness, and so swift is the development of the following scenes that we are surprised into assuming an attitude of secret, perhaps unconscious, complicity with the hero which nothing later in the action can wholly destroy, not even the murder of Lady Macduff and her children. Any account of *Macbeth* which ignores this close relationship between audience and hero as it is established in a theatrical performance will inevitably distort the play's effect, particularly in the extraordinarily concentrated early scenes.

From the structural point of view, what is at once striking is the satisfying simplicity, the formal coherence, of the play as a whole; its elegance, one might be tempted to say, if the word did not suggest a concern somewhat incompatible with Shakespeare's gravity of mood in *Macbeth*. (There is in fact no such real incompatibility, but the notion of elegance has undeniable associations which work to trivialize the idea of finished artistic shaping.) Although a five-act structure is clearly discernible (and is marked out as such in the Folio text), what comes across more clearly in performance as well as in reading is a three-part division, in which Part One ('Duncan') occupies Acts One and Two, Part Two ('Banquo') Act Three, and Part Three ('Macduff') Acts Four and Five. The first and second of these three parts are followed by a marked pause, so that it is possible that they were designed with

196 MACBETH

an interval in mind. On the other hand, Act Three forms a fairly short unit in itself, so that it may be that in performance a short pause divided the Duncan and Banquo actions, while a full interval followed Act Three, thus allowing the play to conform to the two-part structure postulated in Chapter 3. This suggestion is supported by the placing of the appearances of the Weird Sisters. If the Hecate scene (III. v) is omitted as a later, though Shakespearian, addition, they appear in the first and third scenes of Act One and the first scene of Act Four.[1] They therefore open both main parts of the play, and if an interval were to follow the third act, this essential structural arrangement could be made clear to the audience. For the opening of Act Four has an inevitable recapitulatory effect, taking us back to the beginning of the play with its similar witchcraft concerns; and in these parallel openings of the two main parts a design is revealed comparable with the 'structural rhyming' of *Julius Caesar* and *Hamlet*, but with like beginnings as opposed to their like endings.

Despite its clear outlines and its austerely ordered coherence, the scenic forms of *Macbeth* are often subtle and even intricate. Perhaps more than for any other play of Shakespeare's a structural account will resolve itself into a detailed textual commentary: so much of the action is located in the verbal detail of the individual speeches. The fourth scene of the first act, for example, is on the face of it a rudimentary scenic occasion: Duncan hears from Malcolm how Cawdor met his execution; then he welcomes his two victorious generals, Macbeth and Banquo; he goes on to announce that Malcolm is his heir; and finally the King's party leaves for Macbeth's castle at Inverness. Macbeth has only three speeches, but the third is an aside which expresses his dismay at hearing Malcolm proclaimed the heir apparent. This speech, with its treacherous and already murderous thoughts, clarifies the ambiguities of tone and sequence earlier in the scene: the juxtaposition of the former Cawdor's execution and the present Cawdor's welcome, and the framing of Macbeth's arrival and departure with Duncan's words of innocent trust: 'There's no art / To find the mind's construction in the face' and 'It is a peerless

---

[1] I accept J. M. Nosworthy's arguments for the authenticity of the Hecate passages; see *Shakespeare's Occasional Plays* (London, 1965), pp. 25–33. He suggests that they were added by Shakespeare some years after the play's first performance. I have omitted them from my account, since even if they are Shakespeare's, they remain (it seems to me) regrettable excrescences.

kinsman'. It also makes clear that for Macbeth the scene is one of abrupt reversal: his decision, made during the previous scene, to wait passively upon events, has already been shaken by Duncan's announcement; he now leaves Duncan resolved, at any rate temporarily, to take events into his own hands. The scene shows, then, the superimposition of Macbeth's subjective responses on to a public occasion otherwise apparently straightforward; the result is a dramatic and poetic dialogue of considerable local complexity and with an intricate counterpointed rhythm. Yet the scene itself, like all those in *Macbeth* with the exception of that in England (IV. iii), is compressed to the utmost degree. The entire dialogue occupies only fifty-eight lines; eleven speeches are distributed between four speakers (six to Duncan, three to Macbeth, and one each to Malcolm and Banquo) in such a way that in each exchange Duncan is one of the interlocutors. A sense of orderliness and measure is thus felt to be precariously holding its own against the violently anarchic impulses ('my black and deep desires', 51) given secret expression in Macbeth's final speech. The scene is characteristic of the play: as a structural device in itself it does not solicit attention; emphasis falls instead on the potently charged individual utterance.

An analogy may be drawn from music. The term 'chamber music' implies no limitation of scope or stature; and *Macbeth* could be called something analogous so long as the term suggested intense concision rather than smallness of scale or narrowness of scope. It is perhaps the first of those late plays of Shakespeare which seem to succeed best in a small theatre with an intimately placed audience. (*Antony and Cleopatra*, so unlike it in other respects, is like it in this.) In its dramatic mode *Macbeth* obviously lacks the clear or even obtrusive symmetries and the robust rhetorical schemes of the earlier history plays. Its patterning is more often discreetly unassertive, delicate but none the less firm. Some of its finest effects are daringly elliptical, in keeping with the rapid, allusive, above all imaginative character of the play's verbal style. A good example is the hospitality Duncan receives at Inverness, which is dramatized in two scenes. In the first (I. vi), a scene of only thirty-one lines, Lady Macbeth welcomes Duncan. Macbeth is not present, as Duncan notices ('Where's the Thane of Cawdor?', 20); he is kept off stage by Shakespeare probably because he opens the next scene, but also perhaps to keep this encounter as pointedly brief and as uncluttered as possible. The next scene opens with a dumbshow: '*Enter a* Sewer, *and divers* Servants *with dishes and service over the stage*'. This is all we see of the feast in which Duncan is entertained. Macbeth enters to soliloquize: the host is absent from his own feast—he is visibly derogating from his duty. We never see Duncan again. A similar concern for economy marks the dramatist's selection of incidents or occasions for dramatization. Una Ellis-Fermor has some good comments on this matter: the reason why Shakespeare selected certain incidents for dramatization and not other possible ones. The art of the dramatist, she suggests, is engaged in 'selecting those fragments of the whole that stimulate our imaginations to an understanding of the essential experience':

> It would seem that the imagination of audience or reader is thrown forward, by the immense impact of such scenes, upon a track of emotional experience, to come to rest upon the next scene, at the moment in its curving flight at which it can alight without interference or loss of momentum, to be projected again upon another movement, there to be similarly received, diverted, and flung out again upon its track of discovery.[1]

The amount which Shakespeare takes for granted, the great gaps between the scenes which we are obliged to leap (and whose contents we are forced to supply), are the most obvious reason for our sense that, by the end of the play, we have travelled a distance almost incredibly incommensurate with the brevity of the text as performed or read.

II

Shakespeare's use of his main narrative source, Holinshed, has often been studied. Here it is necessary only to recall that he adhered reasonably faithfully to Holinshed's account of Macbeth's murder of Duncan and the subsequent events of Macbeth's reign, suppressing only the fact that for ten years Macbeth ruled so justly that 'he might well haue been numbered amongest the most noble princes that anie where had reigned'.[2] Particularly close to Holinshed is the scene set in England (IV. iii) in which Malcolm tests the loyalty of Macduff. For the circumstances of Duncan's murder

---

[1] Una Ellis-Fermor, *Shakespeare the Dramatist* (London, 1961), p. 95.
[2] *Shakespeare's Holinshed*, ed. W. G. Boswell-Stone (London, 1907), p. 32.

Shakespeare used Holinshed's separate account of Donwald's murder of Duff. Elsewhere in one important detail Shakespeare departs from Holinshed in making Macduff flee to England before his wife and children are murdered; in Holinshed the murders are committed before he leaves Scotland, and his purpose in going to England is 'to reuenge the slaughter so cruellie executed on his wife, his children, and other friends'.

From Holinshed, then, Shakespeare took most of the narrative material, the incidents and circumstances which make up the story of Macbeth as we know it. What he did not find in Holinshed was any indication how to shape this narrative material for the stage. Any reader going to Holinshed from Shakespeare's play will be struck by the gulf between them in form. Holinshed's account is shapeless chronicle matter which, apart from the conversation between Malcolm and Macduff which supplied material for the first part of IV. iii of *Macbeth*, contains little or nothing suggestive of dramatic form.

How did Shakespeare convert Holinshed's narrative into the play as we have it? Any explanation must of course be partial and conjectural; but it would seem that in part at any rate the process resembled that which I have already postulated for *Julius Caesar*. *Macbeth*, like *Julius Caesar*, seems to have derived its basic form—together with a great deal else—from the earlier history plays. It has long been recognized that Shakespeare's Richard III and Macbeth have a good deal in common—at least, in external circumstances, if not in their inner natures. Both are men who murder their way to a throne; both become tyrants, oppressed by guilty dreams, and both end on a battle-field, friendless and universally execrated. Both, in short, are versions of the Renaissance type of the Tyrant. It has also been noticed that the play *Macbeth* has a good deal structurally in common with *Richard III*; the relation between the two has been examined in detail by F. M. Smith.[1] Parallels in incident and phrase are particularly numerous between the last three acts of *Macbeth* and the last two acts of *Richard III*—that is to say, from the point when both men have achieved the throne. So, for example, Smith notes that III. i of *Macbeth*, in which the new king first speaks to Banquo about the surviving sons of the dead king and later in the scene instructs

[1] F. M. Smith, 'The Relation of "Macbeth" to "Richard the Third" ', *P.M.L.A.* 60 (1945), 1003–20.

8120125   O

two murderers, is close in sequence to iv. ii of the earlier play, in which Richard, seen here as king for the first time, speaks to Buckingham about the surviving sons of the dead king and later arranges with Tyrrel to have them murdered. Many of Smith's detailed parallels are convincing, but he has not in fact exposed the fundamental structural design which Shakespeare adapted for *Macbeth*, and he failed to do so because he mistakenly thought that the correspondences between Macbeth and Richard could be traced only from a point after the deaths of the kings who preceded them (Edward IV, Duncan).

As we have seen, *Julius Caesar* was probably formed on the fundamental model of *2 Henry VI*. In the case of *Macbeth*, however, the fundamental model was not a single play but one play and part of another. It was, I suggest, modelled very freely on the career of Richard Gloucester as it was presented in *Henry VI, Part Three* (or the second half of it) and in *Richard III*. All the differences in circumstances between Richard and Macbeth may be taken for granted; what they have in common is their three main crimes, each involving murder. Richard first murders Henry VI in the Tower (*3 Henry VI*, v. vi). His second victim is his brother Clarence: he hires two killers who drown him in a butt of Malmsey (*Richard III*, i. iv). His third major crime is the murder of the Princes in the Tower; Tyrrel is paid to supervise this (iv. ii, iii). Macbeth's crimes follow an exactly similar sequence and pattern. He first murders a king, killing him with his own hands just as Richard had personally killed Henry VI. (It should be noted that in this respect Shakespeare departs from Holinshed's account of Donwald's murder of King Duff: Donwald orders four of his servants to do the deed—he does not personally kill the king.) Macbeth next hires two killers (they are later joined by a third) to kill Banquo. He lastly hires more killers to murder Lady Macduff and her family. Without pressing the similarities too hard, one may find correspondences in each play between the victims and the nature of each of the crimes. Thus the first victim in each case is a king, even a holy king: the piety and virtue of both Henry VI and Duncan are insisted on, and their murder has something especially horrific and even sacrilegious about it. (In Holinshed, Duncan is less admirable than he is in Shakespeare: he is 'so soft and gentle of nature', he had 'too much of clemencie', and the rebel Makdowald calls him 'a faint-hearted milkesop,

more meet to gouerne a sort of idle moonks in some cloister, than
to haue the rule of such valiant and hardie men of warre as the
Scots were'.[1] Each of these phrases might have reminded Shakespeare of his own Henry VI.) The second victim (Clarence,
Banquo) is a brother or colleague of the murderer. In each case
the murderer hires someone else to do the deed (two killers are
involved in both), and both murders have a strong element of the
physically atrocious: Clarence is horribly drowned in wine, while
Banquo is left in a ditch, his throat cut, and 'twenty trenched
gashes on his head'. Finally, the third crime (or group of crimes)
in each case concerns children, so that the terror is modified by
pathos. The dialogue between Lady Macduff and her son has no
exact equivalent in *Richard III*, but Tyrrel's description of the
murder of the Princes (iv. iii. 1–22) has a comparable effect of
arousing pity and indignation. These last crimes are in both plays
the immediate prelude to a turn in the tyrant's fortunes: just after
Richard hears that the Princes are dead he receives news that
Morton has fled to Richmond and that Buckingham is in the field
with a hostile army. Similarly, in the scene following that of the
murder of Macduff's family we are shown Malcolm and Macduff
in England preparing to march against Macbeth.

One small common feature between Richard and Macbeth may
be mentioned, since it has apparently not been noticed. After the
battle of Towton, Edward creates his brother Richard Duke of
Gloucester. Richard asks to be given the title of Clarence instead:
'For Gloucester's dukedom is too ominous' (*3 Henry VI*, ii. vi.
107). In the second scene of *Macbeth* Duncan condemns the traitor
Cawdor to death and gives his title to Macbeth, a similarly
'ominous' transference, as the ironical juxtaposition in this scene
makes clear.

Of course in saying that the career of Richard Gloucester furnished Shakespeare with the basic form of *Macbeth*, we are leaving
a good deal of the play unaccounted for. Shakespeare undoubtedly
drew upon several other earlier works as well. But the fact that
he could find to hand, in the Richard Gloucester plays, a scenario
adaptable to very different purposes, is very suggestive. For it
seems possible that the severe coherence, the 'elegance', of *Macbeth*, is in part due to the fact that it is in the nature of a second try,
a refinement on an earlier attempt. This is not to deny the earlier

[1] Boswell-Stone, op. cit., pp. 18–20.

play its own measure of success. But *Richard* III is probably greater in the part than in the whole: for all the brilliance and exuberance of individual scenes (and the play shows a quite formidable dramatic inventiveness), as a whole it does not achieve any profound unity; it lacks the unwavering control of *Macbeth*. In everything, *Macbeth* is more clear and economical. One way, for example, in which *Macbeth* improves on *Richard III* is in its more logical development of plot. In *Richard III*, Richard's supplanter, Richmond, has no close involvement with any of Richard's victims; he is simply an outsider, who for no clear reason has been providentially chosen to rid the country of a tyrant and rule in his stead. Macduff, on the other hand, stands in the closest possible relation to the last and most helpless victims of Macbeth, and it is fitting that it should be he who personally deprives Macbeth of his life. Malcolm, the figure corresponding to Richmond, plays an altogether more subordinate role. Nevertheless the contribution of *Richard III* to Shakespeare's achievement in *Macbeth* was crucial; more than any other external factor (as far as one can see) it facilitated the transformation of Holinshed's chronicle material into the tragedy as we know it.

But like all the great tragedies, *Macbeth* derives its shape and substance from a number of earlier works, not one alone. *Henry VI, Part Two* has several interesting affinities with *Macbeth*.[1] Duke Humphrey's ambitious wife Eleanor foreshadows Lady Macbeth, and she has dealings with witches. The spirit-raising scene (I. iv) is a clear precursor of the more elaborately spectacular scene of the witches' cavern (*Macbeth*, IV. i). Cardinal Beaufort on his death-bed talks deliriously in his sleep (III. iii), and so anticipates Lady Macbeth betraying her secrets in her sleep-walking scene. Macbeth's reference, in his second soliloquy spoken just before the murder of Duncan, to 'Tarquin's ravishing strides' (II. i. 55) is the clearest sign that *The Rape of Lucrece* also has an intimate affinity to *Macbeth*. M. C. Bradbrook has noted that the deliberations of Tarquin before the rape come extremely close to Macbeth's self-communings before the murder of Duncan. She remarks of both men that 'they commit a violence upon themselves from which they cannot recover', and in the poem's expression of the 'identity between violence and self-violence' she finds the

[1] See G. Wilson Knight, 'The Second Part of "King Henry VI" and "Macbeth" ' (1927), reprinted in *The Sovereign Flower*; F. M. Smith, op. cit., pp. 1012–14.

'central idea, the germ of the play'.[1] It is certainly true that the passage describing Tarquin's guiltily perplexed thoughts before committing himself to the crime (127–54) anticipates the subjective world of Macbeth's early soliloquies more clearly than anything else written before them. Yet the influence of *The Rape of Lucrece* is of course modified by others, working concurrently; it is only one among several.

We have already seen, in previous chapters, that *King John* played its part in the making of *Hamlet* and *King Lear*. Its importance for *Macbeth* is no less clearly demonstrable. One area of the play is particularly relevant: those scenes which concern John's suborning of the murder of Arthur, in III. iii and IV. ii. In the first (III. iii. 19–66), John broaches the idea of the murder with Hubert, but tries to do so in such a way as to make it seem that the idea has occurred independently in Hubert's own mind; John wants to escape the responsibility of actually engaging a murderer. The crucial lines are these:

> Or if that thou couldst see me without eyes,
> Hear me without thine ears, and make reply
> Without a tongue, using conceit alone,
> Without eyes, ears, and harmful sound of words . . .
>
> (48–51)

But Hubert does not understand, and John is forced to be explicit:

> *King John.* Death.
> *Hubert.* My Lord?
> *King John.*   A grave.
> *Hubert.*   He shall not live.
>
> (65)

In the later scene, when John believes Arthur dead, he turns on Hubert in an attempt to escape the responsibility of the crime which he had himself ordered:

> Hadst thou but shook thy head or made a pause,
> When I spake darkly what I purposed,
> Or turn'd an eye of doubt upon my face,
> As bid me tell my tale in express words,
> Deep shame had struck me dumb, made me break off.
> And those thy fears might have wrought fears in me.
>
> (IV. ii. 231–6)

[1] M. C. Bradbrook, 'The Sources of "Macbeth" ', *Shakespeare Survey*, vol, 4 (1951).

Johnson has an admirable comment on these lines:

This account of the timidity of guilt is drawn *ab ipsis recessibus mentis,*
from an intimate knowledge of mankind, particularly that line in which
he says, that *to have bid him tell his tale in express words,* would have
struck him dumb; nothing is more certain, than that bad men use all the
arts of fallacy upon themselves, palliate their actions to their own minds
by gentle terms, and hide themselves from their own detection in
ambiguities and subterfuges.[1]

What Johnson says here of King John is clearly relevant to
Macbeth and his wife, whose use of euphemism, obliquity, heroic
diction, and so on helps to conceal 'from their own detection'
what they are really doing in murdering Duncan. No single scene
in *Macbeth* is closely modelled on any in *King John*; the indebtedness is more a matter of the conception of the subjective process
which leads Macbeth to his crime, but this in itself undoubtedly
affects the shaping of some of the early scenes.[2]

The earliest of the mature tragedies, *Julius Caesar,* is important
for *Macbeth* in a different way. The presentation of the introspective Brutus, particularly in the orchard scene (II. i), has often
been compared with Macbeth's early scenes.[3] But the affinities
between the two plays go deeper than these isolated points of
resemblance would suggest: as so often, specific parallels such as
can be demonstrated verbally are only the tip of an iceberg; larger
affinities may not declare themselves at first sight. The general
development and shape of *Julius Caesar* can be indicated by listing
such topics as conspiracy, murder, retribution; and this sequence
is clearly recalled in *Macbeth*. In *Julius Caesar* the conspiracy stage,
with its self-deceiving euphemisms, comes especially close to
Macbeth, but is more diffusely treated and less intensely felt. But
of perhaps greater significance is the emotional alignment of
Julius Caesar, the way in which Shakespeare manipulates, or
guides, the feelings of the audience. Brutus is at first presented in
such a way as to arouse sympathy, although one is conscious of
something like a cool reserve in Shakespeare's portrayal of him.
In the scenes leading up to and including the assassination and in

---

[1] *Johnson on Shakespeare,* ed. Walter Raleigh (1908), p. 109.
[2] See M. M. Badawi, 'Euphemism and Circumlocution in "Macbeth" ', *Cairo
Studies in English* (1960).
[3] See especially G. Wilson Knight, 'Brutus and Macbeth', in *The Wheel of
Fire.*

the subsequent Forum scene Brutus recedes further from our sympathy, and until the quarrel scene (iv. iii) our feelings seem bafflingly alienated by all the main characters, both conspirators and their opponents. It is only with the reconciliation after the quarrel, when Brutus and Cassius re-pledge their friendship and drink wine together, that our feelings are fully engaged by the simple expression of natural feeling, and from this point to the end of the play we are emotionally committed to Brutus and Cassius in a way in which previously we had been committed to no one. The moments of deepest feeling in *Julius Caesar* come late (all in the last two acts): the drinking of wine, and later in the same scene in Brutus' tent the episode with the boy Lucius, just before the appearance of the Ghost, the final leave-taking of Brutus and Cassius before the battle, and their deaths. Something of this movement of feeling—the withholding of full sympathy while the hero enjoys a form of prosperity (even though in crime), followed by the enlistment of sympathy for him in defeat (it probably owes something to the simpler version in *Richard II*)—is adapted, and greatly improved, in *Macbeth*. It is this movement of feeling which is conflated with the basic scenario provided by the Richard Gloucester plays (and which has no counterpart in *The Rape of Lucrece*), so that it was—we may conjecture—in large part the experience of writing *Julius Caesar* that prompted the decisive change in emotional alignment. Macbeth has Richard Gloucester's capacity for violent crime (but nothing of his heartless gusto) as well as Brutus' introspection, while transcending both in the vehemence and intensity of his moral imagination. What he 'does' is comparable to what Richard 'does'; what he 'is' is more like what Brutus 'is' (and, we may add, Tarquin).

No doubt still other plays contributed qualities to *Macbeth* in ways that are hardly determinable. *Macbeth* would probably not be what it is if it had been written before *Hamlet*, which takes Shakespeare's introspective mode further than anything else to that date. The gradual isolation of Macbeth from his wife, which is so powerfully yet reticently suggested, perhaps owes something to the relationship of Claudius and Gertrude, although examples of husbands who fail to take their wives into their confidence (Hotspur and his wife, Brutus and Portia) had occurred earlier. And of course Shakespeare was further indebted to writings other than his own: the debt to Seneca, for example, is more evident than in any other of the mature tragedies.[1]

III

In this section I shall make a selective commentary on the scenic forms of *Macbeth*. The three main actions already distinguished ('Duncan', 'Banquo', and 'Macduff') each have their own structure and their own peculiar alignment to the audience. In each of them Shakespeare arouses expectation and suspense in a way appropriate to its position in the play as a whole.

Although the first two acts, comprising the 'Duncan' action, contain eleven distinct scenes in all (and we can, if we wish, distinguish two stages corresponding to the first and second acts of the Folio text), the entire action is conceived as a single movement, which clearly needs to be acted without a break. These scenes are primarily concerned with Macbeth's growing decision to murder Duncan, the crime itself, and the discovery of the king's death.

How does Shakespeare engage the feelings of the audience? In her book, *Feeling and Form*, Susanne Langer devotes a chapter to 'The Dramatic Illusion'. She suggests that the 'dramatic mode' is peculiarly concerned with what she calls the 'virtual future', with what the immediate future is about to bring into the present:

It has been said repeatedly that the theater creates a perpetual present moment; but it is only a present filled with its own future that is really dramatic. . . . As literature creates a virtual past, drama creates a virtual future. The literary mode is the mode of Memory; the dramatic is the mode of Destiny.[2]

In formulating this, Mrs. Langer is discussing drama as an art form, drama in general. But in the case of *Macbeth*, at any rate in this first part of the play, the 'virtual future' is not only the mode of the dramatic genre to which *Macbeth* belongs: it is also its *subject*. In these early scenes *Macbeth* is 'about' the immediate future: Macbeth is morbidly or wickedly fascinated by it, and so falls into temptation.

The opening scenes derive some of their impetus from the formal numerical scheme of the Weird Sisters' salutation: *Glamis*,

[1] See Inga-Stina Ewbank, 'The Fiend-like Queen: A Note on "Macbeth" and Seneca's "Medea"', *Shakespeare Survey*, vol. 19 (1966).
[2] Susanne K. Langer, *Feeling and Form*, p. 307.

Cawdor, King. One, two, and—will it be three? The thought, unspoken in Macbeth's mind, is also present in ours. His own suspense, his unbearably keen interest in the 'future', is analogous to ours—hence the unrivalled sense of complicity which *Macbeth* generates in an audience. The *Glamis–Cawdor–King* scheme, once it has been ceremoniously announced by the Weird Sisters in I. iii, is repeatedly echoed in the following scenes: four times in this same scene (I. iii. 71–5, 86–7, 116–17, 119–122), twice in I. v, the scene in which Lady Macbeth first appears and welcomes her husband home (7–12, 51–2):

> Great Glamis! Worthy Cawdor!
> Greater than both, by the all-hail hereafter!

once again, after the murder, at II. ii. 42–3, and finally, in reversed order, in Banquo's soliloquy:

> Thou hast it now—King, Cawdor, Glamis, all
> As the weird women promis'd . . .
>
> (III. i. 1–2)

In the earlier scenes this pattern of an unfinished triad has an irresistible power: it agitates the nerves like an unfinished sentence, and has the effect of making not only Macbeth but ourselves long to complete it. In these scenes, we feel perhaps, in at least part of our minds, such intimate partakers of Macbeth's experience—our sense of complicity (even if largely unconscious) is so strong—that we find it impossible to want him *not* to murder Duncan—the whole movement of the play at this stage seems to cry out for it. There is certainly some truth in the remark that 'we hold our breath in fear lest he should not accomplish the murder. We are all on Macbeth's side . . .'.[1] Another way of putting it is to say that the 'supernatural soliciting' is also a dramaturgical one. This must be one of the reasons why Macbeth is so improbably sympathetic in these early scenes: he wins our allegiance in defiance of all moral scruples largely because his criminal desires are (so to speak) so powerfully reinforced by the dramatic medium. Similarly, when in I. vii, after his great soliloquy, he decides to 'proceed no further in this business', Lady Macbeth replies with three powerful speeches ('Was the hope drunk . . .?', 'What beast was't then . . .'?, 'We fail! . . .'), each of which effectually silences Macbeth or

---

[1] Gilbert Norwood, *Euripides and Shaw* (London, 1921), p. 188.

meets with only feeble rejoinders. (In the first two, she appeals to the recent past; in the third, with an effect of climactic force, she turns to the immediate future.) At this point, although she is counselling treachery and murder, the unscrupulous energy of her speeches comes as such relief to the state of painful tension which we share with Macbeth that, again, in one part of our minds we must welcome her intrusion, egg her on in the task of quashing his scruples, and feel, with him, nothing but a kind of helpless satisfaction in his decision, even though the decision is to proceed with an act against which all his moral feelings protest.

Seen from this point of view, the action from I. iii to I. vii consists of Macbeth's vacillating progress towards the act of murder, a progress marked by increasingly violent fluctuations of will, the climax coming in the final scene of Act One, with, first, his decision *not* to proceed, and then, his submission to his wife's coercion.

The earlier scenes of Act One do not derive structurally from *Richard III*, or *2 Henry VI*, or *The Rape of Lucrece*. The main structural influence here—in I. ii, I. iv, and I. v (and, possibly, in a more indirect form, in I. i and I. iii as well)—is *Henry IV, Part One*. In I. ii the bleeding Sergeant gives Duncan the news of the two military actions which have just been fought: one against the 'kerns and gallowglasses' of the Western Isles, the other against the army from Norway. The Sergeant leaves the issue of the second engagement doubtful; Ross arrives to complete the story, with the news of Macbeth's victory. This very compressed scene seems modelled on the opening scene of *1 Henry IV*. In that scene the King is told by Westmoreland of the Welsh engagement; Westmoreland goes on to speak of a second engagement fought in the north between the Percys and the Scots, but is unable to say how it ended. The King replies that he has already been informed by Blunt: the Scots have been defeated by Hotspur, the 'theme of honour's tongue' (81). Several elements here were carried over into I. ii of *Macbeth*. If Henry IV's long prologue-like opening speech is omitted as irrelevant, both scenes centre on messenger speeches; in both cases *two* military actions are the subject, of which one is associated with the west (Wales, Western Isles), the other with the north (Scotland, Norway); and in each case the conclusion of the second action is left briefly in suspense until disclosed by another speaker. The hero of the day (Hotspur,

Macbeth) turns out later in the play to be a rebel or traitor himself. Moreover the style of the messenger speeches in both scenes has an obviously 'heroic' cast; indeed Westmoreland, like the bleeding Sergeant, has an incomplete line (on the Virgilian pattern). There are further slighter details in common: some of the Scottish names mentioned by Henry (Angus and Menteith, 73) reappear in *Macbeth*; and the word 'broil' is used in both scenes: 'the tidings of this broil' (*1 Henry IV*, I. i. 47), 'the knowledge of the broil' (*Macbeth*, I. ii. 6). It has sometimes been doubted whether this scene in *Macbeth* is by Shakespeare; but the fact that it is closely modelled on an earlier and undoubtedly genuine Shakespearian scene is clearly in favour of its authenticity (which is, in any case, nowadays widely accepted).

If the Falstaff scenes are left aside as irrelevant, the sequence in *1 Henry IV* from I. i to II. iii is followed, very freely, in *Macbeth*. The second court scene of *1 Henry IV* (I. iii) shows the King's reception of the warrior hero Hotspur, but also the first stages of Hotspur's rebellion, with his uncle Worcester as tempter. The corresponding scene in *Macbeth* is I. iv, in which Duncan receives Macbeth, also a warrior hero, but by proclaiming Malcolm the heir apparent provokes Macbeth to indulge further his murderous thoughts. This scene is very different in circumstance from I. iii of *1 Henry IV*; but its essential 'occasion' is comparable. The next Hotspur scene (II. iii) shows Hotspur entering reading a letter about the conspiracy; he soliloquizes, and is then joined by his wife.[1] In the following scene in *Macbeth* (I. v), Lady Macbeth enters reading a letter which describes her husband's encounter with the Weird Sisters; she soliloquizes, and is then joined by her husband. No other scene in Shakespeare opens with a character reading a letter in this way; it seems clear that *1 Henry IV* is still being used as a structural guide, although after this scene its influence apparently ceases.

In this opening sequence, two scenes have not been accounted for: I. i and I. iii. The Weird Sisters appear in both, first for their brief rhyming incantation, and then for their encounter with Macbeth and Banquo. For all its apparent simplicity the first

---

[1] Shakespeare may have taken the idea for Hotspur's entry with a letter from Marlowe's *Edward II*, a play with thematic and verbal links with *1 Henry IV*. Marlowe opens the play boldly with '*Enter Gaveston reading on a letter that was brought him from the King*'. Cf. also Barabas's two entries with a letter at III. iv and IV. iii of *The Jew of Malta*.

scene is an artful construction. The Weird Sisters speak singly in
turn three times before chanting the final couplet in unison. But
the 'rounds' or cycles are progressively diminished, so that the first
one fills five lines, the second two lines, and the third one line. The
scene therefore has a kind of wedge shape, diminishing purposefully to a point. The effect is one of bewildering power contained
within the narrowest possible compass.

This opening scene and i. iii clearly take place during and immediately after the battle in which Macbeth and Banquo defeat
the rebels; the Second Witch makes the occasion of the second
scene clear:

> When the hurlyburly's done,
> When the battle's lost and won.

> (i. i. 3–4)

For this scene of the Witches' encounter with the two victorious
generals, Shakespeare took something from the fifth act of
1 Henry IV, which presents the battle of Shrewsbury: a fight
between the King's supporters and a rebel army, just as is this
battle in *Macbeth*. In order to protect King Henry IV, several of
his supporters have disguised themselves as the King. At the
opening of v. iii the following exchange takes place between the
King's supporter Sir Walter Blunt and the Scottish ally of the
rebels, Douglas:

> *Blunt.* What is thy name that in the battle thus
>   Thou crossest me? What honour dost thou seek
>   Upon my head?
> *Douglas.*   Know, then, my name is Douglas;
>   And I do haunt thee in the battle thus
>   Because some tell me that thou art a king.

> (1–5)

They fight, and Douglas kills Blunt. Hotspur enters, and Douglas
announces: 'All's done, all's won; here breathless lies the King.'
Hotspur quickly undeceives him, since he has had no difficulty
in recognizing Blunt. Angrily Douglas addresses the corpse:

> A fool go with thy soul whither it goes!
> A borrowed title hast thou bought too dear;
> Why didst thou tell me that thou wert a king?

> (22–4)

This curious incident is obviously not very close to the Witches' encounter with Macbeth and Banquo, but something of it seems to have been recalled by Shakespeare and fused with Holinshed's narrative so as to produce the scene as we have it. There is something ceremoniously formal, and even perhaps a little eerie, about the encounter of Blunt and Douglas. The formality is there in the repetition of the phrase 'in the battle thus', while Douglas's use of the word 'haunt', though not necessarily sinister, has supernatural connotations. The imitation king is then killed: 'A borrowed title hast thou bought too dear'—for dressing in the King's 'coat' he pays with his life. Coming from the battle, Macbeth and Banquo are confronted by the Weird Sisters; the encounter is certainly formal and alarming. When, later in the scene, Ross addresses Macbeth as 'Thane of Cawdor', Macbeth replies:

> The Thane of Cawdor lives. Why do you dress me
> In borrowed robes?
>
> (I. iii. 108–9)

The likeness of the remark to Douglas's 'A borrowed title . . .' is clear; and Blunt was literally, it could be said, 'in borrowed robes'. Of course too much cannot be made of the parallel details, but even so Douglas's rhyme 'All's done, all's won' seems recalled in the Weird Sisters' first scene (the rhyme words are identical), and also, a stray detail, the word 'hurlyburly' (I. i. 3) occurs nowhere else in Shakespeare but in *1 Henry IV*: 'hurlyburly innovation' (v. i. 78), a phrase applied to the rebellion which is crushed at Shrewsbury.

The brief scene of Duncan's arrival at Inverness and his welcome by Lady Macbeth (I. vi) possibly recalls, in a very general way, the scene in Seneca's *Thyestes* in which Thyestes and his children are received by Atreus. The essentials of the situation—a host, with murderous intentions, hypocritically welcomes his victims to his home—are present in this scene in *Macbeth*, and both scenes lead on to an (off-stage) feast. Shakespeare's restraint, it goes without saying, is as far as possible removed from Seneca.

The second act of the play takes Macbeth and his wife to the murder of Duncan and beyond; and the keen suspense of the earlier scenes inevitably changes its character. It is not now a matter of the irritable frustration of having a wish denied, but the circumstantial terror involved in committing a secret murder:

not only fear of being discovered, but fear (to apply Johnson's
phrase) of 'their own detection', their own discovery of what in
reality they have done. However, along with the two murderers,
the audience also are forced to consider what it is they have done,
and it is to this end—responsibly imagining the crime—that
Shakespeare's dramatic constructions are directed.

In his soliloquy ('Is this a dagger which I see before me . . .?')
Macbeth dwells in horror on the murder he is about to commit—
for no reason, as it now seems. It shows him projecting around
him images of horror so as to create an unnaturally 'dead' (II. i. 50)
environment which will suit with 'the present horror of the time'.
The following scene (II. ii) dramatizes the murder itself, but does
so by putting the deed off stage. We wait with Lady Macbeth and
share her agitation, but the scene is so contrived that she is also
made to enter Duncan's bedchamber and be herself smeared with
blood. This ensures that she understands the physical reality of
what Macbeth has done; it also encourages the audience to follow
her in imagination to the corpse of the murdered man. Dramatically, Lady Macbeth acts in this scene as a conductor for the
audience's response. Since the scene opens with her alone on
stage, we see the action from her point of view; which is why it is
so effective to have her enter the bedchamber. But her flat un-
imaginative understatements have the effect, so evidently in-
appropriate are they, of arousing the correspondingly sluggish
imaginations of those watching the play.

This scene has its ancestry in earlier Shakespearian drama.
Behind it is the much more externally presented assassination of
Julius Caesar, and behind that the murder of Duke Humphrey in
2 *Henry VI*. The last mentioned is especially relevant. Duke
Humphrey's murder is shown in dumbshow at the beginning of
III. ii; later in the scene, the bed with the dead body on it is
brought on to the stage, Warwick describing in detail the horrible
signs of violence. The incomparably finer effect of the scene in
Macbeth comes from the fact that the murder is left to our imagination; in the circumstances anything as explicit as a dumbshow
would be absurdly self-defeating. Instead, the use of euphemism
and circumlocution ('He is about it', 'Th'attempt, and not the
deed, / Confounds us', 'I have done the deed') powerfully stimulates us to re-enact in imagination the act of murder itself. The
rhythms of the scene—its abrupt whispers and starts, the staccato

passages of dialogue, with the gathering hysteria of Macbeth's
'Sleep no more' speeches, and finally the knocking—bring an
audience as closely as seems possible to an intimate apprehension
of the moments leading up to and after the murder, but in a freely
imaginative way, unembarrassed and undistracted by stage
business.

The knocking at the gate drives the murderers from the stage
and brings on the Porter. The stage direction *Knock*, repeated in
the Folio text no fewer than ten times, is in itself an effective way
of playing on the nerves. But it is of course the idea of the Porter
'devil-portering' it in hell that is Shakespeare's highly original and
economical way of suddenly changing the perspective. He is here
appealing to his audience's memories of mystery cycles, and in
particular to the Harrowing of Hell plays, at the climax of which
there is an alarming knocking at the gate. The porter is sent to
see who is making the noise, and the person knocking reveals
himself to be Christ. The devil-porter at Inverness thus makes a
rapid and startling allusion to a whole area of drama quite different
from the one *Macbeth* itself belongs to. It establishes that Inverness
is at this moment a kind of hell, but it also associates the person
knocking with heavenly judgement. (The knocking is at 'the
south entry': the south was associated with heaven, just as the
north was associated with the devil.) Here it is Macduff who is
seeking entry, and Macduff is finally to prove himself Macbeth's
victorious antagonist.

The scene that follows, with Macduff's discovery of Duncan's
murder and Macbeth's simulated (but also real) horror, is conducted for the most part on a note of full-throated hyperbole.
After the hushed, interrupted dialogues of the murder scene this
comes as a kind of relief. The scene is distantly modelled on that
in *2 Henry VI* which shows the immediate response of the court
to the murder of Duke Humphrey (III. ii), a scene which is over-
long and somewhat ineffectively rhetorical; the present scene in
Macbeth makes its points more briefly. An interesting reminiscence
of the earlier scene is Lady Macbeth's swoon (which I take to be
genuine, not assumed). In *2 Henry VI* King Henry himself swoons,
whereas Margaret, who in some ways corresponds to Lady Macbeth, shows no sign of weakness. Warwick's description of Duke
Humphrey's body is paralleled by Macbeth's more hysterically
heightened account ('Here lay Duncan . . .'). The correspondences

between the two scenes show that the constituents have all been
rearranged to stronger effect: the murderer describes his victim's
body, while his apparently unnaturally nerveless wife betrays a
sudden, but human, loss of self-control.

A brief retrospective choric scene (II. iv) concludes the second
act, and summarily disposes of concern with Duncan.

The third act is Banquo's: not that he is much on stage, but
that the main business of this second action is Macbeth's attempt
to cut off Banquo and his line. The entire act is planned as a single
action. In the first scene two themes are set going which run
through the act until its climax in III. iv: namely, the feast which
Macbeth is to hold 'to-night' and which Banquo is urged not to
miss, and the murder of Banquo, which is to absent him from the
feast. Thus the first part of III. i, in which Banquo is invited to the
feast, is countered by the second part (72 ff.), in which Macbeth
instructs the murderers. The contradictory purposes of this scene
—arranging for Banquo to attend the feast, arranging for him to
miss it—are extended further in the following scene (III. ii), that
between Macbeth and his wife. This passage is a good example
of a characteristic scenic pattern of the play. Macbeth joins his
wife and they briefly talk. The scene may appear to be, from a
structural viewpoint, a mere effusion, with little concern for
design, so simple is its over-all shape. But its true structure is one
of feeling rather than of action: apart from its obvious function—
showing husband and wife in a state of deepening isolation from
each other—what it shows is a series of impulses towards a
sociable, convivial spirit thwarted by remorse and anxiety. The
tone is bleak in the extreme, but the terms of endearment and
good cheer by their very incongruity point up the emptiness of
their achievement: 'Be bright and jovial among your guests to-
night', 'Love', 'dear wife', 'be thou jocund', 'dearest chuck'. (The
word 'jovial' is especially grotesque in this context.) Lady Macbeth's reference to the feast receives a curious reply from her
husband: he enjoins her to be especially courteous to Banquo,
'Present him eminence, both with eye and tongue', as if he really
expected him to be there. This foreshadows the 'schizophrenia'
of the banquet scene—Macbeth's genuine desire for Banquo to
be present coupled with his fear lest he should—and is one further
sign of the divided motivation that runs through the whole of the
third act and contributes to its peculiar structure.

This scene, like I. vi already mentioned, may be modelled in a very general way on one in Seneca's *Thyestes*. This is the scene in which Atreus hints to his confidant that something dreadful is about to be done:

> *Minister.* What deed is in your mind?
> *Atreus.* I know not what. Some deed more wonderful
> Than mind can contemplate, more terrible
> Than any ordinary act of man . . .[1]

Similarly Macbeth hints at the 'deed of dreadful note' that is imminent, to which his wife inquires 'What's to be done?'.

The scene of Banquo's murder (III. iii) is notable for the appearance of the additional Third Murderer. His function is thematic: Macbeth has sought to delegate the murder of Banquo and Fleance to others: this time he will at least not be personally involved. But the placing of his name in the opening exchange—

> *1 Murderer.* But who did bid thee join with us?
> *3 Murderer.*   Macbeth.

—in effect establishes Macbeth's presence; the Third Murderer is a guarantee that Macbeth's imagination forces him to be present at the crime. The point is made obliquely, and justifies the choice of this incident for dramatization.

The scene of the feast (usually called the banquet scene, no doubt by association with Banquo's name) gathers together all the themes of this act and magnificently transcends expectation. For all its comparative brevity it is undoubtedly one of Shakespeare's greatest scenic inventions. The occasion has been prepared for in the three preceding scenes; no other scene in *Macbeth* is given this kind of premonitory treatment. Or one may put it differently by saying that the third act is entirely constructed with a view to this scene: the first three scenes are preliminaries to it. What is so remarkable about it is its primitive power, which is largely to be associated with its hypnotic repetitions, the invoked and simultaneously dreaded appearance and reappearance of Banquo. It is as if Macbeth has unwittingly stumbled upon a secret ritual from which he is unable to extricate himself; he is being played with by some power stronger than himself. One way of analysing

---

[1] Seneca, *Four Tragedies and* Octavia, tr. E. F. Watling (Penguin Books, Harmondsworth, 1966), p. 57.

the structural device that underlies the occasion and contributes to its power is to see the scene as a play-within-a-play that goes wrong. Shakespeare had three times before used this device, twice for comic effect (in *Love's Labour's Lost* and *A Midsummer Night's Dream*), and once in a tragic context in *Hamlet*. The play scene in *Hamlet* (III. ii) seems to have exerted a general shaping influence: its nature can be suggested by saying that in both scenes a king (who is a murderer) and a queen are discountenanced by *shadows*. For Shakespeare the word 'shadow' could mean either 'actor' or 'ghost'.[1] The two scenes have further likenesses: both have a strong sense of occasion, and have been well prepared for in preceding scenes. They are in fact the most highly developed ensemble scenes of their respective plays, and occupy a corresponding third act position. And both trace a similar course in that after their disruptive climaxes they modulate into a quiet duologue (Hamlet and Horatio, Macbeth and his wife) in which the emotional tone has something in it of combined nervous exhilaration and exhaustion.

Of course Macbeth is not literally appearing in a play, although he does announce early in the scene that he will 'play the humble host' (III. iv. 4), and a histrionic element is certainly present as it must be in any display of hypocrisy.[2] The performance he is putting on is a social performance, in the presence of his country's nobility, since the feast is intended to ratify the new social order. What happens in terms of the play-within-a-play is that Macbeth is put out of his part. The dramatic effect—the effect on the audience of *Macbeth*—is extraordinarily intense. For just as at a real-life performance of a play the experience of seeing an actor forget his part can be quite unforeseeably jarring, so the spectacle of Macbeth lapsing into helpless confusion arouses a feeling of

---

[1] That Shakespeare associated actors and ghosts, since both were 'shadows', is borne out by the verbal correspondences in the following two passages, the first of which refers to ghosts, the second to actors:

> By the apostle Paul, shadows to-night
> Have struck more terror to the soul of Richard
> Than can the substance of ten thousand soldiers ...
> $\qquad$ (*Richard III*, v. iii. 216–18)

> ... guilty creatures, sitting at a play,
> Have by the very cunning of the scene,
> Been struck so to the soul ...
> $\qquad$ (*Hamlet*, II. ii. 585–7)

[2] Cf. Anne Righter, *Shakespeare and the Idea of the Play* (London, 1962), pp. 130–1.

acute tragic embarrassment. The embarrassment arises from his involuntary self-exposure; what makes it also tragic is the state of mind which impels Macbeth to do it. For an understanding of the scene it is essential to see that, in wishing Banquo were present, Macbeth is not being merely hypocritical: he is also being completely sincere. What the banquet scene dramatizes so consummately is the granting to Macbeth of his divided and self-contradictory wishes: Banquo both comes and does not come to the feast. In this profoundly satisfying resolution to the themes of Act Three the scene exerts something of the elemental power and the inevitability of great myth. One is surprised that even Shakespeare could have invented it.

In Holinshed the only suggestion for the banquet is the remark: 'He willed therefore the same Banquho, with his sonne named Fleance, to come to a supper that he had prepared for them . . .',[1] but there is no mention of a ghost. It has been suggested that the source of Banquo's Ghost is the account of King Thierry who 'on an evening as he sat at supper' is haunted by the ghost of a man he has slain.[2] These appear to be the only known narrative sources for the scene. There are, however, two scenes in earlier Shakespearian plays which probably helped to shape the banquet scene. The first is II. i of *Richard III*, in which Edward IV tries to effect a reconciliation among the court factions (the Queen and her kinsfolk, Buckingham, and Hastings). When they have all embraced each other, professing forgiveness of injuries and friendship, the sick King reflects:

> A pleasing cordial, princely Buckingham,
> Is this thy vow unto my sickly heart.
> There wanteth now our brother Gloucester here
> To make the blessed period of our peace.
>
> (II. i. 41–4)

At this point Richard Gloucester enters, takes up the theme of loving reconciliation by professing friendship for all those present, and then drops a bombshell by casually mentioning Clarence's death: 'Who knows not that the gentle Duke is dead?' The stage direction is eloquent of the effect of this: '*They all start*'. The

---

[1] Boswell-Stone, op. cit., p. 33.
[2] See H. N. Paul, *The Royal Play of 'Macbeth'* (New York, 1950), pp. 58–9, which cites De Loier's *Treatise of Spectres* (1605).

harmonious *tableau* is shattered. The feature here that Shakespeare recalled can be pinpointed in the cadence of two lines just quoted:

> There wanteth now our brother Gloucester here
> To make the blessed period of our peace.

Two of Macbeth's lines have a similar movement as well as a comparable significance:

> Here had we now our country's honour roof'd,
> Were the grac'd person of our Banquo present . . .
>
> (III. iv. 40–1)

(The position of 'now' is the same, while 'here' is reversed.) Macbeth's feast has a loving-cup, intended to affirm love and concord, while Edward compares Buckingham's vow to a 'pleasing cordial'; both these scenes of professed love and friendship follow immediately upon a savage murder (Clarence, Banquo); finally, the harmony is broken by the arrival of, in one case Richard, in the other the Ghost of Banquo. What this scene in *Richard III* lacks, compared with the banquet scene, is the presence of the supernatural. This is provided by the other scene which seems to have contributed something to the banquet scene: the opening scene of *Hamlet*. The chief point of resemblance here is that the Ghost appears twice, as does the Ghost of Banquo. This is not a trivial detail, for the repeated appearance of Banquo's Ghost is the structural feature which above everything else gives the banquet scene its compelling rhythm: while it lasts it seems that Macbeth could go on indefinitely invoking Banquo's presence and being thrown horribly into confusion when 'Banquo' appears (in this series of two, the number two seems to stand for an indefinite number of times). There is no such suggestion as this in the first scene of *Hamlet*; the Ghost appears twice in this scene, and a third time in Hamlet's presence in I. iv, each visitation being more prolonged until the Ghost makes its full disclosure to Hamlet in I. v. Nevertheless the first scene, considered as a structural unit, is given shape by the Ghost's two appearances, one near the beginning of the scene, the other near the end. The power of the scene to arouse excitement clearly comes from these two appearances, so that it looks as if Shakespeare remembered and adapted the effect to a new purpose in *Macbeth*. There is also one further link between the two scenes. The first scene of *Hamlet* takes place at night and ends at daybreak; so does the banquet scene. Both scenes end with brief indications of the time of day ('But look, the morn, in russet mantle clad . . .'; 'Almost at odds with morning, which is which'), and also with announcements of future purpose: young Hamlet is to be informed, and Macbeth is to visit the Weird Sisters. The banquet scene acquires its complex form from being a conflation of two quite different scenic ideas, and perhaps something of its power derives from this diversity of structural sources.

Two further observations may be made here about Act Three, the second of the three main actions of the play. It is notable that neither Macduff nor Malcolm appears in it; both go out of the action in Act Two, to reappear only in Act Four. Their absence helps to isolate, or concentrate, this central innermost phase of the action: nothing is allowed to distract from the grouping of Macbeth and his wife and Banquo. This clearing of the stage for the middle movement of the play is a feature paralleled in several other tragedies. So, for example, Paris, Cassius (who does not appear in the Forum scene), Laertes, Lodovico, Cordelia, and Aufidius are confined to either the earlier or the later scenes of the play or both.

Both Act Two and Act Three of *Macbeth* end with short choric scenes which comment on the preceding events. Despite some passages of good writing, both scenes may in performance be felt to be slightly tedious, too obtrusively thematic. Shakespeare may have felt it desirable to punctuate each of the two first actions with a scene of this sort simply in order to qualify the exceptionally subjective, almost feverish, nature of the scenes in which Macbeth appears. Moreover, if the play had two intervals (after the second and third acts) or a pause and one longer interval, then each unit as acted would conclude with persons representing the normal and natural order: in the first case, Ross, the Old Man, and Macduff; in the second Lennox and a Lord—the very anonymity of two of these characters denotes their representative status. The Old Man pronounces 'God's benison', while the Lord remarks 'I'll send my prayers with him'. So each of the three actions ends with a promise of the reassertion of the natural order, the third most explicitly with Malcolm as King of Scotland.

The third movement of the play, Macduff's, divides into two phases according to the act-division, but it clearly needs to be

acted without a break: the scene-links between the end of IV. iii
and the beginning of V. ii are particularly marked. The scene of
the Witches' cavern (IV. i) is an occasion for spectacular shows,
while its Stuart symbolism ties the entire play to the reign of
Shakespeare's patron James I. Dramatically, the prophecies of
the raised spirits motivate Macbeth's actions for the rest of the
play; we experience them as giving the play a fresh impetus for
its final movement.

　　The following two scenes are conceived as a single unit; neither
should be considered without the other. They are framed by the
presence of Ross, who appears in the first part of the first and
the second part of the second. In IV. ii the dialogue is carefully
contrived so as to prepare the issues which will be resolved in
the following scene. Accordingly, in the exchange between Lady
Macduff and Ross (1–30) the charge is brought against Macduff
that he is lacking in humanity ('He wants the natural touch');
in the talk between Lady Macduff and her son (30–63) this is
followed up by a second charge: that he is a traitor. The long
scene in England (IV. iii) falls into two clear episodes separated
by a brief interlude describing Edward the Confessor. In the first
Malcolm tests the loyalty of Macduff, in the course of which
Macduff clears himself of the imputation of being a traitor; in the
second, with the arrival of Ross and the news of the slaughter of
his wife and children, he in effect clears himself of the other charge,
that of being without natural feeling. The first episode is closely
based on Holinshed; the second, however, is Shakespeare's invention and is of crucial importance to the play's structure of feeling.
This is the first time in the play that what we see on stage has the
effect of simply moving us; and the occasion has in it something
of solemn formality. The occasion is one of receiving bad news.
Ross is the messenger, who performs his task tentatively and
gradually until the full import breaks upon Macduff. The peak of
feeling is marked by a simple gesture: Macduff pulls his hat over
his brows. Malcolm, playing the role ritually ordained him by the
situation, urges him to 'give sorrow words'; and the action is
finally crystallized in the exchange:

> *Malcolm.* Dispute it like a man.
> *Macduff.*　　　　　　　　　　　　I shall do so;
> But I must also feel it as a man.

(220–1)

MACBETH 221

The charge made against Macduff by his wife, that 'All is the fear, and nothing is the love' (iv. ii. 12), is refuted in the most convincing way possible. In a few moments Macduff will be ready to join the march with Malcolm against Macbeth.

The form of this scene, the reception of bad news, followed by a decision to seek revenge (in Malcolm's words, 'Let grief / Convert to anger'), is possibly recalled from the scene in *3 Henry VI* (II. 1) in which Edward and Richard receive the news of their father York's death at the hands of Clifford and Queen Margaret, a death which occurred shortly after Clifford's savage killing of the child Rutland. As in this scene in *Macbeth*, the victims of the atrocity are an adult and a child (of course, Macduff's other children are also killed, but only one child is presented on stage).[1]

This testing of Macduff's humanity is always a turning-point in a performance of *Macbeth*, since it is the first time that strong tragic emotion is released in the audience: a current of feeling is made available (so to speak) for the dramatist's disposal. What Shakespeare does is to place this feeling at the service of Macbeth and his wife, so that—unfeasible though it may seem in retrospect—the emotion released by Macduff and his family is then transferred, or rather extended, first to Lady Macbeth, and then to the tyrant himself. In this way it can be seen that without the atrocious slaughter of Lady Macduff and her children, which more than anything else in the play makes Macbeth hateful to us, we could not feel that deep tragic sympathy with him which we do feel in the fifth act; for the current of feeling that flows in the fifth act has been set going in the fourth.

The following scene (v. i), that of Lady Macbeth's sleep-walking, inherits (as I have just suggested) the newly awakened mood of tenderness and compassion created by its predecessor. (It is the audience's state of mind that provides the continuity.) In this scene the watchers, the Doctor and the Gentlewoman, are beautifully characterized: very effective is the Gentlewoman's refusal to tell the Doctor what Lady Macbeth has said in her sleep—it makes him, and with him the audience, listen all the more keenly. In her six muttered speeches Lady Macbeth recalls past crimes, but they are all mingled in a disordered sequence. We have to

[1] The passion scene in *Titus Andronicus* (III. i) has a similar sequence (the reception of bad news followed by the decision to seek revenge), and like Macduff Titus is a bereaved father; but in other respects the scene in *3 Henry VI* seems closer.

make sense of them as we can from our knowledge of the action
up to this point. Her speeches have a further function: occurring
at the beginning of the final phase of the play, they prompt us to
glance back at the entire course of the action, rapidly taking stock
of Macbeth's situation before witnessing his destruction.

The sleep-walking scene forms a kind of loop in the narrative:
it interrupts the rhythm set going at the end of iv. iii, which is
taken up again at the beginning of v. ii, a confident, steady
forward march:

> Come, go we to the King. Our power is ready;
> Our lack is nothing but our leave. Macbeth
> Is ripe for shaking . . .
>
> (iv. iii. 236–8)

And v. ii opens: 'The English pow'r is near, led on by Malcolm'.
This brief scene, like its counterpart v. iv, is full of phrases in
the present or future tense and of reiterated uses of the word 'now'.
Everything in these scenes is measured, orderly, serenely purposeful. They alternate with two scenes given to Macbeth (v. iii, v),
the first of which stands out for its nervously excitable, abrupt,
and even convulsive, movement. Macbeth's opening words take
up his position when we last saw him in iv. ii: he is trying to persuade himself that he is incapable of fear; and the choice of his
three interlocutors (as in a morality play) demonstrates his state
of mind. The first is a terrified servant (who stammers and so
hisses the word 'soldiers' like a goose). He is a kind of personified
'Fear', whom Macbeth beats away. The other two are his doctor
and armourer; and Macbeth, divided in mind and purpose, talks
distractedly to both:

> Throw physic to the dogs, I'll none of it.
> Come, put mine armour on; give me my staff.
> Seyton, send out. Doctor, the thanes fly from me.
> Come, sir, dispatch. If thou couldst, doctor, cast
> The waters of my land . . .
>
> (v. iii. 47–51)

This scene presents a purely illustrative episode. In the next scene
in Dunsinane (v. v), Macbeth's great speech responding to the
news of his wife's death is in fact a non-response as far as his
'dearest partner of greatness' is concerned. It states his inability
to feel, and in this is at the opposite pole from Macduff's reception

of the news of *his* wife's death. But the capacity to feel and respond, which in Macbeth has atrophied, has been awakened in the audience; if he has become numbed and calloused, we have not, and Macduff's earlier response—his exemplary *human* capacity to experience emotion—is the immediate reason.

This fifth act (omitting the sleep-walking scene) has sometimes been criticized for being, from a dramatic point of view, a per-functory or piecemeal winding-up of the tragedy.[1] It is in fact a carefully thought out and superbly rhythmical solution to a large structural problem. It should not be seen as a number of separate scenes (seven or more, according to the editor), but as a single comprehensive action comprising several smaller narrative inte-rests. The army from England, led by Malcolm and Macduff, joins up with the Scottish army led by Menteith and others before advancing on Dunsinane. Macbeth leaves the castle and joins battle, killing Young Siward before being killed by Macduff. Shakespeare has a considerable number of 'points' to make, and he does so economically and with an unfaltering sense of the right order; hence, in part, the effect of a ritualistic unfolding: every-thing is taken in its due time. The death of Young Siward, for example, is beautifully placed, and (although based on Holinshed: Shakespeare found it mentioned in the account of Edward the Confessor) is felt to be a necessary part in the solemn, almost ceremonious, action of deposing the tyrant. The winning side must win only at some cost, and the death of Old Siward's son is like a sacrifice. Finally, Malcolm is hailed three times King of Scotland. In this pre-eminently 'elegant' play this triple salutation is no doubt meant to recall the three 'All-hail's' with which the Weird Sisters initially greeted Macbeth.

This long final action (v. ii–viii) possibly owes something to the final scenes of *Richard III*. The eve of Bosworth was one of the most ambitious scenic movements in early Shakespeare. It carried the audience from the pitching of the tents on the evening before battle, through the night with the visitations of the ghosts of Richard's victims (first to Richard, then to Richmond), to the morning of the next day, and finally to the battle orations of Rich-mond and Richard. The battle follows briefly, with Richard's

---

[1] Cf. J. M. Nosworthy: 'The short scenes in Act v, with their numbing couplets and their general air of inferiority, suggest either that Shakespeare was growing bored with the play or that time was running out' (op. cit., p. 13).

death. The structural principle was one of punctilious symmetry in allocation of material, except for Richard's terrified soliloquy after the departure of the ghosts. In *Macbeth* Shakespeare adapts the method of giving attention alternately to the tyrant and to his supplanters, as well as the measured tempo which gives this final phase a movement suggestive of pre-ordained ceremony. Moreover, Shakespeare possibly recalled one particular feature from *Richard III* which contributes signally (as I have just suggested) to the pattern of these final scenes. This is the minor action concerning Young Siward. In *Richard III* Stanley's son is held as hostage by Richard, and since Stanley has finally declared himself on the side of Richmond there is some doubt whether his son will escape with his life. Near the end of the play, after Richard's death, Richmond asks: 'But, tell me is young George Stanley living', and is told that he is after all safe. It may have been the memory of this subsidiary thread in the denouement of *Richard III* that prompted Shakespeare to include the incident of Young Siward.[1] But it is finely in keeping with the deeper tragic feeling of *Macbeth* that the issue of this theme is not a joyful one. Young Siward admittedly dies a fair death, as 'God's soldier', but there is nothing of the jubilant mood of the conclusion of *Richard III*. Macduff is without his wife and children, and Old Siward's son is slain.

[1] Cf. too the incident involving Young Cato, who is killed in battle in the penultimate scene of *Julius Caesar* (v. iv).

8. *Antony and Cleopatra*

I

ANTONY AND CLEOPATRA has suffered perhaps more than any other of Shakespeare's plays by being fitted insensitively into a five-act structural scheme. There are no act-divisions in the Folio text, and the five-act arrangement which is accepted in all modern standard editions does little to bring out the true structural lines of the play. It is, in fact, often declared that the play is simply not very well constructed. 'The events', said Johnson, 'of which the principal are described according to history, are produced without any art of connection or care of disposition.'[1] This is an extreme verdict, and an imperceptive one, but positions more or less approaching it have often been taken in more recent criticism. The best treatment of this aspect of the play remains Granville-Barker's, but even he does not do all that can be done to clarify Shakespeare's intentions.

Plutarch's *Life of Marcus Antonius*, Shakespeare's main narrative source, gives an extremely lively account of Antony but at hardly any point does it look like a natural candidate for scenic transcription. As a narrative it is rambling, episodic, full of compelling circumstantial detail, but lacking in a clearly visualizable shape—and in all this it follows the wavering course of Antony himself. Antony's obsession with Cleopatra provides a stabilizing factor (from the narrative point of view), and increasingly so in his last years, but there are considerable stretches of the story, particularly in the early and middle phases, which could have had little interest for a prospective dramatist, since their tendency is so digressive as to resist clear design. A notable example is the long account of Antony's Parthian campaign. Another is the Timon-like episode of Antony's retirement after Actium: this account of his revulsion from the world after his humiliating fall might have been expected to be of interest to a dramatist, but Shakespeare omits all mention of it. Of course Shakespeare was by no means the only dramatist to be attracted to the story of Antony and

---

[1] *Johnson on Shakespeare*, ed. Walter Raleigh, p. 180.

Cleopatra, but the others, Giraldi, Garnier, Daniel, or (after Shakespeare) Dryden, cut it down to neo-classical size by opening the play shortly before the end: their last day alive is all that we see of the two main characters; the rest is relegated to retrospective narration. Only Shakespeare, apparently, opens his play well before the closing stages, and he is the only one to give any sense of the story as told by Plutarch, with its long time perspectives and all its rich, endlessly qualifying detail. In no other dramatic treatment do we see Antony long before the defeat at Actium as well as after it.

Compared with *Macbeth* (which was possibly written immediately before it), *Antony and Cleopatra* may at first seem a puzzlingly unemphatic play. The structure of *Macbeth*—its general shape, if not its finer details—can be understood after only a single reading: the three stages in the plot correspond to three well-marked stages in Macbeth's career as murderer and usurper, and there is nothing to distract attention from the central idea. The structure of *Antony and Cleopatra*, however, evidently does not declare itself at once; if it did, there would be less criticism of its 'defective construction' (in Bradley's phrase). There is, to begin with, nothing as clear-cut in Antony's story as there is in Macbeth's; nothing corresponding to Macbeth's three main crimes. The clearest, most memorable events in Antony's story are his collapse at Actium and his death. But his love for Cleopatra is not so much an event as a process, a pattern of behaviour rather than a series of decisive actions, and as such it presented Shakespeare with a problem in constructing a plot. Yet a plot of sorts there must be in any play, certainly any play of Shakespeare's, and this is no exception. Rowe's five-act divisions, however, are not much help in discovering what it is.

We have seen earlier that Shakespeare's tragedies and histories are usually divided into two parts, and that the break in continuity, if properly observed, will be found to help articulate the play's meaning. If Granville-Barker is to be believed, however, *Antony and Cleopatra* is without any such feature; there is, he says, 'no juncture where the play's acting will be made more effective by a pause'.[1] Granville-Barker's authority in this matter is not to be lightly disregarded, but it seems fair to suppose that there would have been an interval during a play as long as this; and it seems, moreover, unlikely that Shakespeare would not have taken artistic

[1] Harley Granville-Barker, *Prefaces to Shakespeare*, vol. i, p. 379.

advantage of the fact by constructing his play in a manner which was, apparently, customary with him. In fact, Bradley noticed that the first half or so of the play was different in tone and mood from the second, and this perception—that *Antony and Cleopatra* does fall into two parts or movements—is the first structural observation to be made about it.[1] The play is no exception to the two-part structural principle postulated in an earlier chapter. Granville-Barker conceded that in modern performances an interval might be necessary, and found that four places in the text were possible pausing places : after III. iii (the second scene of Cleopatra with the Messenger), or—better—after III. v (in which Enobarbus and Eros briefly discuss the growing rift between Antony and Caesar), or after III. vi (which shows Caesar's indignation against Antony and Cleopatra and Octavia's unexpected return home), or—which seemed to Granville-Barker least objectionable of the four—after III. vii (with Cleopatra and Enobarbus quarrelling and the launching of the war).[2] Of these suggestions, the third, after III. vi, seems to me conspicuously stronger than the others for the following reasons.

Shakespeare chose to open the play towards the end of Antony's first stay in Egypt with Cleopatra. Plutarch in his narrative has just described the way of life adopted by the lovers 'which they called *Amimetobion* (as much to say, "no life comparable and matchable with it")'.[3] In Shakespeare, Antony's first major utterance, the speech beginning 'Let Rome in Tiber melt' (I. i. 33–40) contains what is probably Shakespeare's version of these words of Plutarch :

> The nobleness of life
> Is to do thus (*embracing*), when such a mutual pair
> And such a twain can do't, in which I bind,
> On pain of punishment, the world to weet
> We stand up peerless.

The point in Plutarch's sequence at which Shakespeare set his plot going is this :

Now Antonius delighting in these fond and childish pastimes, very ill news were brought him from two places. The first from Rome :

[1] A. C. Bradley, 'Shakespeare's "Antony and Cleopatra" ', in *Oxford Lectures on Poetry* (1909), pp. 284–5.
[2] Granville-Barker, op. cit., pp. 379–80.
[3] *Shakespeare's Plutarch*, ed. T. J. B. Spencer, p. 204.

that his brother Lucius and Fulvia his wife fell out first between themselves, and afterwards fell to open war with Caesar, and had brought
all to nought, that they were both driven to fly out of Italy. The second
news, as bad as the first: that Labienus conquered all Asia with the
army of the Parthians, from the river of Euphrates and from Syria unto
the countries of Lydia and Ionia. Then began Antonius with much
ado a little to rouse himself, as if he had been wakened out of a deep
sleep and, as a man may say, coming out of a great drunkenness.[1]

Antony hears the news in the second scene of the play, and leaves
Cleopatra at the end of the third. (All the rest of the first act is
Shakespeare's invention, much of it evoking the *Amimetobion* as
described by Plutarch.) Antony meets Caesar in Rome and agrees
to marry his sister Octavia; the triumvirate settle peaceably with
the rebel Pompey; Antony abandons Octavia in order to return
to Cleopatra, and the mutual hostility between himself and Caesar
flares into war. The war itself and its aftermath in the deaths of
Antony and Cleopatra occupy the rest of the play.

The point at which the play seems to waver, as if to take second
wind, is in the middle of what modern editions call Act Three;
more precisely, at III. iv, III. v, and III. vi. Unless it is seen that
Shakespeare is preparing for a break here and adjusting his tempo
with a particular effect in mind, this part of the play is liable to be
misunderstood. III. iii has shown Cleopatra interrogating the
Messenger about Octavia and being satisfied by his now prudent
replies. The following scene shows Antony and Octavia on the
point of separating: the rift between Antony and Caesar is growing, and Octavia, foreseeing war, feels herself torn between
husband and brother. We next see Eros and Enobarbus exchanging the latest news: Lepidus has been deposed by Caesar, leaving
the world a 'pair of chaps' in Caesar and Antony. The war seems
even nearer. The following scene (III. vi) is significantly longer
than its three predecessors (it really runs together two episodes).
It is also written in a style conspicuously weighty and emphatic:
in his note on *Antony and Cleopatra* Johnson observed that 'the
most tumid speech in the play is that which *Caesar* makes to
Octavia' (presumably III. vi. 42–55).[2] Caesar first describes to
Agrippa and Maecenas the enthronement of Antony and Cleopatra in the market-place of Alexandria. Octavia unexpectedly

---

[1] *Shakespeare's Plutarch*, ed. T. J. B. Spencer, p. 207.
[2] *Johnson on Shakespeare*, p. 180.

appears, and in the course of the following dialogue Caesar speaks
to her on three topics: he upbraids her for her unceremonious
arrival; he lists the 'kings o'th'earth' whom Antony and Cleopatra are levying for war against him; lastly he offers comfort, by
assuring her that the outcome of the conflict is settled:

> Be you not troubled with the time, which drives
> O'er your content these strong necessities,
> But let determin'd things to destiny
> Hold unbewail'd their way.

(III. vi. 82–5)

This extraordinarily confident assertion is the high point of the
scene, and it is on this note, I suggest, that the first movement of
Antony and Cleopatra comes to an end. Caesar's reference to destiny
works as a reminder to the audience of the historical outcome of
the coming war; it makes Antony and Cleopatra seem already
doomed. But the reference is also in keeping with Caesar's characterization in this scene. His efficiency and foresight are at their
most remarkable; whenever his subordinates suggest a course of
action he replies that he has already done it, and his intelligence
of Antony's whereabouts is made to look almost like omniscience:
'I have eyes upon him, / And his affairs come to me on the wind'
(62–3). Behind such remarks lies perhaps an image of Jupiter, who
(in the fourth book of the Aeneid), enthroned in the empyrean
heavens, literally does have eyes upon Aeneas.[1] In this scene, then,
Caesar is at his most godlike, serenely enjoying more than mortal
knowledge. And it is at this point in the action, pausing on the
brink of civil war, that Shakespeare closes—for, *pace* Granville-
Barker, it is not an interruption—his first part. Moreover, if the
test of *liaison des scènes* is applied, the result supports this analysis.
Octavia's arrival in Rome in III. vi links up with her departure
from Athens in III. iv: therefore III. iv, III. v, and III. vi must be
acted as a continuous sequence. But III. vi ends on a note of some
finality and makes no preparation for any specific business in the
immediate future. And in fact a considerable hiatus separates the

[1] In Garnier's tragedy *Antonius*, Octavius Caesar says of himself (in his first speech,
at the beginning of Act Four) that he enjoys godlike power. The Countess of Pem-
broke's version is as follows:

> As Monarch I both world and *Rome* commaund;
> Do all, can all; fourth my command'ment cast
> Like Thundring fire from one to other Pole
> Equall to Jove . . .

scenes leading up to III. vi from III. vii. This scene opens with
Cleopatra and Enobarbus quarrelling; and they are shortly joined
by Antony. This is the first time that we have seen the lovers
together again since Antony's return to Egypt. A good deal has
happened in the interim: the wars have already begun. And the
new sequence, set going in III. vii, continues without interruption
to the end of the play.

Antony and Cleopatra divides, then, into two uninterrupted
scenic sequences. In the first Antony leaves Cleopatra for Caesar,
but in its last scene we learn that he has returned to her. The
second movement opens, like the first, with Antony and Cleopatra together; but this time, despite more than one estrangement,
he remains with her until his death. Both movements end, not
with Antony and Cleopatra themselves, but with Caesar—an
arrangement which reflects the historical process. So the first part
ends with Caesar's injunction to

> let determin'd things to destiny
> Hold unbewail'd their way

while the second ends with his final summing-up in which, again
transcending his merely historical role, he concludes:

> High events as these
> Strike those that make them; and their story is
> No less in pity than his glory which
> Brought them to be lamented.

He speaks here with the detached, yet all-comprehending voice
of the historian, or rather the historical poet; just as in the earlier
scene he spoke of future events as if retrospectively—something
only granted to the historian who lives later than the events which
he describes. Here Shakespeare was in fact using a remark of
Plutarch's: 'for it was predestined that the government of all the
world should fall into Octavius Caesar's hands'.[1]

It should be noted that in dividing his material in this way
Shakespeare was being faithful to what he took from Plutarch.
Shakespeare's first and second movements correspond to two
massive blocks of Plutarch's *Life*, but in Plutarch they are separa-
ted by the long account of Antony's Parthian campaign, which
Shakespeare did not use.[2]

---

[1] *Shakespeare's Plutarch*, p. 245.

[2] In T. J. B. Spencer's very useful *Shakespeare's Plutarch*, the footnotes enable one
to see at a glance that the first movement of Shakespeare's play is for the most part

II

In this section I want to consider how the outlines of *Antony and Cleopatra* may have come into being. So far I have tried to establish that the play falls into two movements, the first of which might be summarized as preliminaries to a war, and the second as the war itself and its immediate consequences. Such a summary deliberately omits all the circumstances of plot and all details of the play's imaginative colouring, since my concern now is with Shakespeare's basic scenario, the fundamental shape which he must have had in mind before working the play out in detail. As with the other mature tragedies already discussed, it seems reasonable to suppose that this basic formal idea was not itself new but was derived from an earlier play. On the present occasion the play which seems to have supplied him with his fundamental layout was the most recently written of his English history plays, *Henry V* (if the usual qualifications are made: other works also made their contribution).[1] I shall argue that if Shakespeare had not first written *Henry V*, *Antony and Cleopatra* as we now have it would hardly have been written either.

The two plays have one obvious structural difference. *Henry V* divides very clearly into five acts; unmistakably so, since every act is preceded by a Chorus. But this difference (which is, I think, relatively superficial) accompanies some deep affinities between the plays. *Henry V* might be summarily described as follows: preliminaries to a war (or, more exactly, a battle), followed by the battle itself and its immediate consequences. In other words,

based on pp. 207–21, and the second on pp. 249–93. There are a few details which complicate this account, and in particular the material for III. vi is taken from pp. 220 and 242–4, but on the whole the two main blocks of source material unmistakably declare themselves.

[1] Ernest Schanzer has pointed out the thematic preoccupations which *Antony and Cleopatra* shares with the two Parts of *Henry IV*. Eastcheap and Westminster are opposed just as are Egypt and Rome; Prince Hal moves between the two settings, just as Antony in his different way is torn between his imperial duties and his love for Cleopatra. See *The Problem Plays of Shakespeare* (London, 1963), pp. 162–7. Schanzer has several interesting structural observations to make, but he does not sufficiently allow for the radical re-configuration of constituents which usually occurs when Shakespeare adapts the forms of his own plays to a new purpose. If Antony is like Prince Hal in some respects, he is like Hotspur or even Falstaff in others. He is closest perhaps to Hotspur in being, like him, rash, generous, passionate, and finally a loser. At one point they use a closely comparable style of rhetoric (they are both calling for trumpets); cf. *1 Henry IV*, v. ii. 98–101 and *Antony and Cleopatra*, IV. viii. 35–9.

if all circumstantial detail is ignored, the main lines of *Henry V*
are so similar to those of *Antony and Cleopatra* that it seems fair
to conjecture that the ground-plan of the earlier history play
served as a model (however we go on to qualify this) for the
later.

This structural kinship—and only the large outline of the two
plays is in question—possibly also extends to the placing of the
main interval, if the following brief analysis is correct. In *Henry V*
the allocation of material between the five acts is as follows: Act
One, London: the decision to make war; Act Two, preparations
on both sides, and the conspiracy of Cambridge, Scroop, and
Grey; Act Three, the siege of Harfleur, and further moves
towards the decisive battle; Act Four, Agincourt; Act Five, the
marriage treaty and settlement. Each act is preceded by a Chorus,
but it does not follow that an interval followed each act. On the
contrary, the Chorus is a means of ensuring continuity between
the acts, smoothing the transitions, and kindling the imagination
of the audience. The whole play, I suggest, may fall into the usual
two parts: the first part ending with III. v, the scene in the French
court. The scene opens with the French King's words: "'Tis
certain he hath pass'd the river Somme'—he does not need to say
who 'he' is. Henry's army is moving further into Picardy, and the
French nobility can no longer delay stirring themselves. The
courtiers respond to the invasion in different ways—contempt for
the English, reluctant admiration for them, impatience with themselves—and the scene reaches its climax with the King's speech
of defiance and resolution (36–55). In it he orders Montjoy the
herald to carry a message of defiance to Henry, and then calls upon
the French nobility to crush the English invaders:

> Charles Delabreth, High Constable of France,
> You Dukes of Orleans, Bourbon, and of Berri,
> Alençon, Brabant, Bar, and Burgundy;
> Jaques Chatillon, Rambures, Vaudemont,
> Beaumont, Grandpré, Roussi, and Fauconbridge . . .

And the scene ends with a confident flourish, a rhyming couplet,
again spoken by the King, which rings out with an effective, if
unsubtle, irony:

> Now forth, Lord Constable and Princes all,
> And quickly bring us word of England's fall.

If this scene were followed by an interval, it would make a very effective place to pause at: on the brink—or, as it turns out, almost on the eve—of the battle of Agincourt. For the scene that follows (III. vi), in the English camp, initiates an unbroken sequence that leads into and beyond the battle (up to the end of Act Four); at no point within this sequence can the performance be interrupted.

I have dwelt on the scene at the French court at this length in order to bring out a similarity between this part of *Henry V* and the corresponding part of *Antony and Cleopatra*. For the scene of Caesar's indignation and reception of Octavia (III. vi) is in some ways—in tone and even in some points of substance—curiously reminiscent of this scene in *Henry V*. The most exact parallel is their heroic-sounding catalogues: the names of the French nobility just quoted, and the 'kings o'th'earth' who are being brought into the war by Antony and Cleopatra. Both scenes are full of a sense of imminent conflict and decisive engagement; they are of the nature of deliberative statements, taking stock of the situation. Of course, in circumstance the scenes are quite different: the French are about to lose the battle, while Caesar knows that he, befriended by 'destiny', cannot lose. Nevertheless, both the French and Caesar are antagonists to the heroes of their respective plays; and in this, their roles are comparable.

The similarities in layout between the two plays and in the (conjectural) placing of the main interval are perhaps sufficient indications that Shakespeare associated them; but there are further affinities, both structural and thematic. Both plays are about two nations (if Rome can be called a nation) separated by sea. In both plays the size of the martial forces is so great that it was not possible for Shakespeare to represent the fighting on stage (as he had in his earlier history plays). In neither play are there any single combats: Antony vainly challenges Caesar to a personal fight, but it is part of the dramatic situation that such things belong to the past. At Agincourt the French nobility was mounted and so impossible to bring on the stage. 'Think, when we talk of horses, that you see them', the Chorus early enjoins, and the Dauphin's talk runs continually on his horse. Actium too was impracticable for Shakespeare's stage, since it was a sea-engagement and a particularly huge one. So the famous battles in which Henry and Antony participate are necessarily off-stage affairs. In *Henry V* the nearest we get to the fighting is the encounter of Pistol, the Boy, and a French soldier; in *Antony and Cleopatra* all we see is a freshly wounded soldier, Scarus ('I had a wound here that was like a T, / But now 'tis made an H'), but we are shown no hand-to-hand fighting. Further, in both plays the distances involved were so great that the antagonists seldom met. As a result, considerable use is made of ambassadors, heralds, and messengers, who are sometimes given key roles in individual scenes, (e.g. Montjoy the herald, or the various messengers who have dealings with Cleopatra, like the unnamed Messenger who announces Antony's marriage, and later, Thyreus, Proculeius, and Dolabella). Henry V and the French King do not confront each other until the last scene of the play, a point which Burgundy makes clear:

> that I have labour'd . . .
> To bring your most imperial Majesties
> Unto this bar and royal interview,
> Your mightiness on both parts best can witness.
> Since then my office hath so far prevail'd
> That face to face and royal eye to eye
> You have congreeted . . .
>
> (v. ii. 24–31)

Similarly Cleopatra and Octavius Caesar meet only in the last scene, near the end of the play. Cleopatra says of Caesar she 'would gladly / Look him i'th'face' (v. ii. 31–2), and shortly before her death her wish is granted. This diffused spaciousness, particularly in *Antony and Cleopatra*, created special problems for the dramatist, and no doubt contributed to the somewhat detached mood of the later play, a mood capable of contemplative and poetic intensity, but not of the near-melodramatic impetus of such plays as *Hamlet* and *Othello*.

The comparison between the two plays can be usefully taken further. In *Henry V* the striking structural innovation, for Shakespeare, is the use of a Chorus throughout the play. The function of this Chorus is not primarily to inform the audience of what it does not already know, but to work on the audience's imagination, and to help it to rise to the greatness of the occasion. The high point of the play is the 'Saint Crispin's Day' speech immediately before the battle. In its crucial lines Henry appeals to the immortality which the victors of Agincourt will find in the memory of Englishmen:

He that shall live this day, and see old age,
Will yearly on the vigil feast his neighbours,
And say 'To-morrow is Saint Crispian'.
Then will he strip his sleeve and show his scars,
And say 'These wounds I had on Crispian's day'.
Old men forget; yet all shall be forgot,
But he'll remember, with advantages,
What feats he did that day. Then shall our names,
Familiar in his mouth as household words—
Harry the King, Bedford and Exeter,
Warwick and Talbot, Bedford and Gloucester—
Be in their flowing cups freshly remember'd.
This story shall the good man teach his son . . .

                                        (IV. iii. 44–56)

The whole play leads up to this moment, when the audience in the theatre watching *Henry V* realizes that it is itself the posterity invoked by Henry, and that the attention it gives the play itself constitutes the fame promised by Henry to his soldiers. *Henry V* is not perhaps so much 'about' Henry himself and his reign as about what was for the Elizabethans the most famous of English victories. A more accurate name for the play would be *Agincourt*.

In *Antony and Cleopatra* Shakespeare did not of course use a Chorus. But in subtler, more exacting ways the play requires its audience, as did *Henry V*, to contemplate the events shown in a mood suitable to the occasion—not a great event out of the national calendar, but an episode from an alien civilization. Like *Henry V*, *Antony and Cleopatra* is peculiarly concerned with the fame of its chief characters and events. The earlier play had been about the most famous of English victories; the later is about the most famous lovers in history (not in myth or legend, but in history; the historical concern is essential). In *Henry V* it is largely the courteous, reverent-voiced Chorus that guides the audience into a suitable frame of mind. In *Antony and Cleopatra* the devices used to this end are more various and less obtrusive; most of them can be included under the headings of style and structure.

The verbal style of the play has often been described, evidently because readers have felt that an instrument so beautiful and so supple deserved some attention in its own right. It has an incandescence, a fastidious delicacy, and a soft resonance that arouse continuous pleasure, and have a good deal to do with a quality of the play that has often been commented on: the comparative absence of pain or distress in its effect on the audience. In this context, however, it may be suggested that the verbal style of the play has a specific purpose: it performs much the same function as the Chorus in *Henry V*. It awakens in the audience a certain attitude to the events it is witnessing on stage. Indeed some passages in the Choruses have a brilliancy and warmth which clearly anticipate the style of *Antony and Cleopatra*; the following lines, for example:

> Suppose that you have seen
> The well-appointed King at Hampton pier
> Embark his royalty; and his brave fleet
> With silken streamers the young Phoebus fanning.
> Play with your fancies; and in them behold
> Upon the hempen tackle ship-boys climbing;
> Hear the shrill whistle which doth order give
> To sounds confus'd; behold the threaden sails,
> Borne with th'invisible and creeping wind,
> Draw the huge bottoms through the furrowed sea,
> Breasting the lofty surge. O, do but think
> You stand upon the rivage and behold
> A city on th'inconstant billows dancing . . .
>
> (Act III, Prol. 3–15)

This, though more buoyant and overtly enthusiastic, might be compared with Enobarbus' description of Cleopatra (which in fact recalls this Chorus in one or two details, e.g. 'silken tackle'). The style of *Antony and Cleopatra* diffuses over the entire play, in ways perceptible even where elusive of analysis, something of the author's own attitude to his material, which is, as far as possible, to be conveyed to the audience during the performance. A brief example will illustrate this. After his disgrace at Actium, Antony sends his schoolmaster as ambassador to Caesar. The schoolmaster introduces himself with these words:

> Such as I am, I come from Antony.
> I was of late as petty to his ends
> As is the morn-dew on the myrtle leaf
> To his grand sea. (III. xii. 7–10)

The dignified utterance is not unsuitable to the speaker, but its stylistic grace distances the moment, turning it into an object for our detached, almost aesthetic, scrutiny, but in a way that does not preclude sympathy for the speaker or being moved by his situation. Any number of other examples could be cited, such as the anonymous Centurion's remark, after Enobarbus' death: 'Hark!

the drums / Demurely wake the sleepers.' Such writing is a constant stimulus to a certain kind of imaginative activity in the audience. The directive to respond in a certain way is not as forthright as the Chorus's 'Think, when we talk of horses, that you see them', but it is of a related kind.

The uniquely expressive poetic style of *Antony and Cleopatra* is one means by which the audience is aroused to a high pitch of imaginative attention. Another aspect of the play which reflects the same intention in the author is structural—which returns us to our main concern. We have seen that Shakespeare seems to have adapted from *Henry V* the fundamental layout of his action, in which the decisive battle—Actium instead of Agincourt— occurs in the position usually designated as the fourth act. In most other structural respects, however, *Antony and Cleopatra* is very different, and in nothing more so than in that feature which has so often caused adverse critical comment : the unusual preponderance of short scenes. In modern editions of the play as many as forty-two separate scenes are numbered. Some of these scenes, particularly in the battle sequences, are as short as one or two speeches of a few lines each; they stand as sharp reminders that what we have to deal with is a play, primarily a script for acting, not a poem to be read. Granville-Barker helped to dispose of the late Victorian prejudice against such sequences by appealing to the conditions of the stage Shakespeare was writing for (and since Granville-Barker's day there have been a number of fairly successful productions of the play, usually designed with minimal stage scenery). To some extent Shakespeare's technique of short scenes can be explained with reference to his subject : unless he adopted the neoclassical solution, with its unities of time and place, he was committed to an action which included at least Rome and Alexandria among its locations and with frequent jumps from one to the other. But this explanation is only a partial one; it does not account for the whole play, and it does not explain why Shakespeare seems purposely to have constructed his plot so that the stage is repeatedly being cleared as one group of persons in one locality makes way for another group in another. A dramatist of Shakespeare's experience could easily have reduced the number of scenes if he had wanted to. It seems far more likely that he decided to turn to artistic advantage something which was already inherent in his subject.

What his purpose was can be inferred from the effect his technique of short scenes has on the audience. At a performance we become aware that our attention is being solicited in a certain way: in the first half of the play particularly, we are being required to look and watch, take notice, compare, essentially to let our understanding play over the scene. What we are not required to do is to become emotionally engaged to any great depth; indeed the structure of the scenes forbids it. For the action is continually breaking off without enlisting any strong emotional allegiance. Not, of course, that the dramatic material is dull or lifeless; it is, on the contrary, everywhere vivacious, full of personality and quick human awareness. But the rapid succession of little scenes, together with the emotional instability of some of its characters, breeds a sense of irony, even of comedy (again, especially in the first half) which does not allow an emotional response, although —such is the complexity of the play's mode—it does not rule out what might be called an intense affectionate involvement. In the second part of the play, however, the effect is different. The technique of short scenes continues to be used, but now with a far greater effect of continuity, as attention focuses unsparingly on the process of Antony's decline. Indeed in the scenes from III. vii to the end of the play we have the impression of something like unity of place: Actium–Alexandria–the Monument are all sufficiently ill defined to be acceptable as different spots in more or less the same locality, an effect quite different from the clearly denoted and far-flung localities of the first half: Egypt, Rome, Misenum, Syria, Athens. Time too is used in a different way in the second part: it is now no longer possible to ignore it (as it had been in the first), but as far as the lovers are concerned time is now limited and passes with increasing rapidity. It is quite in keeping with this emphasis on continuity that the action of the second part engages the audience's emotions to a far higher degree. The scenic juxtapositions still generate a play of irony, especially where Cleopatra is concerned, but the irony is now deeper, more gravely coloured, more simply tragic, than that of the blander critical mood of the earlier scenes.

To sum up this brief description of the play in terms of its style and structure: it combines intimacy with detachment.[1] The style,

---

[1] Although probably too early to have been designed expressly for the indoor Blackfriars playhouse (which the King's Men took over in 1608), the play may have been written with the strong possibility of that event kept in mind. (That it

allusive and particularized ('A certain queen to Caesar in a mattress') permits an intimacy of imaginative response; yet the technique of short scenes enforces a certain detachment. The constant interruptions to the dialogue and the restless shifting of points of view have the effect of encouraging reflection and a tentative evaluation of what is going on before us. The play's irony is of a humane, tolerant kind, not ever as harsh and reductive as that of, say, *Troilus and Cressida*. We are induced to assume a contemplative posture: unsparingly observant but sympathetic, and finally acquiescent. We have the means of passing judgement, but we refrain from doing so. This is the vision of the historical poet, as Shakespeare conceived it in this play.

III

There is one further feature of *Antony and Cleopatra* which deserves attention: the character of Enobarbus. He is not only the play's strongest supporting character; he also embodies a structural device of great importance to the play's dramatic effect.

As Antony's bluff soldierly counsellor, Enobarbus probably owes something in general conception to Lyly's Hephaestion in *Campaspe*. His role is to oppose his commander's love-in-idleness by exalting the military life over amorous entanglements. But in the way Enobarbus is presented, and especially in the relationship he early establishes with the audience, Shakespeare was probably drawing on the earlier Tudor tradition of the Vice. Not, of course, that there is anything seductively vicious about Enobarbus' point of view: quite the reverse. But he can be said to represent a structural principle of opposition to the dominant values of Egypt, just as the Vice habitually called in question the dominant values of the play in which he appeared.[1] Like the Vice, but in a smoother, more sophisticated way, Enobarbus enjoys a sense of *rapport* with the audience, since he carries with him an attitude of offhand informality which—in the first movement of the play, at least—frequently arouses laughter. He corresponds to that element

was acted at the Blackfriars we know from the Lord Chamberlain's record of 1669: see Irwin Smith, *Shakespeare's Blackfriars Playhouse* (London, 1966), pp. 503–4; but the list of plays 'formerly acted at the Blackfriars' also includes such works as *Richard III* and *King John* which were obviously intended in the first place for the public theatres.)

[1] See Bernard Spivack, *Shakespeare and the Allegory of Evil* (New York and London, 1958).

of controlled indecorum which is so important in the early stages of a play in enlisting the creative co-operation of the audience. The value of his presence can be judged by imagining the play (and particularly the first two acts) without him: if he were not there, something that contributes to the play's sense of inner perspective—its spatial, three-dimensional quality—would be missing. But it is not enough to speak of him, as is often done, simply as a 'choric' figure. The contribution of the Vice and his dramatic descendants is much more a matter of generating dramatic energy, arousing a fruitful spirit of irreverence, mockery, and humour, all of which are vitalizing agencies. Antony and Cleopatra themselves derive a good deal of their reality from Enobarbus' quizzical presence.

The Bastard Faulconbridge in *King John* is the character who seems to have served as Shakespeare's chief model for Enobarbus; and he shows even more clearly the strength of the Vice tradition. In the first two acts of *King John* his diction is low and familiar; he is given two long monologues, which bring him close to the audience—closer than anyone else in the play; and his mockery of the 'great ones', particularly in the scenes before Angiers, gives the play when acted a good deal of its life. Enobarbus is more quietly drawn, but in the triumvirate scene (II. ii) his rude interjections cause Antony to silence him (just as, to take another example of indecorous behaviour in the same Vice tradition, Prince Hal silences Falstaff in the camp scene of *1 Henry IV*: 'Peace, chewet, peace!', v. i. 29). And in his later squabble with Cleopatra, Enobarbus uses a trick of the Vice which had had a long stage history. Cleopatra is asserting her right to be at Antony's side in the war:

> *Cleopatra.* Is't not denounc'd against us? Why should not we
> Be there in person?
> *Enobarbus.* (*Aside*) Well, I could reply:
> If we should serve with horse and mare together
> The horse were merely lost; the mares would bear
> A soldier and his horse.
> *Cleopatra.* What is't you say?
> *Enobarbus.* Your presence needs must puzzle Antony . . .
>
> (III. vii. 4–10)

The Vice often made an improper remark which, when challenged, he covered up with an innocent gloss, as Enobarbus does here.

But these elements of the Vice account for only a few lineaments in Enobarbus' personality. His loyalty and integrity he shares with the Bastard, and like him he is considerably changed by events in the second part of the play. In the first part Enobarbus is largely the sardonic, often amusing, commentator, but in the second his tone is changed. He is now no longer detached, but tragically involved in Antony's fall, and in this development he follows the Bastard. As a structural device for guiding the emotional responses of the audience, Enobarbus' commentary, at first satirical, later more gravely and distressfully implicated, is crucially important.

There is one other matter which throws light on the growth of Enobarbus as a character, and indirectly on the development of the play as a whole. The following two sentences in Plutarch formed the basis of Shakespeare's treatment: 'Furthermore, he dealt very friendly and courteously with Domitius, and against Cleopatra's mind. For, he being sick of an ague when he went and took a little boat to go unto Caesar's camp, Antonius was very sorry for it, but yet he sent after him all his carriage, train, and men; and the same Domitius, as though he gave him to understand that he repented his open treason, he died immediately after.'[1]

What Shakespeare does is to present the full process by which Enobarbus reaches his decision to leave Antony, stressing the painful conflict between a loyalty which may become, or seem to become, 'mere folly', and a disloyalty which may seem approved by reason. In the scene of his death, Enobarbus appeals to night and the moon to 'witness' his repentance. He now believes that if the world is to remember him it will be simply as a deserter:

> O Antony,
> Nobler than my revolt is infamous,
> Forgive me in thine own particular,
> But let the world rank me in register
> A master-leaver and a fugitive!
>
> (IV. ix. 18–22)

Like the other chief characters of the play, Enobarbus is very aware of the way he will be remembered, if at all, by posterity. Here at his death he expects the verdict of history to be

[1] *Shakespeare's Plutarch*, pp. 252–3.

uncompromisingly harsh: Enobarbus the deserter. The sad irony is that that is how he was in fact remembered by the one historian who noticed his existence. In Plutarch he figures in the passage just quoted as the deserter who seemed to repent because he died of an ague. Shakespeare's play, however, bears full 'witness' to the complexity of the facts and of the issues involved—and also of the difficulty of making any judgement except one based on sympathy. (There is no mention of an ague: Enobarbus seems to die of remorse.) The place Enobarbus 'earns i' th' story' is not, in the play, the one he expects.

It may be that Shakespeare had in mind a remark about fame made by the younger Pliny: 'Summam enim rerum nuntiat fama, non ordinem', which Herrick translated:

> 'Tis still observ'd, that Fame ne'er sings
> The order, but the Sum of things.[1]

Whereas Fame remembers only what crudely happened, what is made publicly known, the poet—in this case, Shakespeare—is concerned with what precedes 'the Sum of things', the full process which led up to the final *tableau*: what Enobarbus was like before the final desertion which earned him Plutarch's attention.

IV

A more detailed commentary follows on the scenic forms of *Antony and Cleopatra*.

The first movement opens with an emphatic *tableau* scene. As often in such scenes there are two 'presenters', one of whom bids the other to watch, with an implied injunction to the audience: 'Look where they come', 'Take but good note', 'Behold and see'. (An example in a recent play would be Lady Macbeth's sleep-walking—a *tableau* of the guilty mind—which also has two 'presenters'.) Antony, Cleopatra, and their train take up their position, and the lovers assume a characteristic posture, one in which they are remembered in fame: they embrace, and Antony rejects a messenger. Cleopatra's repeated taunting that Antony should hear the messengers and Antony's refusal to do so form a completely

[1] See *Poetical Works of Robert Herrick*, ed. L. C. Martin (Oxford, 1956), p. 245. Martin gives the source in Pliny as *Ep.* iv. 11. 15. 'Herrick', he notes, 'therefore means by "Sum" (l. 2) the upshot, and by "order" the processes or incidents leading to it' (p. 551).

typical action, something invented by Shakespeare to subserve the *tableau*. The entire scene can be contemplated in pictorial terms, and a caption might be supplied: Antony neglects Empire for Love. Shakespeare is probably also remembering Lyly's *Campaspe*, which dealt with a theme relevant to his present concerns: Alexander the Great in love. The scenes between Clytus and Parmenio, the soldiers who disapprove of Alexander's amorous idleness (I. i, III. iv, and especially IV. iii) may have prompted Shakespeare's use here of the hostile pair Demetrius and Philo (just as Lyly's Hephaestion strongly anticipates Enobarbus).

The following two scenes establish the languid, aimless atmosphere of gossip and chatter out of which Antony has to extricate himself. The rapid comings and goings of the characters suggest a world of thoughtless mobility: Cleopatra's appearance and wilful departure within a few moments epitomize a way of life hostile to sober reason. The news of Fulvia's death and of the threat posed by Sextus Pompeius mark the point at which Shakespeare takes up Plutarch's narrative sequence. Gradually Antony's newly formed purpose to leave Egypt makes headway and has the effect of imposing direction on these scenes.

Throughout this first movement (until III. vi), the play's scenic contours are very lightly moulded; much of the writing, though always precise and allusive, is curiously unemphatic. There is little passionate conviction and therefore no strong dramatic climax. Cleopatra provides an element of histrionic self-consciousness, but her wilfulness and duplicity have a cooling effect; the big scene she stages before Antony's departure (I. iii) is almost like a play-within-a-play, but her extravagant attitudes and mannered shifts of tone rob it of warmth—we watch it with an eye to her artistry, with something of Demetrius' and Philo's acid detachment. Throughout this part of the play Shakespeare makes do with very little in the way of firm plot, although the allusiveness of the dialogue helps to conceal this. Only two scenes have a strong sense of present occasion: the meeting of the triumvirate (II. ii) towards which the earlier scenes have been building up, and the feast on Pompey's galley (II. vii), which also receives careful preparation. The marriage between Antony and Octavia, which is the immediate outcome of the triumvirate's meeting, is referred to but scarcely dramatized; but Shakespeare skilfully makes it the *raison d'être* of the two scenes with Cleopatra—which is all she is given in this part of the sequence. (As Granville-Barker noted, a difficulty in Shakespeare's material here was that Cleopatra had nothing to do but wait for Antony's return.) Most of the other scenes have a peripheral relation to the main subject, Antony himself: thus Caesar and Lepidus discuss Antony (i. iv), so does Cleopatra (i. v), so do Pompey and Menas (ii. i). When Antony arrives in Rome (ii. ii), the play seems to take on a solider substance, which continues until the galley scene. Immediately after it (iii. i), Ventidius appears in Parthia, and again turns the subject towards Antony; and in two of the last scenes in this sequence (iii. v, iii. vi) Antony is again the off-stage subject of discussion. Despite the great resourcefulness of the writing, there is undoubtedly something wanting in dramatic substance in some of these scenes, perhaps too much in the way of ante-room drama; we may feel that we are too seldom at the growing-point of action. This is certainly a common response of reader and spectator; but it may be that Shakespeare's intention in this part of the play is, in a special sense, a narrative one (as it was in *Henry V*). In this play he is to a great extent submitting himself to the arbitrary particulars of history, telling us what happened, not imposing a clear pattern on to events—but all the time inducing in us a special way of looking at those events.

At the same time Shakespeare places his simple, often elementary, scenic forms in a sequence which takes extremely careful account of time and place. After the first minor climax, Antony's departure from Cleopatra (i. iii), Antony's journey from Egypt to Rome is traced in such a way that we are made conscious of the distance involved—a way of taking up the pointed reference to 'space' in Antony's first major speech in i. i ('Here is my space'). So instead of having Antony arriving in Rome at the end of i. iv (in which Caesar and Lepidus first appear), Shakespeare has Caesar urging Antony, in an apostrophe, to leave Cleopatra, and then, in the brilliantly written little scene that follows, shows Cleopatra with nothing to do except write to and receive messages from Antony. Her idle musing ('Where think'st thou he is now?') places him at some medial point *en route*, while her words 'That I might sleep out this great gap of time / My Antony is away' are invented with a purpose, because this in a way is what she does—as a character she is absent from the stage until ii. v. Her final words ('He shall have every day a several greeting, / Or I'll unpeople Egypt') push us forward in the sequence by making us look ahead to Antony. The next scene introduces Pompey and Menas; but Antony's journey is still in progress, since a messenger announces 'Mark Antony is every hour in Rome / Expected. Since he went from Egypt 'tis / A space for farther travel' (he has had time to go even further than Rome). Space is repeatedly being defined in terms of time, and time in terms of space : so here 'A space for farther travel', just as previously Cleopatra had referred to 'this great gap of time'. Later an otherwise otiose scene (II. iv) of ten lines is included simply in order to recall to us the journeying involved from Rome to Misenum and to insist once more on the space-time dimension.

This way of stressing geographical distances and the time taken to traverse them alerts us to what was after all for the persons of the history an irreducible and unignorable reality—the physical milieu in which they lived and which they took for granted. It reminds us that these persons were actual human beings, not mere characters in a story. As in *Henry V*, with its concern to bring 'the vasty fields of France' vividly before our inner vision, so here Shakespeare seems intent on stretching our historical imaginations to the utmost, making us *see* that that is how it was for them then. And certainly, the curious aimlessness, the seemingly over-generous detail, of this first part of the play does very effectively evoke something of the wasteful drifting movement of the life-process (which is very much part of Shakespeare's artistic concern throughout the play). In this use of structural syntax, with its nice sense of the temporal measurement of space, *Antony and Cleopatra* is possibly the most sensitive of all the plays; in its care for the nuances of scenic sequence lies much of its formal excellence.

The confrontation of Antony and Caesar (II. ii) makes the first, though moderate, climax of this part of the sequence; it is the longest scene so far. It has been prepared for ever since I. ii, and is handled with the reticence, the lack of loud emphasis, characteristic of this play. Seeing Antony back in Rome among Romans in itself gives the audience a kind of relief; the anxiety aroused by the play's opening *tableau* is now momentarily eased. The occasion is one of some solemn formality, yet the gravity of the meeting is undermined by the play's firmly unheroic, human-scaled view of its characters, with Enobarbus (until he is silenced) calling attention to some of the meaner realities underlying it. Irony plays over the entire scene, not least in the mischievous juxtaposition of its two parts: the public part issuing in the political marriage of Antony and Octavia, the private part that follows when Enobarbus describes Cleopatra. In performance this scene is felt to be robustly planned, for all its quiet irony and sophisticated restraint. One reason is perhaps that Shakespeare has adapted it, very freely, from the lively sequence in *King John* (II. i), in which the forces of England and France, drawn up in opposition before the walls of Angiers, are temporarily reconciled by means of a political marriage. The situation in the two plays is remarkably similar at this point, so similar that Shakespeare was able to take *King John* as a model for this part of the sequence. Octavia corresponds to Blanch, and Enobarbus to the Bastard Faulconbridge, the honest sardonic spectator of the unpalatable goings-on.[1] Everything is more delicate in the later play; nothing is strident or blatant; the irony is less explicit. (At the same time the whole Angiers sequence is an impressively sustained piece of political satire, written with an engaging warmth of indignation.) At the end of the scene, in the place occupied by the Bastard's monologue on 'Commodity', Enobarbus speaks his description of Cleopatra on the Cydnus—an adroit placing of the elaborate passage in Plutarch, which was too good not to use.

Two brief scenes follow, and then Cleopatra herself is shown receiving the news of Antony's marriage (II. v). The scene is a brilliantly devised one-act play; it has real shape, which is grounded upon a strong sense of occasion. Structurally it is simply another on the model of such earlier scenes as I. iv, I. v, and II. i: two persons talk; a messenger enters and delivers his message; they all go out. But this time Shakespeare enlivens the occasion by making the messenger an important character in the scene, so that the delivery of the message itself constitutes the dramatic action. The 'germ' of the scene is again one from *King John*. King John and Philip of France have patched up a peace by arranging a marriage between Blanch, niece to John, and the Dauphin Lewis; in doing so, Philip has deserted the cause of Constance and Arthur. In the scene in question (III. i. 1–74), which immediately follows the scene

---

[1] In a later scene (III. iv. 12–20), Octavia speaks in terms very like those used by Blanch; cf. *King John*, III. ii. 327–36.

before Angiers, the unwelcome news is broken to Constance by Salisbury. In each case the outraged woman turns on the innocent messenger and tells him he has been made ugly by his ugly mission. Constance says to Salisbury:

> Fellow, be gone: I cannot brook thy sight;
> This news hath made thee a most ugly man.
>
> (III. i. 36–7)

while Cleopatra says to the Messenger:

> Go, get thee hence.
> Hadst thou Narcissus in thy face, to me
> Thou wouldst appear most ugly.
>
> (II. v. 95–7)

What was tragic in Constance's situation becomes urbane comedy here.[1]

The following two scenes complete the Pompey action: the first, the meeting of the triumvirate with Pompey, acts in effect as a prologue to the second, the feast on Pompey's galley. The feast scene (II. vii) is the last of the high points in this first movement; a self-contained convivial occasion, but also one which brings to a focus the ironies more diffusely expressed in the preceding scenes: the dignified roles of the triumvirs clashing with their drunken vulnerable private selves, and the conviviality of the feast menaced by ambitious treachery. As in the case of the previous strong scenes in this part of the sequence, the scene is apparently modelled on an earlier one. The scene in question is the feast (or ball) scene in *Romeo and Juliet* (I. v), whose structure is closely followed. This scene opens with servants conversing; then Capulet welcomes the guests and sets them dancing; Romeo sees Juliet and asks a servant her name; he is overheard by Tybalt, who is about to attack him when he is restrained by Capulet; Romeo and Juliet meet, speak, and kiss; the guests depart, leaving Juliet with the Nurse who informs her of Romeo's name and family. Pompey's feast scene is similarly composed of a series of brief actions. It opens with two servants; the company enters, Antony supplying a flow of talk; Pompey is drawn aside by

---

[1] In his article 'Elizabeth I, Jodelle and Cleopatra', *Renaissance Drama*, New Series, vol. 2 (1969), Kenneth Muir notes that Cleopatra's physical attack on the Messenger is adapted by Shakespeare from Plutarch's account of her ill-treatment of her treasurer Seleucus.

Menas, who suggests killing the triumvirs; Pompey refuses; the feast grows to its climax with the bacchic song; the company departs, leaving Enobarbus with Menas. In a way similar in each case, the host crushes a murderous threat to the festive mood. Both scenes are roughly equal in length and comparable in shape: from the servants' talk the feast grows to a climax and then diminishes to a duologue, rueful in tone. The dialogue is well orchestrated in brief, charged exchanges, distributed among several speakers, with quick transitions from group to group.

The following six short scenes take us up to the interval (if the former analysis was correct). The first two (III. i and III. ii) dispose of the triumvirate part of the action. In the first, Ventidius' triumph in Syria presents what one would expect to be a major spectacle in severely muted terms. The stage pictures at this point in the sequence reinforce the play's political irony, which is now at its most mordant (though even here not really harsh, but softened by understatement). For Pompey's drunken feast in all its indecorous informality is given more theatrical emphasis than the triumph that follows, which is presented in an oblique peripheral way. The next scene shows the triumvirate for the last time; the occasion is one of dispersal, with Caesar bidding farewell to Octavia and Antony (the two men never meet again), and Lepidus at this point retiring from the action altogether.[1] The sequence here is the most lightly dramatized of the whole play: little seems to be happening, yet suddenly everything has happened. Cleopatra hears Octavia described, and decides to wait ('All may be well enough', III. iii. 46)—a moment which is the still point in the sequence. For the following three scenes each suggest an accelerating movement: the stress is on haste, great events are imminent, and finally (III. vi) things seem to be happening simultaneously, with extraordinary suddenness: Antony is back with Cleopatra, Octavia with her brother, and Caesar is gathering his strength for the coming war. And finally (as we have

---

[1] In this farewell scene there is possibly a slight reminiscence of the parting sequence in *Troilus and Cressida* (IV. ii, iv). Cf. Troilus' 'As many farewells as be stars in heaven' (IV. iv. 43) and Lepidus' 'Let all the number of the stars give light / To your fair way!', which is followed by repeated farewells (III. ii. 65–6). Cressida's behaviour in this sequence at moments anticipates Cleopatra's in her first scene with the Messenger; both hear bad news and extravagantly refuse to believe it; cf. Cressida's 'And is it true that I must go from Troy? . . . What, and from Troilus too? . . . Is't possible?', and Cleopatra's 'Is he married?' (II. v. 89).

seen) he speaks with the superhuman confidence of a man of destiny.[1] In the second movement of the play everything will be conceived from a different viewpoint.

In this second movement we follow, throughout a single unbroken sequence, the fortunes of Antony and Cleopatra from the day of the first battle to their deaths. Editors mark the sequence off into twenty-four separate scenes, most of them short, only three of which receive the emphasis of substantial length: the temptation of Cleopatra by Thyreus (III. xiii); Antony's death, which occupies two scenes, but which is a single continuous action (IV. xiv, xv); and the final scene, Cleopatra's death (V. ii), by far the longest of the whole play.

The greater part of this sequence (III. vi to IV. xii) is taken up with the wars between Antony and Caesar. In Plutarch these wars extended over a considerable period (Antony's Timon-like retreat occurring in the middle); but Shakespeare compresses the process so as to make it seem more like a three-day battle, although the duration of the action is in fact left indefinite. What we see happening are three military engagements, of which the first and third are disastrous defeats for Antony, while the second is a briefly enjoyed victory which serves temporarily to raise his morale. For this plot sequence Shakespeare used an early play as a structural guide. The play was the *Henry VI, Part One*, of which the relevant scenes were the sequence showing the struggle between the English and French for Orleans (I. ii, iv, v. vi, II. i). In I. ii we are shown the French army, led by Charles the Dauphin, being defeated by the English. Later in the scene Joan la Pucelle makes her first appearance, and persuades the Dauphin to support her. In the next battle, the French, inspired by Joan, defeat the English, and even Talbot is forced to retreat. But a reversal quickly follows: Orleans is recovered by the English, and the French are put to flight. In this sequence the Dauphin corresponds to Antony, and Joan to Cleopatra, so that the series is in both cases one of defeat, followed by victory, followed by defeat. Of course the scale of the military action is very much larger in *Antony and Cleopatra*, and the likenesses are obscured by circumstantial

[1] With Caesar's prophetic note here, cf. Pandulph's speech to the Dauphin: 'Now hear me speak with a prophetic spirit . . .' (*King John*, III. iv. 126 ff.). If my analysis is correct, both speeches come at the end of the first movement of their respective plays. They both predict accurately, though in general terms, what is to happen in the second part.

differences; but that Shakespeare did in fact recall the Orleans
sequence is further supported by verbal and thematic correspondences. The obvious point of contact in both plays is that a military
leader allies himself with a woman, who is—in different ways—
associated with 'witchcraft' (Pompey associates Cleopatra with
'witchcraft' at II. i. 22, and Antony refers to her as a 'witch' at
IV. xii. 47); and Joan is like Cleopatra in that she is said to be
unchaste. In scenic terms the plays come closest together in their
treatment of the victory and the second defeat. The French capture of Orleans is followed by a scene of triumph in which the
Dauphin, Joan, and the other French leaders appear *'on the walls'*
of Orleans, and the Dauphin rapturously eulogizes Joan:

> A statelier pyramis to her I'll rear
> Than Rhodope's of Memphis ever was . . .
>
> (I. vi. 21–2)

(This reference to a Greek courtesan in Egypt is notable.) They
go off to 'banquet royally', and a quiet sentry scene follows, with
a Sergeant instructing his men to keep in touch with him at 'the
court of guard' (II. i. 4). The corresponding scene in *Antony and
Cleopatra* shows Antony returning to Cleopatra after his victory
and greeting her with the most clangorously sonorous rhetoric
in the play

> Trumpeters,
> With brazen din blast you the city's ear . . .
>
> (IV. viii. 35–6)

which is then immediately followed by a quiet night scene with
sentries: the Centurion, like the Sergeant, refers to the 'court of
guard' (IV. ix. 2). Both groups of sentries contrast their own state
with the quiet of sleepers in their beds, and the Centurion's
remark

> Hark! the drums
> Demurely wake the sleepers
>
> (29–30)

is perhaps anticipated in the speech of Reignier's in the corresponding scene:

> 'Twas time, I trow, to wake and leave our beds,
> Hearing alarums at our chamber doors.
>
> (II. i. 41–2)

Finally, when the French suffer a second defeat, the Dauphin puts the blame on to Joan:

> *Charles.* Is this thy cunning, thou deceitful dame?
> Didst thou at first, to flatter us withal,
> Make us partakers of a little gain
> That now our loss might be ten times so much?
> *Pucelle.* Wherefore is Charles impatient with his friend?
>
> (II. i. 50–4)

After his final defeat Antony similarly turns against Cleopatra, but with far greater violence:

> *Antony.* O this false soul of Egypt! this grave charm— . . .
> Like a right gipsy hath at fast and loose
> Beguil'd me to the very heart of loss.
> What, Eros, Eros!
>
> *Enter* CLEOPATRA.
>
> Ah, thou spell! Avaunt!
> *Cleopatra.* Why is my lord enrag'd against his love?
>
> (IV. xii. 25–31)

Both men believe that the woman has cheated them by granting them some gain before plunging them into utter loss. Both women seem genuinely taken by surprise—indeed the tone and movement of Joan's and Cleopatra's reply are unmistakably similar. So much for the main structural model for the battle sequences in *Antony and Cleopatra*.

In this second movement of the play the individual scenes, considered as editorial units, are often without much striking structural design; there is little or nothing like the symmetries and the obtrusively artful matching and contrasting of the early history plays, nor on the other hand anything like the more profoundly wrought patterning of such a scene as the banquet scene in *Macbeth*. But this absence of a certain kind of formality is not inadvertent, certainly not a sign of failure. On the contrary, one purpose of the sequence is to avoid obtrusive patterning, to convey something of the day-to-day, even minute-to-minute, feel of experience without interposing the large formal constructions of conventional drama between the spectators and the happenings themselves.[1] A comparison with *Macbeth* may make this clearer.

---

[1] Cf. Hazlitt's comment on the play: 'The characters breathe, move, and live . . . [Shakespeare] does not present us with groups of stage-puppets or poetical machines making set speeches on human life, and acting from a calculation of ostensible

In the last act of *Macbeth* Shakespeare uses a technique of short scenes in some ways like that of *Antony and Cleopatra*. But the whole process of Macbeth's isolation and destruction is presented in an ordered, measured way suggestive of ceremony or ritual. Nothing is unexpected or out of place: Malcolm, for example, does not meet with an unexpected set-back, but everything goes according to plan. Even the loss of Young Siward may be felt to be fitting. In the present sequence in *Antony and Cleopatra*, however, there is nothing of the pre-ordained movement of ceremony, but instead the kind of haphazard succession of seemingly arbitrary happenings which is characteristic of phenomenal experience. We are made aware of fortune's mutability, the impossibility of predicting what the next day will bring, and also of the ceaseless play of mood in the human personality, the quick-changing feelings of living men and women. A remark of Canidius' at the end of the first scene in this sequence alerts us to this sense of the unrepeatable present moment of experience:

> With news the time's with labour, and throes forth
> Each minute some.
>
> (III. vii. 80–1)

It also perhaps suggests something of the play's bifocal historical vision: we know how these events issued since we know the end of the story, but we are also partially suppressing our knowledge in order to share imaginatively the characters' own human ignorance of the future. The fact that Caesar and the soothsayer are more than once given a foreknowledge of the larger outcome of things does not essentially modify the play's otherwise mundane realism.

But one question needs to be raised. If these scenes are trying to convey an illusion of wayward random experience, how is it that they avoid lapsing into mere formlessness? Of all the genres which use language, drama can perhaps least dispense with strong structural bracing. Part of the answer must be that Shakespeare exploits the audience's knowledge of the historical outcome (as I have just suggested). The first thing we know of Antony and

motives, but he brings living men and women on the scene, who speak and act from real feelings, according to the ebbs and flows of passion, without the least tincture of the pedantry of logic or rhetoric. Nothing is made out by inference and analogy, by climax and antithesis, but everything takes place just as it would have done in reality, according to the occasion.' (*The Characters of Shakespeare's Plays*, 1817.)

Cleopatra is that they were famous lovers who were defeated (they would probably not be famous if they had not been defeated). With Antony's coming defeat taken for granted (and the earlier presence of the Soothsayer and Caesar's remark about 'determin'd things to destiny' are inescapable reminders of the end), Shakespeare's material in this sequence is in one respect already formed: there is a given *terminus ad quem*. This allows Shakespeare the opportunity to work within a demarcated space, a limited area within which the random irruptions of chance can be admitted without prejudice to the sequence's containing form. We can therefore follow the meandering course of Antony to his death without feeling that we are merely meandering. But another reason is that some degree of system has in fact been imposed on the events of history as found in Plutarch; there is clear evidence of artistic selection and patterning. The adaptation of the three-battle sequence in *1 Henry VI* has already been mentioned. Here the aftermath of the two defeats is given extended treatment: the first in the scenes concerning Thyreus and his attempt to corrupt Cleopatra (III. xii, xiii), the second in Antony's preparations for suicide and his eventual death in Cleopatra's Monument (IV. xiv, xv). But there is nothing to suggest any facile symmetry.

But the fullest answer to the question 'What keeps these scenes from lapsing into formlessness?' is simply that, for all their concern with rendering the random flow of events, they are in fact themselves exquisitely ordered: the sequence is a marvel of minute plotting—and any illusion of life-likeness should not be confused with the reality of formidable artistry. Every small episode is in its place; the order of the sequence cannot be changed without loss. For example, at the end of III. xiii Enobarbus announces in a soliloquy (it is in the last lines of a long scene): 'I will seek / Some way to leave him'. The announcement comes with a beautiful quietness; it has long been expected, but when it comes it comes as a surprise. However, with Antony's next appearance (IV. ii) it also comes as a surprise that Enobarbus is still with him. The scene opens: 'He will not fight with me, Domitius?' And throughout this brief scene, in which Antony puzzles Cleopatra by his emotional behaviour with his servants, Enobarbus acts as usual—as the one who is closest to Antony and understands him best. The following three brief scenes see the passing of night and the coming of morning: the soldiers hear music under the earth; Cleopatra helps Antony to arm and sees him go out to battle; and Antony then hears from a soldier of Enobarbus' desertion. In sending his treasure after him, Antony shows unexpected forbearance and magnanimity. We next (IV. vi) see Caesar preparing for the battle, confident as always ('Our will is Antony be took alive') and speaking more largely of the final outcome:

> The time of universal peace is near.
> Prove this a prosp'rous day, the three-nook'd world
> Shall bear the olive freely.

The *pax Romana* seems imminent. But the rest of the scene shows Enobarbus' remorse and shame at Antony's generosity. The next scene opens the second battle action—but, quite unexpectedly, Antony is in luck: Agrippa calls a retreat, and 'Caesar himself has work'. Antony and Scarus emerge briefly from the fighting, and reappear (IV. viii) for the most heroic passage in the entire play, in which they march with the victorious army back into Alexandria, met on the way by Cleopatra. The whole of this sequence (III. xiii to IV. viii) has both the sequaciousness and the unpredictability of actual experience. Thus Enobarbus reappears once after he has decided to leave Antony; so Caesar's confident pronouncement is placed immediately before his temporary defeat; so too after the ominous withdrawal of the god Hercules from Antony's side and Cleopatra's murmured admission of her loss of faith in Antony, Antony's day turns out to be victorious. The entire sequence is a succession of small surprises, none of which is forced; it is all natural-seeming and convincing—life is like this.

The technique of short scenes is essential to the effect: for it helps to focus our attention on to the notion of causality, but with a sharp awareness of the true intricacy of the working of cause and effect. There is here a Montaignian sense of the complexity of the process of flux, which the precise ordering of the often very circumscribed scenic units helps to define; indeed without this technique it is hard to see how Shakespeare could have conveyed this sense of combined continuity and discontinuity.[1] Moreover the

---

[1] One may observe that a writer like Sterne, for example, another close reader of Montaigne and also anxious to render the precise feel of experience, is driven to construct a narrative sequence formed of comparably brief units (this is especially noticeable in *A Sentimental Journey*).

dialogue of these scenes—the topics of conversation—is such as to confirm us in our concentration on the process of causality and sequence. Nothing distracts us from attending to the present moment and the next, what is and what will be: Caesar, says Antony, makes him angry

> harping on what I am,
> Not what he knew I was

(III. xiii. 142–3)

and the remark brings out sharply Antony's doomed attempt to swim against the current of time. Cleopatra is more realistic: seeing Antony go out to battle, she says merely, 'Then, Antony—but now' (IV. iv. 38). Granville-Barker is admirable on this battle sequence, and he concludes: 'We have been ideal spectators, we know what happened, and why; and just such an impression has been made on us as the reality would leave behind. It is a great technical achievement, and one of great artistry too.'[1] We might recall from *Henry V* the Chorus's 'Follow, follow!', and the repeated injunctions to the audience to supply continuity to the action:

> Still be kind,
> And eke out our performance with your mind.

We can now resume the commentary on the second movement. The tone is set at the outset (III. vii. 1 ff.) by the bickerings of Cleopatra and Enobarbus and the repeated warnings, all unheeded, made to Antony by the professional soldiers. The occasion of the scene (a common one in Elizabethan drama, of course) is the immediate prelude to a battle. But here the tone is one of ominous indecorum—discord, foolhardiness, and the presence of women. The fight itself is passed over with all possible brevity—stylized marchings, and sounds off—until the re-entry of Enobarbus, followed by Scarus, and then by Canidius, so that connected dialogue can be resumed. All three soldiers are appalled by the shame of Antony's flight; their horror serves as a prelude to the appearance of Antony himself, reserved for the next scene. Antony's entry (III. xi) is thus well prepared for. The scene can be regarded as a *tableau* illustrative of despair, as Antony repeatedly urges his attendants to flight and sinks to the ground in silence; and when

[1] Granville-Barker, op. cit., p. 399.

the servants draw Cleopatra to him, the dialogue is got going
again only with difficulty. There is something nakedly direct in
this exhibition of Antony's shame. Nothing comes between us
and Antony's sober awareness of his loss of honour.

> *Antony.* No, no, no, no, no.
> *Eros.* See you here, sir?
> *Antony.* O, fie, fie, fie!
>
> (III. xi. 29–31)

Moreover the fact that his shame is at this moment being dramatized, being publicly re-enacted, makes its own contribution to
our imaginative experience. Antony has, so to say, the eyes not
only of his contemporaries upon him but of posterity as well. In
watching the tragedy we are helping to perpetuate his humiliation
along with his fame, but, under Shakespeare's guidance, doing so
with an informed sympathy.

The next action is initiated in III. xii : Caesar dispatches Thyreus
with the task of seducing Cleopatra from Antony. The hint of
intrigue gives Shakespeare the chance to develop a scene much
more extended than any earlier in this sequence. Like most of the
longer scenes in the play this one gives an important role to a
messenger, who to a certain extent acts as a surrogate for an
absent personage; in this case, Caesar. Caesar's scheme actually
fails : Thyreus does not succeed in seducing Cleopatra. But the
failure seems merely nominal, since she receives him graciously,
their talk being broken off only by Antony's unexpected return.
In one sense the entire scene, for all Antony's violent 'passion',
accomplishes nothing : Antony declares himself 'satisfied' by
Cleopatra's highly coloured self-defence, and they go off together
to 'one other gaudy night'. Yet Enobarbus' story, at least, enters
a crucial phase : his murmured asides are like an interrupted but
essentially continuous soliloquy, which lends the scene an invalu-
able spatial dimension; and it is with an effect of firmness and
decisiveness, making a complete contrast with Antony's vacil-
lations, that he ends the episode with the quiet announcement,
'I will seek / Some way to leave him.' So in effect Caesar seduces,
not Cleopatra, but Enobarbus—a brilliant Shakespearian interpretation of a few sentences in Plutarch.[1]

---

[1] Enobarbus' soliloquies and asides in this sequence (III. x to III. xiii) seem to
recall something of Exeter's soliloquies in *1 Henry VI* (II. i. 187–201; IV. i. 182–94).

There follows a series of short scenes, each enriched with sharp phrasing and with occasional memorable incident, but none of them given the deeper emphasis of extended development. These scenes (IV. i–x) magically suggest the swift passage of time, as day gives way to night, night to day, and day to night again, and as we change from one camp to the other. Antony is at his most moody and volatile, now embarrassingly pathetic (IV. ii), now romantically valiant as he goes forth to battle (iv), now sadly but superbly magnanimous as he sends Enobarbus' treasure after him (v), and then radiantly heroic after his moment of victory (viii). But each mood is held only for a moment. We are given glimpses, snapshots, of the experience as it was, while the *full* experience—the full sum of moments lived through—defies imagination. Sound-effects are magnificently used to evoke the unreal insubstantiality of the minute-to-minute experience. Antony's return to Cleopatra after his victory gives rise to superb hyperbolical rhetoric and ear-splitting trumpets, which are then immediately followed by the noiseless night scene of Caesar's soldiers, with the whispered exchanges of the guards, Enobarbus' quiet death, and the exquisite drum-effect ('Hark! the drums demurely wake the sleepers'). (Earlier in this sequence, III. x. 33–7 and IV. vi. 12–39, the theme of desertion and betrayal recalls some passages in *King John*, v. iv; for the bad treatment Caesar metes out to those who have deserted to him from Antony is very similar to the Dauphin's proposed treachery to the English lords who have defected to him. Unlike the Bastard Faulconbridge, his closest prototype in the earlier play, Enobarbus does desert his master, but his feelings of guilt align him with the English lords.)

The final part of this Actium sequence begins with Antony in slightly hysterical high spirits (IV. x. 3–4). Shortly after, he reappears with Scarus (IV. xii) and, a little oddly, goes off promising to bring back news ('I'll bring thee word / Straight how 'tis like to go'). This arrangement is a little surprising, since it makes Antony act as messenger to his own subordinate (it finds a later parallel in Antony's tribute to Eros: 'Thy master dies thy scholar', IV. xiv. 102). At this point, then, he goes off stage, to return a few moments later with an abrupt lack of ceremony. Everything is over: 'All is lost!' And suddenly, by what seems an immensely rapid transformation, the battle setting and all its paraphernalia are removed (Scarus leaves, never to return), and Antony is alone, in a state of agonized dissolution. The feeling represented here is so unendurably intense that even Shakespeare's words may seem at first almost inadequate, and the dramatization itself seems to resort to something like mime: Cleopatra appears and quickly disappears while Antony rages on and on without restraint. The whole scene is a curiously simple, even formless, exhibition of passion. It is, one should note, quite unlike such scenes of passion as the last phase of Othello's temptation scene or Lear's scene before Gloucester's castle (or the passion scene in Act Three of *Titus Andronicus*). Those scenes carry the audience with the protagonist by carefully gradated degrees up to a maximum pitch of feeling; they are rhetorically shaped to a climax. This scene, however, is not so shaped, intentionally not, since the concern is not now to engage our feelings in any profoundly upheaving way, but rather to make us see Antony—certainly with sympathy, but in a contemplative spirit—in the ineffable moment of his final collapse. The very abruptness of the 'passion' ensures our comparative detachment. We *watch* it, understanding it. (The model for this scene seems to be the reception of the defeat of Agincourt by the French lords, the exactly corresponding point of *Henry V*. In this scene, IV. v, the 'passion' is shared between four speakers; Orleans cries 'tout est perdu!', like Antony; and the keynote is shame, 'Reproach and ever lasting shame', 'O perdurable shame!', 'Shame, and eternal shame, nothing but shame!' The final line is exactly in Antony's mood: 'Let life be short, else shame will be too long.')

After a few moments—Cleopatra and Charmian come and go—the mood has changed. For Antony, no doubt, several hours have passed; for us it is literally two or three minutes, and another adjustment is required of us. Antony's reappearance (IV. xiv) initiates the sequence which is ended only with his death and Cleopatra's lament. The impression made by this scene is again that Antony is doing a solo act, supported for brief passages by subordinate interlocutors (Eros, Mardian, Dercetas, and soldiers), but essentially engaged in a long monologue. The scene is more an effusion than a construction, following the wavering stream of Antony's thoughts and what happens to happen. There are, of course, brief passages which rise to formality: Antony's opening description of the clouds and their likeness to himself, Mardian's announcement of Cleopatra's death, and the leave-taking of

Antony and Eros which leads up to Eros' sudden suicide. But otherwise there is little obvious patterning; one has instead the sense that this is simply how it was—in all its digressive uncertain onward movement, its private, informal tone, and its capacity for lifelike anticlimax (Antony tries and fails to make a clean job of his suicide). Antony has 'lost command' and lost his way, and the scene itself reflects something of his feeling of deliquescence, his loss of a sense of direction; he has become passive and feminine, weaker than his servants, impractical and ineffective. Shakespeare is in fact (as Dover Wilson noted) keeping very close to Plutarch here: this scene and the next (iv. xv) are substantially straight-forward dramatizations of Plutarch; whatever verbal heightening Shakespeare contributes, the historical narrative is being allowed to speak for itself. Cleopatra's personality dominates and energizes the Monument scene which follows, so that although Antony is by now wholly quiet and acquiescent, his death is given dramatic emphasis by her lament, swoon, and words of resolution. But still the dramatist is submitting himself to the events of history rather than imposing his own patterns; and this is so, to a large extent, until the end of the play.

The next scene (v. i) makes the transition to the final movement with as little delay as possible—Caesar receives the news of Antony's death (so dealing with the immediate past); he then prepares for the capture of Cleopatra (so dealing with the immediate future). His apostrophe to Antony (35–48)—matching the one he had made to him in his first scene (i. iv. 55–71)—serves to dispose summarily of Antony before turning to the new interest, Cleopatra and her fate.[1] Towards the end of this scene, we are given more details of Caesar's efficiency: he momentarily forgets what Dolabella is doing, but quickly recovers himself, 'Let him alone, for I remember now / How he's employed' (69–72). Caesar's efficient messenger service has been well established earlier in the play; he is always, it seems (as at iii. vi. 19–31), sending fast messengers

[1] The decisiveness with which we are disengaged from Antony here is not unlike the way in which, at a similar point in 1 Henry VI, Talbot is dismissed from our concern as soon as he is dead and interest turns to a new group of characters, Margaret and Suffolk. This play is one with which, as we have seen, Antony and Cleopatra has other connections. What fundamentally relates the two plays—and Henry V may be added to the group—is the idea of fame: 1 Henry VI celebrates the famous Talbot and the notorious Maid of Orleans, while Henry V and Antony and Cleopatra are similarly irradiated by the fame of their great personages and events.

out on business. His brief lapse here prepares for the way in which Cleopatra and her women outwit him at the end:

> *1 Guard.* Caesar hath sent—
> *Charmian.*   Too slow a messenger.

Much of the final scene (v. ii) follows Plutarch closely, but a few details seem to derive from Shakespeare's earlier work, and they may be best mentioned here before the scene as a whole is described. Cleopatra's 'dream' of Antony (76–100) may owe something to Lady Percy's speech on her dead husband Hotspur (*2 Henry IV*, ii. iii. 9–45). We have already seen that Shakespeare at times associates Antony with Hotspur, and both these speeches are alike in that the man who survives in the memory of the woman who loved him is not quite as he was in life, but exalted and purified of imperfections. One or two verbal parallels give support to this comparison. Lady Percy says of Hotspur's honour:

> For his, it stuck upon him as the sun
> In the grey vault of heaven . . .   (ii. iii. 16–19)

Her words momentarily anticipate Cleopatra's

> His face was as the heav'ns, and therein stuck
> A sun and moon . . .   (79–80)

(with their use of 'heav'ns', 'sun', and 'stuck'). Secondly, the Clown who brings Cleopatra the asps is presented in a way that strikingly recalls the Clown in Shakespeare's first Roman tragedy *Titus Andronicus* (iv. iii, iv), who enters carrying a basket containing pigeons. His role is similarly circumscribed, and makes a comparable effect of pungent anachronism (both make references more obviously suitable to a Christian than to a pagan context). Finally, Cleopatra's death seems to owe something essential in conception to the death of Cassius (*Julius Caesar*, v. iii).[1] In his last scene Cassius has moments which anticipate the deaths of both Antony and Cleopatra. Like Antony he makes a last request of his bondman—that he should stab him. When he is dead, Titinius places the wreath of victory on his brow, Titinius here matching Charmian, who adjusts Cleopatra's crown; both Titinius and Charmian then take their own lives. Cassius and Cleopatra are

---

[1] Their thematic resemblances are worked out by G. Wilson Knight in *The Imperial Theme* (London, 1954 reprint), pp. 90–2.

therefore both pointedly crowned in death; and in both scenes the dramatic effect is one of placing the dead person on exhibition. For Brutus and his friends come to look at Cassius (' Look whe'r he have not crown'd dead Cassius!'), just as Octavius and his men finally look at Cleopatra.

This last scene is from one point of view a brisk succession of short episodes, with Cleopatra on stage throughout receiving a series of visitors.[1] Proculeius and his men gain entry to the Monument and prevent Cleopatra from killing herself. Dolabella has a private conversation with her; she tells him of her 'dream' of Antony, and he informs her that Caesar intends to lead her in triumph. At this point Caesar himself appears, and confronts Cleopatra for the first time. She behaves with apparent submissiveness, but her treasurer discloses that she has kept back some of her treasure. As soon as Caesar has left, Cleopatra hastens preparations for her death; when the Clown too has gone, she dies with her women, so outwitting Caesar.

Such a bare summary conveys, of course, nothing of the scene's power, nor does it hint at its peculiar dramatic nature. The first thing to be noted about it is that it is by far the longest scene in the play, and there can be little doubt that it is so by intention. The clue to the scene's great power, its capacity to arouse keen tension, is given in Cleopatra's opening speech, and particularly in the words

> and it is great
> To do that thing that ends all other deeds . . .
>
> (4–5)

For the scene is an *ending*; and it puts an end to everything—to 'all other deeds'. Moreover it derives much of its power from its position in this particular play: it puts an end not only to Cleopatra's life, but to the very long play we have been witnessing, with its quite exceptional number of short scenes, its restlessly shifting points of view, and the changing fortunes of its volatile characters. We have been shown life in its perpetual mobility—

---

[1] This final scene is comparable in form with the second movement of *Timon of Athens*, with Timon in the wilderness similarly receiving a series of visitors and, like Cleopatra, concluding the movement with his own death. One of Shakespeare's sources for *Timon* was Plutarch's *Life of Marcus Antonius*—an obvious reason why he should associate the two plays.

> This common body,
> Like to a vagabond flag upon the stream,
> Goes to and back, lackeying the varying tide,
> To rot itself with motion
>
> (I. iv. 44–7)

—so that it is inevitably with feelings of relief and pleasure that we approach a point of rest,

> that thing that ends all other deeds,
> Which shackles accidents and bolts up change . . .

There are, therefore, strong dramaturgical reasons why this long last scene should arouse, as many critics have testified, such feelings of satisfaction. The entire play, with its ceaseless wave-like motion, has mounted an unobtrusive assault on the nerves, but in doing so it has finally placed the audience in an entirely suitable frame of mind for this final movement in which Cleopatra abjures 'the fleeting moon' and scorns a world subject to fortune as 'not worth leave-taking'. There is of course much else in the scene, but the profound effect it makes simply as an *ending* is perhaps the primary one.

In order to make such an effect, its length is necessary; a series of short disjunct scenes could not have achieved it. What we must have is the opportunity to focus at length on a single occasion, without interruption, so as to be able to feel the contrast when it comes between movement and stillness (like seeing a train come gradually to rest at a terminus). This is why the scene's destination—Cleopatra's death—is announced in its opening speech: we must be clear as to what we are approaching, so that everything that intervenes—the brief visits of Proculeius, Dolabella, Caesar, Dolabella again, and the Clown—can be contemplated for what they are: Cleopatra's *last* transactions with the world. When at last the Clown goes (and Cleopatra impatiently bids him farewell four times), we have a powerful and moving sense of being nearly home (and the *contemptus mundi* sentiments which, in this scene, briefly invest Cleopatra contribute their own pressure).

But the scene is not only an ending. It is also a contest of wits, with Cleopatra and Caesar as antagonists, the issue being whether Cleopatra is to be led in Caesar's triumph. The middle episodes of the scene, therefore, present us with an alternative possibility to the one we in fact know must happen; but none the less, the vividness of the alternative works as a reminder that for the persons concerned the issues are still not settled, nothing has yet hardened into the fixed lines of the story as told by the historian. Cleopatra could even now fail to achieve, or so the dramatist makes us feel, the end which will turn her defeat into what is felt to be a last-minute victory.

A further reason why this last episode has such power to move and even thrill an audience is that in it we witness a metamorphosis. Cleopatra changes before our eyes from a living human being into an inanimate work of art, 'a wonderful piece of work' which men can gaze at as they would at a painting or a piece of sculpture. The metamorphosis is in fact the reverse of what happens at the end of *The Winter's Tale*: there we witness a 'statue' becoming a woman, here a woman becomes a 'statue'. In Cleopatra's case the sense of the marvellous aroused by the change is very largely due to her extraordinary vitality, which has been so variously evoked throughout the play. Now all that life is translated into this stillness and coldness. But some of the force of the scenic effect derives from the way in which Shakespeare's theatre used *tableaux*. Cleopatra's death is the most deliberate and ceremonious in all Shakespeare's plays, and the *tableau* formed by the dead women is held for fifty lines. With the Romans we look at the formally arranged group; and in no other death scene do we contemplate the dead in so nearly aesthetic a way. This is not, however, like most of Shakespeare's *tableau* scenes, merely a figurative or metaphorical one: a stage picture composed of living persons, who for the moment are standing still; instead, it is, so to speak, a literal *tableau*, in which the persons have carefully arranged themselves for exhibition while they were 'alive', and have then by 'dying' become inanimate objects. They are, for dramatic purposes, as dead as if they were graven images.

Cleopatra's metamorphosis from woman into icon throws light on Shakespeare's purpose in the play as a whole as well as on the poetic and historical vision which he has sought to transmit. Enobarbus concludes his description of Cleopatra's first meeting with Antony with an anecdote not found in Plutarch and apparently invented by Shakespeare:

> I saw her once
> Hop forty paces through the public street;
> And, having lost her breath, she spoke, and panted,

> That she did make defect perfection,
> And, breathless, pour breath forth.
>
>   (II. ii. 232–6)[1]

What this trivial, but oddly memorable, little incident helps to
bring out is Cleopatra's reality as a living person: though out of
breath, she 'pours breath forth', making 'defect perfection'—but
it is her *breath* that our attention is drawn to. A few scenes later,
Cleopatra is interrogating the Messenger about Octavia. To her
question 'What majesty is in her gait?', he replies:

> She creeps.
> Her motion and her station are as one;
> She shows a body rather than a life,
> A statue than a breather.
>
>   (III. iii. 18–21)

For Shakespeare 'life' and 'breath', 'living' and 'breathing' are
almost synonymous terms. A statue, on the other hand, is a
breathless copy of a human being. ('What fine chisel / Could ever
yet cut breath?' says Leontes, standing before Hermione's
'statue'.) The contrast between 'breather' and 'statue' seems to
have been much in Shakespeare's mind during the writing of a
play so much concerned with the private experiences of long-
famous personages: the once breathing and intensely animate
lives of those who have since become statues standing with fixed
postures in the Temple of Fame.[2]

The distinction between the man as he was in life and as he is
to become in fame or history was in any case one which Shakespeare would have met in Plutarch. In his *Life of Alexander*
Plutarch says that his intent

is not to write histories, but only lives. For the noblest deeds do not
always show men's virtues and vices; but oftentimes a light occasion,
a word, or some sport, makes men's natural dispositions and manners
appear more plain than the famous battles won wherein are slain ten
thousand men, or the great armies, or cities won by siege or assault.[3]

---

¹ The Folio reading 'powre breath forth' is regularly emended in modern editions
to 'power breathe forth'. Besides being unnecessary, the emendation produces an
awkward inversion; it also obscures the paradox of 'having lost her breath' and
pouring breath forth.
² The contrast between 'man' and 'statue' is present in Marston's Roman tragedy
Sophonisba (printed 1606): 'Statue, not man!' (III. ii. 22; ed. A. H. Bullen). Shakespeare may have drawn on this play for a few details of *Antony and Cleopatra*; see
J. M. Nosworthy, *Shakespeare's Occasional Plays*, p. 9.
¹ Quoted by T. J. B. Spencer, *Shakespeare's Plutarch*, p. 7.

By the sixteenth century the fame of the 'Noble Grecians and Romanes' had reached its high point: Montaigne speaks of 'that great and farre-spreading lustre of the Romane names, which still are tingling in our eares, and never out of our mindes';[1] and Shakespeare's Roman tragedy obliges its audience to include in its dramatic experience an awareness of the fame of the hero and heroine which will considerably affect their response to the drama. Accordingly, in his final speech, Caesar speaks of Antony and Cleopatra no longer as their antagonist but with the sympathetic voice of the detached historian:

> No grave upon the earth shall clip in it
> A pair so famous.
>
> (v. ii. 356–7)

Not only, his words suggest, are Antony and Cleopatra history's most famous lovers: they are so famous that they cannot die. Despite the fact that they were in an obvious sense defeated, it might be said of them what the young Prince in *Richard III* said of another famous Roman, Julius Caesar:

> Death makes no conquest of this conqueror;
> For now he lives in fame, though not in life.
>
> (III. i. 87–8)

[1] Montaigne, tr. Florio, from 'A Defence of *Seneca* and *Plutarch*' (Everyman edn., 1910), vol. ii, p. 454.

Index

PRINTED IN GREAT BRITAIN
AT THE UNIVERSITY PRESS, OXFORD
BY VIVIAN RIDLER
PRINTER TO THE UNIVERSITY